# ESSENTIAL CC
# ENVIRONMEI

MW00628271

Aligning global governance to the challenges of sustainability is one of the most urgent environmental issues to be addressed. This book is a timely and up-to-date compilation of the main pieces of the global environmental governance puzzle.

The text is comprised of 101 entries, each defining a central concept in global environmental governance, presenting its historical evolution, introducing related debates, and including key bibliographical references and further reading. The entries combine analytical rigor with empirical description. The book:

- offers cutting-edge analysis of the state of global environmental governance;
- raises an up-to-date debate on global governance for sustainable development;
- gives an in-depth exploration of the current international architecture of global environmental governance;
- examines the interaction between environmental politics and other fields of governance such as trade, development, and security;
- elaborates a critical review of the recent literature in global environmental governance.

This unique work synthesizes writing from an internationally diverse range of well-known experts in the field of global environmental governance. Innovative thinking and high-profile expertise come together to create a volume that is accessible to students, scholars, and practitioners alike.

**Jean-Frédéric Morin** is Professor of International Relations at the Université libre de Bruxelles, Belgium, where he teaches international political economy and global environmental politics.

**Amandine Orsini** is Professor of International Relations at the Université Saint-Louis - Bruxelles, Belgium. She teaches introduction to international relations, international organizations, and global environmental politics.

"This volume provides an essential glossary of critical terms and concepts in the field of international environmental politics for diplomats, analysts and students. The interdisciplinary array of expert authors provides terse and authoritative overview of the key concepts and debates that have defined the field of international environmental governance over the years. The entries carefully survey the intellectual ecosystem of the concepts applied to understanding and managing our global environmental crisis."

*– Peter M. Haas, Professor of Political Science,*
*University of Massachusetts Amherst, USA*

"In a truly unique way, this book helps to connect the dots and navigate between the concepts, ideas and schools of thought in global environmental policy today. As environmental issues climb higher on the global agenda, I would highly recommend this book to all who wish to better understand the insights of sustainable global governance."

*– Connie Hedegaard, European Union Commissioner*
*for Climate Action*

"The global community is at a crossroads in respect to addressing climate change. A solid understanding of global environmental governance empowers people to better shape positive democracy that determines a safer future. This book makes a valuable contribution to societal understanding and societal change. Those who care about the world we leave to our children should take inspiration from its many and varied contributors drawn from so many disparate but interlocking disciplines."

*– Christiana Figueres, Executive Secretary, United Nations*
*Framework Convention on Climate Change*

# ESSENTIAL CONCEPTS OF GLOBAL ENVIRONMENTAL GOVERNANCE

*Edited by Jean-Frédéric Morin and Amandine Orsini*

LONDON AND NEW YORK

First published 2015
by Routledge
2 Park Square, Milton Park, Abingdon, Oxon OX14 4RN

and by Routledge
711 Third Avenue, New York, NY 10017

*Routledge is an imprint of the Taylor & Francis Group, an informa business*

*British Library Cataloguing-in-Publication Data*
A catalogue record for this book is available from the British Library

*Library of Congress Cataloging-in-Publication Data*
Essential concepts of global environmental governance /
edited by Jean-Frédéric Morin and Amandine Orsini.
pages cm
1. Environmental policy – International cooperation. 2. Environmentalism –
International cooperation. 3. Environmental protection – International
cooperation. 4. Environmental responsibility – International cooperation.
5. Global environmental change – International cooperation.
I. Morin, Jean-Frédéric, editor. II. Orsini, Amandine, editor.
GE170.E77 2014
363.7'01561 – dc23
2014001736

ISBN: 978-0-415-82246-6 (hbk)
ISBN: 978-0-415-82247-3 (pbk)
ISBN: 978-0-203-55356-5 (ebk)

Typeset in Baskerville
by Florence Production Limited, Stoodleigh, Devon, UK

Printed and bound in the United States of America by Edwards Brothers Malloy
on sustainably sourced paper.

To Léa, Julie, Anaïs, and Naomie.

# CONTENTS

CONTENTS

CONTENTS

ix

# CONTENTS

# PREFACE
## 101 shades of green in a pink jacket

Pink is a rather surprising color for the cover of a book on global environmental governance. Of course, it is not an innocuous choice, but a deliberate editorial statement. It is meant to illustrate three key assumptions underlying this book. First, we perceive global environmental governance as a unique—and at times surprising—academic field, full of innovative concepts, out-of the-box ideas, and unexpected findings. Second, global environmental governance is not an exclusively "green" field populated by a homogeneous group of activists, but rather a diverse field fueled by several hot debates and heated controversies. Third, global environmental governance has broad impacts on our societies, going well beyond environmental concerns and covering issue-areas such as security, trade, agriculture, health, and gender relations.

*Essential Concepts of Global Environmental Governance* does not only have a unique cover, but a unique format as well. It is organized as an encyclopedia, with 101 independent and short entries presented in alphabetical order. Each entry defines a concept of global environmental governance, provides an original and critical review of the literature on it, and suggests key references for further reading.

We believe this non-linear format suits particularly well students' practices and needs. At times, they can use the table of contents or the index to quickly find the specific information they are looking for. At other times, they can navigate through the book following their mood and explore its content by jumping from one entry to the other with the help of the cross-referencing system. This flexibility favors a learning process by which students progressively connect the dots and expand their knowledge system according to their interests, starting with what they already know.

This flexibility is not achieved at the expense of quality. Entries are written by renowned scholars and comply with the most rigorous academic standards. In total, more than 110 academic experts from 75 different institutions and 18 different countries contributed to this volume. Beyond their geographical diversity, the contributors come from various academic disciplines, including sociology, law, economics, geography, philosophy and political science, proposing different analytical lenses on global environmental governance.

Eclecticism is also reflected in the list of entries. While the encyclopedia covers the classical and well-established concepts of the field, it also discusses emerging and innovative ideas. The aim here is to celebrate the diversity and richness of global environmental governance.

Hoping that our aim is achieved, we warmly thank all our contributors for their enthusiasm and professionalism in cooperating on this project, while accepting strict guidelines, short deadlines and demanding suggestions for revisions. If editing the textbook was so pleasing, it was thanks to the contributors' forebearance and professionalism.

We also thank members of the advisory board of this book, who commented on a first version of this project at a workshop organized in November 2012. Members of this advisory board are Frank Biermann (University of Amsterdam), Peter Dauverge (University of British Colombia), Marc Pallemaerts (Université libre de Bruxelles), Patricia Faga Inglecias Lemos (University of Sao Paulo), Philippe Le Prestre (Université Laval), Hiroshi Ohta (Waseda University), Sebastian Oberthür (Vrije Universiteit Brussel), Kate O'Neill (Berkeley), Susan Owens (Cambridge University), Hélène Trudeau (Université de Montréal), and Chen Yugang (Fudan University).

A special thanks goes to Sebastian Oberthür (Vrije Universiteit Brussel) and Marc Pallemaerts (Université libre de Bruxelles) for their support and encouragement in initiating this project. Without their impulse, it is unlikely that it would have taken shape.

The project benefited from the financial assistance of the Université libre de Bruxelles as well as from the invaluable research assistance of Alexandra Hofer and Laurent Uyttersprot. We thank them and hope they enjoyed working on this project as much as we did.

Finally, we would like to thank our students. They were always in our mind and provided the purpose and the meaning for this book.

Jean-Frédéric Morin and Amandine Orsini,
Brussels, January 2014

# ABBREVIATIONS

| | |
|---|---|
| ABS | Access and benefit sharing |
| ALBA | Bolivia, Venezuela, Ecuador, Nicaragua, and Cuba |
| AOSIS | Alliance of Small Island States |
| ASEAN | Association of Southeast Asian Nations |
| ATS | Antarctic Treaty System |
| BASIC | Brazil, South Africa, India, and China |
| BINGO | Business initiated nongovernmental organization |
| BRICS | Brazil, Russia, India, China, and South Africa |
| CANZ | Canada, Australia, and New Zealand |
| CBD | Convention on Biological Diversity |
| CBDR | Common but differentiated responsibility |
| CCAMLR | Convention on the Conservation of Antarctic Marine Living Resources |
| CDM | Clean Development Mechanism |
| CDP | Carbon Disclosure Project |
| CFC | chlorofluorocarbons |
| CHM | Common heritage of mankind |
| CITES | Convention on International Trade in Endangered Species of Wild Fauna and Flora |
| COP | Conference of the Parties |
| CSD | Commission on Sustainable Development |
| CSR | Corporate social responsibility |
| DDT | dichloro-diphenyl-trichloroethane |
| ECOSOC | Economic and Social Council of the United Nations |
| EEC | European Economic Community |
| EKC | Environmental Kuznets curve |
| EMS | Environmental management systems |
| EROI | Energy return on investment |
| ES | Ecosystem service |
| EU | European Union |
| EU ETS | EU Emissions Trading System |
| FAO | Food and Agriculture Organization |
| FCPF | Forest Carbon Partnership Facility |

| | |
|---|---|
| FSC | Forest Stewardship Council |
| GATT | General Agreement on Tariffs and Trade |
| GDP | Growth Domestic Product |
| GEF | Global Environment Facility |
| GEG | Global Environmental Governance |
| GEO | Global Environmental Outlook |
| GMO | Genetically modified organism |
| GPG | Global public good |
| GPI | Genuine Progress Indicator |
| GRI | Global Reporting Initiative |
| HCFC | Hydrochlorofluorocarbon |
| HFC | Hydrofluorocarbon |
| IBSA | India, Brazil, and South Africa |
| ICRW | International Convention for the Regulation of Whaling |
| IEA | International Energy Agency |
| ILO | International Labor Organization |
| IMF | International Monetary Fund |
| IOM | International Organization for Migration |
| IOPC | International Oil Pollution Compensation |
| IPCC | Intergovernmental Panel on Climate Change |
| IPR | Intellectual property rights |
| IRENA | International Renewable Energy Agency |
| ISEW | Index of Sustainable Economic Welfare |
| ISO | International Organization for Standardization |
| ITPGRFA | International Treaty on Plant Genetic Resources for Food and Agriculture |
| IUCN | International Union for Conservation of Nature |
| IWC | International Whaling Commission |
| JUSCANZ | Japan, United States, Canada, Australia, and New Zealand |
| JUSSCANNZ | Japan, United States, Switzerland, Canada, Australia, Norway, and New Zealand |
| LDC | Least developed country |
| MEA | Multilateral environmental agreement |
| MOP | Meeting of the Parties |
| NAAEC | North American Agreement on Environmental Cooperation |
| NAFTA | North American Free Trade Agreement |
| NGO | Nongovernmental organization |
| ODS | Ozone-depleting substances |
| OECD | Organisation for Economic Co-operation and Development |

| | |
|---|---|
| OPEC | Organization of Petroleum Exporting Countries |
| PES | Payments for ecosystem services |
| PIC | Prior informed consent |
| POP | Persistent organic pollutant |
| RAINS | Regional Acidification Information System |
| REDD | reducing emissions from deforestation and forest degradation |
| RFMO | Regional Fishery Management Organization |
| SADC | Southern African Development Commumity |
| $SO_2$ | Sulfur dioxide |
| SPS | Agreement on the Application of Sanitary and Phytosanitary Measures, to the World Trade Organization |
| STS | Science and technology studies |
| TEC | Transnational environmental crime |
| TNC | Transnational corporation |
| UN | United Nations |
| UNCCD | United Nations Convention to Combat Desertification |
| UNCED | United Nations Conference on Environment and Development |
| UNCLOS | United Nations Convention on the Law of the Sea |
| UNDP | United Nations Development Programme |
| UNEP | United Nations Environment Programme |
| UNESCO | United Nations Educational, Scientific, and Cultural Organization |
| UNFCCC | United Nations Framework Convention on Climate Change |
| UNHCR | UN High Commissioner for Refugees |
| US | United States of America |
| WBCSD | World Business Council for Sustainable Development |
| WCED | World Commission on Environment and Development |
| WTO | World Trade Organization |
| WWF | World Wildlife Fund |

# TIMELINE OF SELECTED INTERNATIONAL ENVIRONMENTAL AGREEMENTS

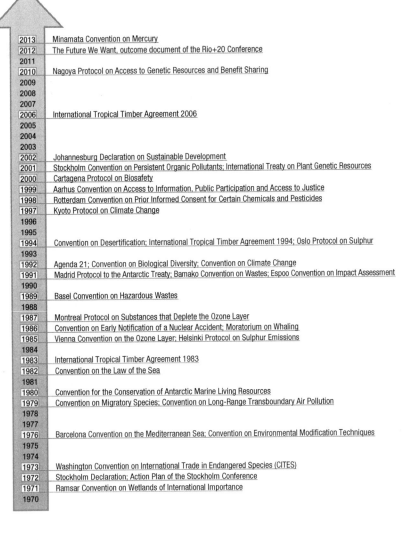

|  |  |
|---|---|
| 2013 | Minamata Convention on Mercury |
| 2012 | The Future We Want, outcome document of the Rio+20 Conference |
| 2011 | |
| 2010 | Nagoya Protocol on Access to Genetic Resources and Benefit Sharing |
| 2009 | |
| 2008 | |
| 2007 | |
| 2006 | International Tropical Timber Agreement 2006 |
| 2005 | |
| 2004 | |
| 2003 | |
| 2002 | Johannesburg Declaration on Sustainable Development |
| 2001 | Stockholm Convention on Persistent Organic Pollutants; International Treaty on Plant Genetic Resources |
| 2000 | Cartagena Protocol on Biosafety |
| 1999 | Aarhus Convention on Access to Information, Public Participation and Access to Justice |
| 1998 | Rotterdam Convention on Prior Informed Consent for Certain Chemicals and Pesticides |
| 1997 | Kyoto Protocol on Climate Change |
| 1996 | |
| 1995 | |
| 1994 | Convention on Desertification; International Tropical Timber Agreement 1994; Oslo Protocol on Sulphur |
| 1993 | |
| 1992 | Agenda 21; Convention on Biological Diversity; Convention on Climate Change |
| 1991 | Madrid Protocol to the Antarctic Treaty; Bamako Convention on Wastes; Espoo Convention on Impact Assessment |
| 1990 | |
| 1989 | Basel Convention on Hazardous Wastes |
| 1988 | |
| 1987 | Montreal Protocol on Substances that Deplete the Ozone Layer |
| 1986 | Convention on Early Notification of a Nuclear Accident; Moratorium on Whaling |
| 1985 | Vienna Convention on the Ozone Layer; Helsinki Protocol on Sulphur Emissions |
| 1984 | |
| 1983 | International Tropical Timber Agreement 1983 |
| 1982 | Convention on the Law of the Sea |
| 1981 | |
| 1980 | Convention for the Conservation of Antarctic Marine Living Resources |
| 1979 | Convention on Migratory Species; Convention on Long-Range Transboundary Air Pollution |
| 1978 | |
| 1977 | |
| 1976 | Barcelona Convention on the Mediterranean Sea; Convention on Environmental Modification Techniques |
| 1975 | |
| 1974 | |
| 1973 | Washington Convention on International Trade in Endangered Species (CITES) |
| 1972 | Stockholm Declaration; Action Plan of the Stockholm Conference |
| 1971 | Ramsar Convention on Wetlands of International Importance |
| 1970 | |

# ADAPTATION

## Eric E. Massey

*Vrije Universiteit Amsterdam, Netherlands*

Adaptation refers to attempts on the part of individuals and societies to respond to, moderate, or benefit from impacts brought about by human induced climate change, for example building dikes to prevent flooding or enjoying longer growing seasons. Impacts include extreme temperatures and temperature variability, sea-level rise and significant changes in weather patterns leading to more frequent and extreme weather related events such as environmental **disasters**. If left unattended, climate change could seriously disrupt socioeconomic and ecological systems (IPCC 2007). In order to ensure that countries started to address the issue of climate impacts and take steps to adapt, the 1992 Convention of the **climate change regime** states that signatory parties should: "facilitate adequate adaptation", "cooperate in preparing for adaptation" and "assist developing countries . . . in meeting the costs of adaptation" (UNFCCC 1992: Article 4). This last provision was based on arguments that developed countries were largely responsible for climate change and that the impacts would fall disproportionately on the poorer, **least developed countries** and especially **indigenous peoples and local communities** (IPCC 2007). Such assistance for adaptation via financial flows, knowledge support and technology transfer could be seen as a means of promoting environmental **justice**.

As countries began to adapt, varying concepts of what adaptation means and entails in the realm of global and environmental governance have developed. At one end of the spectrum, the dominant paradigm as put forth by the United Nations envisions adaptation as a technocratic process to reduce the risks and vulnerabilities from climate impacts and increase societal resilience so as to preserve or improve the socioeconomic status quo of countries. Under this way of thinking, adaptation can be seen as a form of **sustainable development** and subsequently a component of **ecological modernization**. Since climate change will affect all sectors, public and private, concerns for impacts should be integrated or mainstreamed into the management of each sector. For example, each government ministry or department of a country may develop their own adaptation strategies. Additionally, because climate impacts will vary from place to place and be most manifest at lower levels of governance, it is often argued in the academic literature as well as in governments that local communities should be

1

responsible for implementation while national and international organizations provide support and assistance.

At the other end of the spectrum, especially in the academic literature, adaptation (or rather the need to adapt) can be seen as a means for social transformation and not simply for protecting what exists (Adger et al. 2006). Because climate change was brought about by a lack of good environmental governance, adaptation presents the opportunity to "reflect upon and enact change in those practices and underlying institutions that generate root and proximate causes of risk" (Pelling 2011: 21). Adaptation here is a social process to create new governance structures that can avoid past externalities and their subsequent cases of social and environmental injustices.

## References

Adger, Niel, Jouni Paavola, Saleemul Huq, and Mary Mace (Eds.). 2006. *Fairness in Adaptation to Climate Change*. Cambridge, MA, MIT Press.
IPCC (Intergovernmental Panel on Climate Change). 2007. *Impacts, Adaptation and Vulnerability*. Cambridge, Cambridge University Press.
Pelling, Mark. 2011. *Adaptation to Climate Change: From Resilience to Transformation*. New York, Routledge.

# AID

## Åsa Persson
*Stockholm Environment Institute, Sweden*

Whereas formal definitions of environmental aid based on activities (e.g. nature conservation measures, subsidies of cleaner cooking stoves) have been developed by organizations such as the Organisation for Economic Co-operation and Development (OECD) for statistical purposes, it can also be simply defined as bilateral or multilateral financial or technical assistance to developing countries which has a likely positive environmental impact (regardless of the objective of the aid activity) (see Hicks et al. 2008). Environmental aid from public sources is a core feature of contemporary global environmental governance, both for strategic reasons, in that it can act as a concession or side payment for getting recipient countries to participate in international environmental governance, and **effectiveness** reasons, in that it can enhance the capacity of recipient countries to ensure the **compliance and implementation** of international **regimes** and provide **global public goods**.

Environmental aid emerged as a topic in the 1980s when negative environmental impacts of aid projects, among others led by the **World Bank**, were first highlighted, and subsequently addressed through impact **assessments** procedures. In the 1990s, especially after the 1992 Rio conference, a more proactive approach emerged where environmental protection became the main or a significant objective of aid. According to official data from the OECD Development Assistance Committee, bilateral aid with environmental sustainability as a principal purpose has increased threefold since 1997 and reached around 11 billion US dollars in 2009/10 (OECD 2012). If sectorial aid where the environment is a "significant" objective is included, the total amount increases to around 25 billion. The most important sectors were water and sanitation, energy, transport, agriculture, and rural development.

Some independent analyses have also estimated the magnitude of environmentally negative or "dirty" aid. Hicks et al. (2008) found that in the 1990s, aid with likely positive environmental impact was outweighed by aid with likely neutral or negative impact by a factor of seven and three, respectively. Using the same database, a more recent study shows that the ratio of "dirty" to "environmental" was still roughly three in 2008 (Marcoux et al. 2013). The trend is one of gradual improvement, but still poor overall performance.

Why do donors offer environmental aid? It has been found that donors' economic and political interests are the drivers of environmental aid rather than altruism (see example from the whaling issue in Miller and Dolšak 2007). National wealth, strong environmental advocacy groups and post-materialist values appear to improve the environmental impact of a donor's aid, but also "green and greedy" environmental technology lobbies, in particular when it comes to addressing global environmental problems rather than local ones (Hicks et al. 2008). Mitigating global environmental problems directly benefits donor countries as well, which has sometimes raised concern among recipient countries that funds are diverted from urgent local environmental problems. Provision of environmental aid to address global environmental problems may also be perceived by donors as more cost-effective or politically more feasible than taking stronger domestic action. According to environmental aid statistics, the trend is increased aid for global problems.

There are two complementary strategies for environmental aid; specialized environmental aid, disbursed through specific environment-related bilateral and multilateral funds and programs, some of which are operated by the **Global Environment Facility**; and the integration (or mainstreaming) of environmental concerns into all kinds of aid. For the latter purpose, donor agencies have developed various tools, ranging from project-level impact assessment to tools for more strategic decision-making (Persson 2009). While the advantages of effective integration of environmental concerns in mainstream aid are clear, there have also been concerns arising from the general proliferation of issues and objectives to be mainstreamed into aid (e.g. gender, human rights, HIV/AIDS) and that it means a de facto delegation of critical value judgments to implementing agencies as opposed to political decision-makers.

Starting in the 1980s, critique was voiced against the perceived use of "green" conditionality, i.e. that donors required environmental commitments on the part of recipients even though they were not necessarily the immediate priorities of the affected communities (Mori 2011). In 2005, the Paris Declaration on Aid Effectiveness was agreed, in an effort to reframe the relationship between donors and recipients, including sensitivities surrounding conditionality. Key principles included stronger recipient country ownership, donor harmonization and results-based management—and a related trend is to use broader budget support programs rather than specific projects. It is difficult to assess whether these principles and trends will be largely positive or negative for the environmental impact of aid, as it depends to a large extent on detailed **compliance and implementation** arrangements.

A debate that has been reinvigorated by recent negotiations surrounding climate finance under the **climate change regime** is that of additionality of resources. The 1992 Rio summit (see **Summit diplomacy**) served to put the spotlight on global environmental public goods, with the adoption of several international conventions. Financial assistance to help developing countries implement such conventions became a new focus of environmental aid. However, developing countries have questioned whether such assistance is indeed "new and additional" to existing official development assistance budgetary commitments, as stipulated in several key texts. It has been argued that such assistance should be considered as a form of restitution, reflecting the historical responsibility of developed countries and the **common but differentiated responsibility** principle, rather than as aid. Concern surrounding additionality is one of the driving forces behind recent initiatives for increased transparency in aid allocation and aid results, such as the International Aid Transparency Initiative and the database AidData.

The ultimate question is whether aid—in general and environmental aid in particular—is effective? This is an ongoing debate with strong divergence, including more pessimistic views expressed by scholars such as Dambisa Moyo and William Easterly and more optimistic ones by Paul

Collier and Jeffrey Sachs. Part of the challenge is nuancing the question; what do we mean by **effectiveness** and success (e.g. GDP growth or other metrics) and under what particular conditions aid either works or not.

## References

Hicks, Robert, Bradley Parks, J. Timmons Roberts, and Michael Tierney. 2008. *Greening Aid? Understanding the Environmental Impact of Development Assistance.* Oxford, Oxford University Press.

Marcoux, Christopher, Bradley Parks, Christian Peratsakis, J. Timmons Roberts, and Michael Tierney. 2013. "Environmental Aid and Climate Finance in a New World: How Past Environmental Aid Allocation Impacts Future Climate Aid." *WIDER Working Paper.* Helsinki, UNU-WIDER.

Miller, Andrew R. and Nives Dolšak. 2007. "Issue Linkages in International Environmental Policy: The International Whaling Commission and Japanese Development Aid." *Global Environmental Politics* 7(1): 69–96.

Mori, Akihisa. 2011. "Overcoming Barriers to Effective Environmental Aid: A Comparison between Japan, Germany, Denmark, and the World Bank." *Journal of Environment and Development* 20(1): 3–26.

OECD (Organisation for Economic Co-operation and Development). 2012. *Development Co-operation Report 2012.* Paris, OECD.

Persson, Åsa. 2009. "Environmental Policy Integration and Bilateral Development Assistance: Challenges and Opportunities with an Evolving Governance Framework." *International Environmental Agreements* 9(4): 409–429.

# ANTARCTIC TREATY REGIME

## Alan D. Hemmings
*University of Canterbury, New Zealand*

The Antarctic Treaty System (ATS) comprises the 1959 Antarctic Treaty, the 1972 Convention on the Conservation of Antarctic Seals, the 1980 Convention on the Conservation of Antarctic Marine Living Resources (CCAMLR), the 1991 Protocol on Environmental Protection to the Antarctic Treaty (Madrid Protocol), and measures in force under these instruments. Three of these apply to the area south of 60° south. CCAMLR northern boundary approximates the Antarctic convergence, a biologically rich zone where Antarctic waters meet the waters of the sub-Antarctic. The ATS is one of the longest established **regimes** (Dodds 2012).

Its purpose is international governance of the region, since although seven states claim territorial sovereignty over parts of the continent, these claims are not generally recognized and many see Antarctica as **common heritage of mankind**.

Thirty states plus the European Union are decision-making parties, and twenty-six more are non-decision-making parties to one or more ATS instruments. A number of intergovernmental organizations (such as the Council of Managers of National Antarctic Programs, United Nations Environment Programme (UNEP) and Food and Agriculture Organization (FAO)), **nongovernmental organizations** (such as the Scientific Committee for Antarctic Research, Antarctic and Southern Ocean Coalition and the International Association of Antarctica Tour Operators), and hybrid organizations such as International Union for Conservation of Nature (IUCN) have observer status. The three pillars of the ATS are peaceful purposes (avoiding militarization), environmental protection and freedom of scientific enquiry. The latter two and operational management of human activities underway in the region are the focus of measures adopted by the ATS (Hemmings 2011). Responsibility for whaling lies entirely outside the ATS, with the **International Whaling Commission**.

Current ATS foci include: the vexed issue of establishing large marine protected areas in Antarctic waters alongside commercial interests in fishing (see **Fisheries governance**); addressing safety, search and rescue around the Antarctic tourism industry; managing emergent bioprospecting activities; and sustaining international Antarctic **science** and associated logistics collaboration, particularly around globally significant climate change research.

While the ATS historically claims **effectiveness**, in ensuring peaceful order and addressing management issues around the conduct of activities and the environment, it is long-lived in international relations terms and faces challenges if it is to continue to effectively manage the region (Hemmings et al. 2012). Globalization challenges its Antarctic exceptionalism model of governance, wherein issues were addressed through specific instruments negotiated under the ATS. Increasingly, there are pressures to leave regulation to market forces or administrative action, or to global instruments. Increasing scale, pace and complexity of technology-enabled Antarctic activities, less constrained by Antarctica's remoteness and harshness than in the past, require improved ATS institutional integration and instrumental coverage. Further, the architecture of the ATS has its foundations in the Cold War and rising international powers such as Brazil, China, India and South Africa, and the broader post-colonial system of **emerging countries**, few of which are presently within the ATS, will need to be assured that it now serves their interests too (Hemmings 2013).

## References

Dodds, Klaus. 2012. *The Antarctic: A Very Short Introduction*. Oxford, Oxford University Press.

Hemmings, Alan D. 2011. "Environmental Law—Antarctica." In *The Encyclopedia of Sustainability, Vol. 3: The Law and Politics of Sustainability*, Eds. Klaus Bosselmann, Daniel S. Fogel, and J.B. Ruhl, 188–194. Great Barrington, Berkshire Publishing.

Hemmings, Alan D. 2014. "Re-justifying the Antarctic Treaty System for the 21st Century: Rights, Expectations and Global Equity." In *Polar Geopolitics: Knowledges, Resources and Legal Regimes*, Eds. Richard Powell and Klaus Dodds, 55–73. Cheltenham and Northampton, Edward Elgar.

Hemmings, Alan D., Donald R. Rothwell, and Karen N. Scott (Eds.). 2012. *Antarctic Security in the Twenty-First Century: Legal and Policy Perspectives*. London, Routledge.

# ARCTIC COUNCIL

## Olav Schram Stokke

*University of Oslo and Fridtjof Nansen Institute, Norway*

The Arctic Council is an international soft-law institution established in 1996 to address issues of environmental protection and Sustainable Development in the Arctic. Its membership comprises eight states with **sovereignty** over territory north of the Arctic Circle—Canada, Denmark/Greenland, Finland, Iceland, Norway, Russia, Sweden, and the US (see **Regional governance**). Several transnational **indigenous peoples and local communities** associations, such as the Inuit Circumpolar Council and the Saami Council, have permanent participant status, which includes full consultation in all Council meetings and activities, but decisions are taken by the member states. This unusually prominent role of indigenous-peoples' organizations was integral to Canada's initiative for the Arctic Council and weighs heavily in the Council's self-presentation. Numerous non-Arctic states, international bodies, and **nongovernmental organizations** participate as observers. Biannual ministerial meetings adopt declarations directing Council activities, with implementation overseen by the members' Senior Arctic Officials. Working groups in areas such as environmental monitoring, biodiversity protection, and sustainable development prepare **assessment** reports and other studies, sometimes involving non-binding recommendations on such matters as environmental toxics, climate change, oil and gas activities, and shipping (Koivurova and VanderZwaag 2007). Ad hoc task forces have dealt with, among other things, the development of legally binding agreements (adopted by the member states, not the Council) on Search and Rescue (2011) and Marine Oil Pollution Preparedness and Response (2013). A permanent **secretariat** has been operational since 2013, as has a Project Support Instrument for improving regional capacities in areas such as integrated **hazardous waste** management.

These institutional developments reflect the importance of global processes for Arctic governance. The initiatives that generated the Council exploited a window of opportunity opened by the late-1980s thaw in East–West relations. Subsequent willingness to fund increasingly ambitious projects and program activities has been fuelled by the perception that a well-functioning circumpolar body, with Russia and its Western neighbors under a common umbrella, can promote regional Security objectives (Stokke and Hønneland 2010).

The Council's 2013 acceptance of six observer applications, including those from **emerging countries** such as China and India, reflects acknowledgment that many activities that produce Arctic environmental challenges occur outside the region or fall under the full or partial jurisdiction of non-Arctic states. Examples include discharges of greenhouse gases, persistent organic pollutants, and heavy metals, as well as Arctic shipping. Handling such challenges requires regulatory action beyond the Arctic Eight, typically in global institutions such as the **Persistent Organic Pollutants Convention**, the **climate change regime**, and the International Maritime Organization. Welcoming non-regional states into Council activities may make it easier for the Arctic states to achieve regulatory advances in broader institutions crucial to the **effectiveness** of Arctic governance.

The structure of the Arctic Council has grown firmer and its activities have expanded to cover knowledge building, capacity enhancement, and norm development. While the **Law of the Sea Convention** ensures that the five Arctic coastal states predominate in the management of regional natural resources, including fish, oil, and gas, and **regimes** with broader membership are weightier for environmental and shipping regulation, the Council is well placed to promote **institutional interactions** among these levels of governance.

## References

Koivurova, Timo and David L. VanderZwaag. 2007. "The Arctic Council at 10 Years: Retrospect and Prospects." *University of British Columbia Law Review* 40(1): 121–194.

Stokke, Olav Schram and Geir Hønneland (Eds.). 2010 [2007]. *International Cooperation and Arctic Governance.* London, Routledge.

# ASSESSMENTS

## Joyeeta Gupta

*University of Amsterdam, Netherlands*

Environmental assessments have evolved from individual literature review papers, through single organization assessments (e.g. World Resource Institute reports), to structured and regular representative assessments (e.g. Intergovernmental Panel on Climate Change (IPCC)). These latter assessments are sometimes linked to international policy processes. Environmental assessments are produced by joint expert participation and analysis of the existing issue-specific **science** (Clark et al. 2006) with policy implications (Mitchell et al. 2006). It may include collation and analysis of data and responses to specific questions. It can, but mostly does not, include original research. However, it triggers original research subsequently published in journals and referred to in the assessments.

These assessments can potentially bridge the science-policy gap between their respective communities (Caplan 1979; Woodhouse and Nieusma 2001; **boundary organizations**). This gap includes differing assumptions, goals, methods, and reward system. There is also uneven North–South coverage (Annan 2003). Assessments can be classified linearly in a science-policy interface ladder (Gupta, forthcoming). The bottom rung is an informal science-policy interface as on biofuels (where there is neither systematic review of biofuel science nor a centralized governance process) moving up through structured, formalized, regular assessments provided to a formalized negotiating process as in climate change.

Assessments are very diverse. On forests, the Global Forest Resource Assessment of the Food and Agriculture Organization (FAO) uses completed questionnaires from member countries and expert consultations and feeds into the ongoing FAO work. In the **ozone regime**, there are Advisory Panels on Science, Environment, Technology, and Economics that also address specific questions. In 1988 the World Meteorological Organization and the **United Nations Environment Programme** established IPCC. This formal body assesses the scientific literature and derives policy relevant conclusions under a strictly organized regime of writing and responding to the scientific and government review processes. IPCC interacts closely with the UN **climate change regime** negotiations (see also **Treaty negotiations**). Since 1995, UNEP has published five Global Environmental Outlooks (GEOs), less formalized and structured than IPCC but simpler and more communicative. Since 2003, tri-annual World Water Development Reports have been published by UN-Water and United Nations Educational, Scientific, and Cultural Organization (UNESCO) to advise the water community. There are a few one-time assessments such as the 1995 Millennium Ecosystem Assessment, followed fifteen years later by the Intergovernmental Platform on Biodiversity and Ecosystem Services (Larigauderie and Mooney 2010). The **Desertification Convention** is without such assessments that suggest policy options (Bauer and Stringer 2009; Grainger 2009).

The more structured, formalized, regular assessments assess the available global knowledge, structure the information into usable knowledge, point to knowledge conflicts and gaps and prepare simple summaries for policymakers. However, they cannot compensate for patchy global knowledge, cover all languages, and tend to focus on "peer reviewed" journals, thus excluding grey literature including **nongovernmental organizations, business and corporations** assessments, and civic knowledge (Bäckstrand 2003). Moreover, they may focus on best practices and panaceas as opposed to contextual knowledge. Finally, as these assessments become influential, they come under heavy scientific and journalistic scrutiny.

## References

Annan, Kofi. 2003. "A Challenge to the World's Scientists." *Science* 299(5612): 1485–1485.

Bäckstrand, Karin. 2003. "Civic Science for Sustainability: Reframing the Role of Experts, Policy-Makers and Citizens in Environmental Governance." *Global Environmental Politics* 3(4): 24–41.

Bauer, Steffen and Lindsay C. Stringer. 2009. "The Role of Science in the Global Governance of Desertification." *The Journal of Environment and Development* 18(3): 248–267.

Caplan, Nathan. 1979. "The Two-Communities Theory and Knowledge Utilization". *American Behavioral Scientist* 22(3): 459–470.

Clark, William C., Ronald B. Mitchell, and David W, Cash. 2006. "Evaluating the Influence of Global Environmental Assessments." In *Global Environmental Assessments: Information and Influence*, Eds. Ronald B. Mitchell, William C. Clark, David W. Cash, and Nancy M. Dickson, 1–28. Cambridge, MA, MIT Press.

Grainger, Alan. 2009. "The Role of Science in Implementing International Environmental Agreements: The Case of Desertification." *Land Degradation and Development* 20(4): 410–430.

Gupta, Joyeeta. Forthcoming. "Science and Governance: Climate Change, Forests, Environment and Water Governance." In *The Role of Experts in International Decision-Making*, Eds. Monika Ambrus, Karin Arts, Helena Raulus and Ellen Hey, in press. Cambridge, Cambridge University Press.

Larigauderie, Anne and Harold A. Mooney. 2010. "The Intergovernmental Science-Policy Platform on Biodiversity and Ecosystem Services: Moving a Step Closer to an IPCC-like Mechanism for Biodiversity." *Current Opinion in Environmental Sustainability* 2(1–2): 9–14.

Mitchell, Ronald B., William C. Clark, David W. Cash, and Nancy M. Dickson. 2006. *Global Environmental Assessments: Information and Influence*. Cambridge, MA, MIT Press.

Woodhouse, Edward J. and Dean A. Nieusma. 2001. "Democratic Expertise: Integrating Knowledge, Power, and Participation." In *Knowledge, Power and Participation*, Eds. Matthijs, Hisschemöller, Jeery R. Ravetz, Rob Hoppe, and William N. Dunn, 73–95. New Brunswick, NJ, Transaction Publishers.

# AUDITS

## Olivier Boiral
*Université Laval, Canada*

## Iñaki Heras-Saizarbitoria
*University of the Basque Country, Spain*

Environmental audits can be defined as systematic, documented, and, as far as possible, impartial evaluations of environmental practices and compliance with standards, regulations, specifications, or any other pre-established requirements related to environmental issues. As such they are tools for **compliance and implementation**. Environmental audits can focus on a large variety of issues such as sustainable forest management or environmental risks (Hillary 1998). Nevertheless, over the last decade, two forms of environmental audits have become center stage: the verification of environmental management systems (EMS) and the auditing of environmental or sustainability reports (Boiral and Gendron 2011).

First, the audits of EMS generally focus on the conformance of **business and corporations** with an established standard, such as ISO 14001, which is the most widespread with more than 250,000 certified organizations in 2011. This standard is based on the implementation of management principles: structure, resources, and responsibilities of the

EMS, policy and objectives, etc. The certification process, which is sometimes considered as a self-regulation mechanism (Prakash and Potoski 2006), assumes that the conformance of the EMS with the ISO standard has been verified by external and supposedly independent auditors. Nevertheless, organizations can also conduct internal audits based on ISO 14001 to improve their internal practices.

Second, the verification of environmental or sustainability reports focuses on conformance with a **reporting** standard, notably the Global Reporting Initiative, which is the most widely used. The auditing process—often called assurance or external assurance process—is supposed to verify the application of various reporting principles and indicators that are generally not limited to environmental issues. This assurance process is often conducted by auditing firms also involved in financial audits, and it aims to ensure the accuracy, reliability, and **transparency** of the released information.

Although the focus and scope of environmental audits may be very different, the principles underlying the certification process are quite similar. Just as **labeling and certification** in general, environmental audits are primarily intended to inspire trust among stakeholders and to reinforce organizations' social legitimacy. This quest for legitimacy through external audits reflects the emergence of an "audit society," which is characterized by common rituals of verification and an obsession with control (Power 1997). The use of environmental audits as trust-providing mechanisms also raises critical questions that remain largely underexplored (Boiral and Gendron 2011): to what extent can commercial issues underlying the auditing practice undermine the alleged independence of third-party auditors? What are the impacts of the current lack of regulatory and professional guidance on the quality of environmental audits? What are the real impacts of these external audits on organizations' internal practices?

### References

Boiral, Olivier and Yves Gendron. 2011. "Sustainable Development and Certification Practices: Lessons Learned and Prospects." *Business Strategy and the Environment* 20(5): 331–347.

Hillary, Ruth. 1998. "Environmental Auditing: Concepts, Methods and Developments." *International Journal of Auditing* 2(1): 71–85.

Power, Michael. 1997. *The Audit Society: Rituals of Verification.* Oxford, Oxford University Press.

Prakash, Aseem and Matthew Potoski. 2006. *The Voluntary Environmentalists: Green Clubs, ISO 14001, and Voluntary Environmental Regulations.* Cambridge: Cambridge University Press.

# BIODIVERSITY REGIME

## G. Kristin Rosendal

*Fridtjof Nansen Institute, Norway*

The Convention on Biological Diversity (CBD) (1992) builds on a threefold, interacting objective: the conservation of biological diversity, the sustainable use of its components, and the fair and equitable sharing of the benefits arising out of the utilization of genetic resources (see **Conservation and preservation**). The CBD is comprehensive in scope, as biodiversity is defined as species and ecosystems worldwide, as well as the genetic diversity within species. The CBD has nearly universal ratification, with the notable exception of the US. It is governed by a conference of the parties and supported by a **secretariat** and a Subsidiary Body on Scientific, Technical, and Technological Advice. Since 2010, biodiversity related treaties are being sought that are bolstered with stronger scientific pull through the Intergovernmental Panel on Biodiversity and Ecosystem Services which works as a **boundary organization**. The CBD parties are obliged to develop national biodiversity strategies, integrate biodiversity conservation in all sectors, and establish systems of protected areas. The CBD is equipped with a monitoring mechanism—national **reporting** and an incentive mechanism—the **Global Environment Facility**.

Spurring CBD negotiations were increased awareness and agreement that the rate of species extinction was extremely high compared to the natural average rate along with loss of genetic diversity in domesticated plants, with risks of reduced food security. A steady input of genetic material provides genetic variability necessary for overcoming disease outbreaks or adjusting to climatic changes. This coincided with increased economic interests as the value of genetic resources was acknowledged in the life sciences and as gene technology made patenting more feasible in these sectors (Kate and Laird 1999).

The bulk of terrestrial species diversity is found in tropical, mainly developing countries, which gave them a pull in the CBD negotiations and enhanced the conflict level. Developing countries had a normative breakthrough in their demand for economic compensation (1) for costly biodiversity conservation work; and (2) for lack of revenues from technology-rich users, tending to patent genetic material that they access free of charge in the South (Rosendal 2000). CBD parties designed Access to genetic resources and equitable Benefit Sharing (commonly abbreviated as ABS) to avoid misappropriation (biopiracy) of genetic resources (Shiva

1997) and as a prerequisite for conservation and a sustainable use of biodiversity. The CBD reconfirmed national sovereign rights to genetic resources (see **Sovereignty**) and sought to balance intellectual property rights (IPR) through the principles that access to genetic resources shall be on mutually agreed terms and be subject to prior informed consent (Swanson 1995). It has, however, proved difficult to transform the CBD principles into practical policies (Le Prestre 2002). Particularly, while the bulk of developing countries have enacted ABS legislation to secure a share of the benefits from use of their genetic resources, hardly any users have enacted compatible legislation to support ABS (Gehl Sampath 2005). This includes unsuccessful calls for disclosure of origin of genetic material used in patent applications (Tvedt 2006).

The CBD has been elaborated with two protocols. First, the Cartagena Protocol on Biosafety (2000) builds on a **precautionary principle** approach and establishes an advanced informed agreement procedure to help countries make decisions before agreeing to import genetically modified organisms. Precaution and biosafety clash with "sound science" principles of the **World Trade Organization** (Falkner and Gupta 2009). Second, the 2010 Nagoya Protocol re-establishes the CBD objective of benefit sharing between providers and users of genetic resources and aims to remedy the lack of **compliance and implementation** of the ABS regime. Enhanced ABS implementation is unlikely without compatible user measures to ensure a fairer distribution with provider countries (Oberthür and Rosendal 2014).

In addition to the direct economic values of genetic resources, biodiversity as a whole provides **ecosystem services**, such as local water and climate regulation, building materials and firewood, pollination and soil fertility. There are also cultural, recreational, and intrinsic values of biodiversity (see **Ecocentrism**), which may not be suitable for commercialization. The ecosystem approach of the CBD recognizes that humans are an integral component of ecosystems. As the greatest threat to biodiversity lies in land use change, this approach recommends management to reduce market distortions, which undervalue natural systems and provide perverse incentives and subsidies (EC 2008). Annual losses of biodiversity could deprive people of ecosystem services worth an annual US$250 billion (MEA 2005).

The balance between ABS and IPR remains contested and has been central to the US remaining a non-party to the CBD. Also contested are safeguarding rights linked to **indigenous peoples and local communities'** traditional knowledge of biodiversity (Posey and Dutfield 1996). Increasingly studied are the **institutional interactions** between the CBD and relevant international instruments. This includes processes to enhance policy coherence and avoid turf wars between biodiversity-related conventions such as the **CITES**, and—more contested—the Food and Agriculture Organization (Chiarolla 2011), the **climate change regime** (UNEP 2009), and the **World Trade Organization** (Pavoni 2013).

## References

Chiarolla, Claudio. 2011. *Intellectual Property, Agriculture and Global Food Security— The Privatization of Crop Diversity.* Cheltenham and Northampton, Edward Elgar.

EC (European Communities). 2008. *The Economics of Ecosystems and Biodiversity.* European Communities. Wesseling, Welzel and Hardt.

Falkner, Robert and Aarti Gupta. 2009. "The Limits of Regulatory Convergence: Globalization and GMO Politics in the South." *International Environmental Agreements* 9: 113–133.

Gehl Sampath, P. 2005. *Regulating Bioprospecting: Institutions for Drug Research, Access and Benefit Sharing.* New York, United Nations University.

Kate, Kary ten and Sarah Laird. 1999. *The Commercial Use of Biodiversity: Access to Genetic Resources and Benefit-Sharing.* London, Earthscan.

Le Prestre, Philippe (Ed.). 2002. *Governing Global Biodiversity: Evolution and Implementation of the Convention on Biological Diversity.* Ashgate, Aldershot.

MEA (Millennium Ecosystem Assessment). 2005. *Ecosystems and Human Well-Being: Biodiversity Synthesis.* Washington, World Resources Institute.

Oberthür, Sebastian and G. Kristin Rosendal (Eds.). 2014. *Global Governance of Genetic Resources: Access and Benefit Sharing after the Nagoya Protocol.* London, Routledge.

Pavoni, Riccardo. 2013. "The Nagoya Protocol and WTO Law." In *The 2010 Nagoya Protocol on Access and Benefit Sharing in Perspective*, Eds. Elisa Morgera, Matthias Buck, and Elsa Tsioumani, 185–213. Leiden, Martinus Nijhoff.

Posey, Darrel A. and Graham Dutfield. 1996. *Beyond Intellectual Property: Toward Traditional Resource Rights for Indigenous Peoples and Local Communities.* Ottawa, International Development Research Centre.

Rosendal, G. Kristin. 2000. *The Convention on Biological Diversity and Developing Countries.* Dordrecht, Kluwer Academic Publishers.

Shiva, Vandana. 1997. *Biopiracy: The Plunder of Nature and Knowledge.* Cambridge, MA, South End Press.

Swanson, Timothy (Ed.). 1995. *Intellectual Property Rights and Biodiversity Conservation.* Cambridge, Cambridge University Press.

Tvedt, Morten Walløe. 2006. "Elements for Legislation in User Countries to Meet the Fair and Equitable Benefit-Sharing Commitment." *Journal of World Intellectual Property* 9(2): 189–212.

UNEP (United Nations Environment Programme). 2009. *The Natural Fix? The Role of Ecosystems in Climate Mitigation.* Birkeland, Norway.

# BOUNDARY ORGANIZATIONS

## Maria Carmen Lemos
*University of Michigan, United States*

## Christine Kirchhoff
*University of Connecticut, United States*

The concept of a "boundary" for science emerged when scientists increasingly felt the need to demarcate scientific from other non-scientific activities. And while a hard boundary protected **science** from fraud or pseudo-science, it was less effective in areas where the production of science aimed to go beyond the identification and framing of a problem (i.e. basic science) to inform the design of solutions to address it (i.e. applied science). The existence and need for this boundary became increasingly contested as societies came to perceive the potential of science to solve humanities' greatest and most politicized problems. The emphasis shifted from a total separation of science and decision-making towards a blurred boundary (Jasanoff 1990) that bridged science and decision-making while providing protection from both the undue influence of politics on science ("politicization of science") and the excessive domination of science in the design and implementation of policy ("scienticization of policy").

Boundary organizations embody both a process and a structure whose primary purpose is to bridge and stabilize the gap between science and its practical application. As bridgers, boundary organizations facilitate the co-production of science and policy by sustaining collaboration between scientists and non-scientists and by brokering and tailoring scientific knowledge to different decision environments (Kirchhoff et al. 2013). For example, the Subsidiary Body on Scientific, Technical and Technological Advice to the Convention on Biological Diversity (see **Biodiversity regime**) is a boundary organization aiming to bring science into the policy process to protect global biodiversity. As stabilizers, boundary organizations provide a forum that fosters the participation of multiple perspectives, the convergence of multiple knowledge systems and the creation of peer communities around specific issues while allowing participants to remain within their professional boundaries and constituencies. Similarly, the Intergovernmental Panel on Climate Change (IPCC) plays this role in the **climate change regime** by helping to create a "fragile international knowledge order" including a broad range of scientific organizations and political and social actors from numerous countries and a variety of issue areas (Hoppe et al. 2013: 288). Both bridging and stabilizing are necessary for usability; without one or the other usability suffers. For example, as a stabilizer, the IPCC functions well; but, as a bridge to policy it is hamstrung by a variety of challenges being in a highly politicized arena where climate is a "wicked" problem (Hoppe et al. 2013).

Boundary organizations have at least three characteristics. First, they create a legitimizing space and sometimes incentivize the production and use of "boundary objects"—mechanisms, processes, material things, and even epistemologies that transcend the science/non-science divide and provide a means for producers and users of science to collaborate while maintaining their separate identities (Guston 2001; Star and Griesemer 1989). Second, boundary organizations involve information producers, users, and mediators in "boundary work"—efforts undertaken to protect science from political activities and pseudo-science (Gieryn 1983). Third, boundary organizations reside between producer and user worlds, maintaining accountability to each while supporting a combined scientific and social order (Guston 2001).

## References

Gieryn, Thomas F. 1983. "Boundary-work and the Demarcation of Science from Non-science: Strains and Interests in Professional Ideologies of Scientists." *American Sociological Review* 48(6): 781–795.

Guston, David H. 2001. "Boundary Organizations in Environmental Policy and Science: An Introduction." *Science, Technology, and Human Values* 26(4): 399–408.

Hoppe, Rob, Anna Wesselink, and Rose Cairns. 2013. "Lost in the Problem: The Role of Boundary Organizations in the Governance of Climate Change." *Wiley Interdisciplinary Reviews: Climate Change* 4(4): 283–300.

Jasanoff, Sheila. 1990. *The Fifth Branch: Science Advisers as Policymakers*. Cambridge, MA, Harvard University Press.

Kirchhoff, Christine J., Maria C. Lemos, and Suraje Dessai. 2013. "Actionable Knowledge for Environmental Decision Making: Broadening the Usability of Climate Science." *Annual Review of Environment and Natural Resources* 38: 393–414.

Star, Susan L. and James R. Griesemer. 1989. "Institutional Ecology, 'Translations' and Boundary Objects: Amateurs and Professionals in Berkeley's Museum of Vertebrate Zoology 1907–39." *Social Studies of Science* 19(3): 387–420.

# BUSINESS AND CORPORATIONS

## Doris Fuchs and Bastian Knebel

*University of Münster, Germany*

Business actors play a pivotal role in global environmental governance. They are active individually, as more or less formal roundtables, coalitions or associations, as well as via business initiated (and funded) **nongovernmental organizations** (BINGOs), at all levels of governance. Associations took a dominant role in the past, especially at the national and regional (European) levels. In the run-up to the 1992 Earth Summit, the World Business Council for Sustainable Development (WBCSD) was created to organize and steer business **participation** in global environmental governance. Today, however, a substantial share of business influence generates from the activities of individual or small groups of transnational corporations (TNCs), which have realized that their interests frequently diverge from the interests of small and medium sized businesses and are able to invest enormous resources in political activities by themselves. Thus, TNCs lobby national and regional government institutions as well as intergovernmental organizations, and are present at all relevant international environmental **treaty negotiations**. Of course, the interests of different TNCs do not always converge either, and scholars have shown that business influence is relatively more limited in those instances in which corporations lobby on more than one side (Falkner 2008).

Traditionally, business actors primarily influenced political output indirectly, especially via lobbying, or political agendas via the always-implicit threat to move jobs in the case of unfavorable political developments. In the last decades, however, they have started to increasingly show up as autonomous rule-setters or as partners of governments in (global) governance (Fuchs and Vogelmann 2008). The growing visibility of corporations in global environmental governance via public–private **partnerships** or **private regimes**, for instance in terms of voluntary **labeling and certification** schemes, indicates an acquisition of political authority and legitimacy without precedent.

Scholars and politicians evaluate such activities of firms ambiguously. While they all recognize an interest in protecting a firm or sector's reputation as well as the wish to pre-empt more stringent public regulation as likely drivers behind the development of private environmental governance initiatives, they disagree on their implications. Some observers argue that private actors effectively and efficiently help overcome international problems of collective action, and contribute to the production of **global public goods** (Glasbergen 2010). They see private firms taking responsibility and hope for financial resources for environmental objectives in times of rising public debt.

Other observers, however, doubt whether these initiatives reflect any actual greening of global business and strengthening of global environmental governance. Instead, they argue that image concerns and the motivation to pre-empt public regulation frequently lead to a restriction of private environmental governance to green washing activities (Utting 2002). Statistical analyses have failed to find evidence of a positive influence of the Responsible Care program and membership on the rate of environmental improvement among its members, for example, and shown that dirtier firms have actually been more likely to participate in the program (King and Lenox 2000). Critical observers also point out that business investment in environmental governance is (only) likely in cases in which win–win situations exist, e.g. improvements in energy efficiency leading to a reduction of production costs. Likewise, Dupont's advantage vis-à-vis its competitors in the development of substitutes for CFCs allowed it to be an advocate for the Montreal Protocol or the **ozone regime**. Numerous areas of environmental concern and constellations of interests exist, however, in which the costs of addressing environmental problems outweigh the economic benefit to business actors.

Prominent examples of private rule-setting activities and associated criticisms are the ISO 14000 series of environmental management standards and standards for "sustainable" forestry (see **Audits**). The ISO 14000 standard has been criticized for weak environmental prescriptions and yet was adopted by the International Standards Organization in 1996 and soon recognized by other international governmental organizations (Clapp 1998). Private forestry standards, in contrast, started in a promising way, when a coalition of business, trade unions, **indigenous peoples and local communities**, and environmental **nongovernmental organizations** developed the Forest Stewardship Council's (FSC) **labeling and certification** scheme. However, coalitions of business actors soon developed competing labels with weaker standards (e.g. the Sustainable Forestry Initiative of the American Pulp and Paper Association), which provide a source of confusion to consumers and serve to undermine the effectiveness of the FSC label (Gale 2002).

For a long time, the power of business and corporations remained underexposed in theoretical accounts of global environmental governance. But, recent work provides useful analytical perspectives on this crucial question (see also **Critical political economy**). Fuchs (2013), for example, introduces a three-dimensional framework that allows for a theoretically grounded analysis of business power across various fields of governance and differentiates between business' instrumental, material structural, and ideational structural (discursive) power. Exercising instrumental power, business actors influence policy outputs via lobbying or campaign financing. From a material structuralist perspective, corporations derive agenda-setting power, i.e. influence the input side of the political process from their status in institutional arrangements, especially their financial and technological resources and control over investments, jobs, and market access. Importantly, these resources also place them in the position to create, implement, and enforce their own rules and standards. In turn, ideational structuralist approaches, often referred to as discursive approaches, reveal the normative conditions of corporate power. Ideational power shapes societal perceptions and values. Here, business actors have increasingly promoted new discourses, such as **corporate social responsibility**, to polish their public image. They also run media campaigns sometimes conducted by BINGOs, whose creation has become a part of corporate actors' tool set in global environmental governance as well. BINGOs have exercised considerable influence in international climate negotiations, for instance (Levy 2004).

In sum, business actors in general and corporations in particular have become decisive actors in global environmental governance. Their power challenges not only national **sovereignty** but also international regulatory approaches and democracy in general.

## References

Clapp, Jennifer. 1998. "The Privatization of Global Environmental Governance." *Global Governance* 4(3): 295–316.

Falkner, Robert. 2008. *Business Power and Conflict in International Environmental Politics.* Basingstoke, Palgrave.

Fuchs, Doris. 2013. "Theorizing the Power of Global Companies." In *Handbook of Global Companies*, Ed. John Mikler, 77–95. New York, Wiley-Blackwell.

Fuchs, Doris and Jörg Vogelmann. 2008. "Business Power in Shaping the Sustainability of Development." In *Transnational Private Governance and Its Limits*, Eds. Jean-Christophe Graz and Andreas Nölke, 71–83. London, Routledge.

Gale, Fred. 2002. "*Caveat Certificatum.*" In *Confronting Consumption*, Eds. Thomas Princen, Michael Maniates, and Ken Conca, 275–300. Cambridge, MA, MIT Press.

Glasbergen, Pieter. 2010. "Global Action Networks: Agents for Collective Action." *Global Environmental Change* 20(1): 130–141.

King, Andrew and Michael Lenox. 2000. "Industry Self-Regulation without Sanctions." *Academy of Management Journal* 43(4): 698–716.

Levy, David. 2004. "Business and the Evolution of the Climate Regime: The Dynamics of Corporate Strategies." In *The Business of Global Environmental Governance*, Eds. David Levy and Peter Newell, 73–104. Cambridge, MA, MIT Press.

Utting, Peter (Ed.). 2002. *The Greening of Business in Developing Countries*. London, Zed Books.

# CARRYING CAPACITIES PARADIGM

## Nathan F. Sayre and Adam Romero

*University of California at Berkeley, United States*

Carrying capacity can be defined as *the quantity of some X that can or should be supported or conveyed by some Y*; in most of its many applications, exceeding a carrying capacity is considered damaging to $X$, $Y$, or both.

Scholars in many fields have discarded the concept of carrying capacity, but it persists and has in recent decades proliferated in debates about human populations and the environment on which they depend at the **scale** of Earth or significant subunits thereof. Although the term itself is not always used, carrying capacity is thus a pivotal idea for **population sustainability** and **sustainable development**.

The carrying capacities paradigm can be defined as the suite of methods, concepts, and assumptions that inform and support the view that human–environment interactions can and should be understood in terms of the $X{:}Y$ ratios that carrying capacities describe or prescribe. Developing and improving methods to measure and communicate such ratios is often central to debates about the limits to growth, **ecosystem services**, biocapacity, and natural capital. But the origins and implications of the paradigm's supporting concepts and assumptions frequently pass unexamined.

At its origins, the paradigm married the concerns of neo-Malthusians regarding world population with the methods of systems analysis and **scenarios**. Neo-Malthusianism arose around the time of World War II; its marriage to systems analysis dates to the rise of computers in the post-War period. The most influential example is *The Limits to Growth* (Meadows et al. 1972), the landmark report of the Club of Rome's Project on the Predicament of Mankind.

After defining the predicament as reconciling economic and population growth with the limits of a finite world, the Club—a think-tank of "world citizens" from business, politics and academia—turned to Professor Jay

Forrester of the Massachusetts Institute of Technology to develop "a formal, written model of the world" based on "the scientific method, systems analysis, and the modern computer" (Meadows et al. 1972: 21). Forrester's models had originally been developed to understand industrial and corporate dynamics, but were subsequently applied to cities and the world. In his own report on the world model, Forrester (1971) concluded that industrialization was the prime driver of both population growth and environmental problems, and that developing countries therefore might best avoid future problems by not industrializing.

Although far more sophisticated than Malthus's principle of population, *The Limits to Growth* model relied, like Malthus, on the mathematical disparity between arithmetic and geometric (or exponential) growth. Exponential or "nonlinear" growth involves complicated positive feedbacks among subsystems; left unchecked, the authors warned, "the limits to growth on this planet will be reached sometime in the next one hundred years. The most probable result will be a rather sudden and uncontrollable decline in both population and industrial capacity" (Meadows et al. 1972: 23).

*The Limits to Growth* sparked raging debates in scholarly and policy realms, and its authors have twice published updated reports based on current data and model refinements (Meadows et al. 1992, 2004). But the basic conceptual framework has persisted while tools for quantifying the $X$s and $Y$s of carrying capacity have proliferated. These include the "IPAT formula"—Impact = Population × Affluence × Technology—to account for the relative impact of economically unequal populations, and ecological footprint analysis, which measures humanity's impacts in terms of the number of planets identical to Earth needed to supply our demands and absorb our wastes indefinitely (Wackernagel and Rees 1996). Values over 1.0 indicate and quantify "overshoot," and were reached in the late twentieth century. Ecological footprint analysis can also be conducted at smaller scales, and online "calculators" now enable consumers, investors, firms, cities, and nations to measure their footprints in real units of land and water. Scholarly subfields have emerged to measure "biocapacity" and identify ecological indicators of human impacts, such as the percentage of Earth's annual terrestrial and aquatic net primary production that is used or degraded by human activities.

Criticisms of the carrying capacity paradigm have also persisted, mainly among economists and other proponents of **liberal environmentalism** and **ecological modernization**. Some have challenged the quality of the models used in *The Limits to Growth* and subsequent studies. Others have simply dismissed the paradigm's advocates as

Cassandras whose predictions of collapse have failed the test of time. The recent world economic crisis and growing evidence of anthropogenic climate change, on the other hand, have buttressed the paradigm's supporters, who point out that Cassandra was, in fact, correct.

Overlooked in the debates are the underlying concepts and assumptions of the carrying capacities paradigm itself. From systems analysis, it inherited a commitment to models that were necessarily bounded and closed, so that they could be constructed and run as complex programs of equations and algorithms (see **Thermoeconomics**). This was (and arguably still is) seen as the cutting edge of scientific and technological practice, but it can account neither for un-modeled exogenous factors, nor for endogenous qualitative change in the model components and variables themselves.

Even more serious are the conceptual difficulties internal to the concept of carrying capacity itself. It would seem impossible, by definition, that humanity's ecological footprint could exceed 1.0 Earths. Proponents aver that lags in system response permit such a scenario. But this begs the question. Any $X:Y$ ratio derived from logic or models is an idealist postulate, empirical violations of which necessitate the invocation of some mediating factor or opposing force (e.g. Malthus's "misery and vice") that simultaneously enforces the putative limits—if not immediately, then in some indefinite future—and explains (away) the disparity between the ideal and the real. Exploiting the combination of positive and normative in its very definition, carrying capacity becomes immune to empirical test (Sayre 2008).

Over-shoot, in systems analysis, refers not to the measured disparity between burden and capacity, but to the failure of effective feedback mechanisms to enforce the postulated limit. Proponents of the carrying capacities paradigm are, in effect, trying to function as such a mechanism by alerting society to the growing environmental and social ills of industrial capitalism. It is a salutary ambition, but the rhetorical power of quantitative science does not appear sufficient to the task.

## References

Forrester, Jay W. 1971. *World Dynamics*. Cambridge, Wright-Allen Press Inc.

Meadows, Donella H., Dennis L. Meadows, Jorgen Randers, and William W. Behrens III. 1972. *The Limits to Growth*. New York, Universe Books.

Meadows, Donella H., Dennis L. Meadows, and Jorgen Randers. 1992. *Beyond the Limits*. Post Mills, Chelsea Green Publishing.

Meadows, Donella H., Jorgen Randers, and Dennis L. Meadows. 2004. *Limits to Growth: The 30-Year Update*. White River Junction, VT, Chelsea Green Publishing.

Sayre, Nathan F. 2008. "The Genesis, History, and Limits of Carrying Capacity."
*Annals of the Association of American Geographers* 98(1): 120–134.
Wackernagel, Mathis and William E. Rees. 1996. *Our Ecological Footprint.*
Philadelphia, PA, New Society Publishers.

# CITES

## Daniel Compagnon

*Sciences Po Bordeaux, France*

The Convention on International Trade in Endangered Species of Wild
Fauna and Flora (CITES) tackles one of the sources of biodiversity
depletion, the global trade in wildlife and wildlife products booming with
globalization that is worth billions of dollars every year. Although not all
of these animals and plants are in imminent danger of extinction, unlike
the black rhino, the Asian tiger, or the African elephant, the widely
publicized International Union for Conservation of Nature (IUCN) Red
List of Threatened Species released annually since 1963 vindicates the
need of international cooperation to regulate trade in wildlife.

A draft text adopted by the IUCN congress in 1963 led to the
agreement signed in Washington on March 3, 1973. The CITES came
into force on July 1, 1975, and there are now more than 175 parties to
it. Adopted in the wake of the 1972 Stockholm conference, it is one of
the few multilateral environmental agreements, where the United States—
on the basis of its robust domestic conservation legislation—still plays the
role of a lead state, and one reflecting from the onset predominantly
Western concerns about wildlife protection.

More than 33,000 species are listed on Appendix 1 (banning trade),
Appendix 2 (allowing limited trade with a quota system), or Appendix 3
(voluntary listing by at least one range state to monitor trade) with different
sets of countries involved, and various political and economic implications.
Therefore, it is more a collection of species-specific sub-regimes within
a common framework. CITES has been shaped by norms and ideas
as much as power relations or economic interests: the concept of
"endangered species" for instance was constructed through intense
debates between **conservation and preservation** (Mofson 1997)
approaches in the protection of emblematic species such as the African
elephant and big whales (Epstein 2006).

Relying on a system of import/export permits enforced by the member
states' customs and police, CITES is a relatively **effective** agreement in

terms of outputs and outcomes, but its impact has remained limited only because the causal relationship between trade and species extinction is problematic in most cases (Curlier and Andresen 2001), as illustrated by the controversy over the polar bear at the 2013 Conference of the Parties (COP). There are also several loopholes in the treaty: as a two-third majority vote is required for (de)listing, a small number of range states and partners in trade can exert a veto power. In addition, a member state can enter reservations alleging vital national interests within 90 days of the decision's adoption, and is then considered a non-party for such listing.

In practice, few of the 30–50 listing decisions voted at an average COP session are really controversial and in most cases outvoted states, even powerful ones, tend to accept unsavory listing decisions (Sand 1997), to preserve the credibility of the institution. Even the most discontented parties—such as the Southern Africa states after the 1989 elephant ivory ban—tend to remain in the regime and attempt to change it from within (Mofson 1997).

Although a species listing allocates costs and benefits to different parties and, therefore, is open to bargaining, coalition building, and veto power, CITES passed numerous decisions through a logic of arguing rather than bargaining. CITES procedures tend to favor decisions based on reasoned arguments, as population **assessment**s are usually disputed. The COP adopts or rejects proposals put forward by the **secretariat**, based on scientific information and a large deliberation process, in line with the reinforced listing criteria adopted in 1994 at COP 9 in Fort Lauderdale. When such consensus is built, the bargaining power of stakeholders has limited impact even on reservations entered (Gehring and Ruffing 2008).

CITES' impact is limited by the lack of **compliance and implementation** on the ground especially in least developed countries (LDCs), where legislation is inadequate, and state enforcement capacities often very weak (Compagnon et al. 2012). While a growing number of African states are unable to curb well-armed transnational gangs of poachers, an affluent middle class in Asian **emerging countries** boosts the demand while the Internet provides an easier and faster conduit for global criminal networks (Zimmerman 2003).

## References

Compagnon, Daniel, Sander Chan, and Ayçem Mert. 2012. "The Changing Role of the State." In *Global Environmental Governance Reconsidered*, Eds. Franck Biermann and Philipp Pattberg, 237–263. Cambridge, MA, MIT Press.
Curlier, Maaria and Steinar Andresen. 2001. "International Trade in Endangered Species: The CITES Regime." In *Environmental Regime Effectiveness: Confronting*

*Theory with Evidence*, Eds. Edward L. Miles, Arild Underdal, Steinar Andresen, Jørgen Wettestad, Jon Birger Skjaerseth, and Elaine M. Carlin, 357–378. Cambridge, MA, MIT Press.

Epstein, Charlotte. 2006. "The Making of Global Environmental Norms: Endangered Species Protection." *Global Environmental Politics* 6(2): 32–54.

Gehring, Thomas and Eva Ruffing. 2008. "When Arguments Prevail Over Power: The CITES Procedure for the Listing of Endangered Species." *Global Environmental Politics* 8(2): 123–148.

Mofson, Phyllis. 1997. "Zimbabwe and CITES: Illustrating the Reciprocal Relationship between the State and the International Regime." In *The Internationalization of Environmental Protection*, Eds. Miranda A. Schreurs and Elisabeth C. Economy, 162–187. Cambridge, Cambridge University Press.

Sand, Peter H. 1997. "Whither CITES? The Evolution of a Treaty Regime in the Borderland of Trade and Environment." *European Journal of International Law* 8(1): 29–58.

Zimmerman, Mara E. 2003. "The Black Market for Wildlife: Combating Transnational Organized Crime in the Illegal Wildlife Trade." *Vanderbilt Journal of Transnational Law* 36: 1657–1689.

# CLIMATE CHANGE REGIME

## Harro van Asselt

*Stockholm Environment Institute, Sweden*

Climate change gained prominence on the international political agenda in the 1980s, in part due to an emerging scientific consensus about the anthropogenic causes of the problem, and in part because of heightened public awareness. The commencement of **treaty negotiations** in 1990 exposed the diverging viewpoints of developed and developing countries on international climate policy (Bodansky 1993). The 1992 United Nations Framework Convention on Climate Change (UNFCCC) did not resolve the underlying tensions between countries but delivered a compromise through a framework agreement that postponed the more difficult challenges, including questions related to its overall ambition and the distribution of efforts. All countries acknowledged that developed countries had emitted the bulk of greenhouse gases during their rapid industrialization processes and that these countries should lead by reducing their emissions and provide financial and technological assistance to developing countries for environmental **justice**. However, the Convention neither included legally binding emission reduction targets nor did it specify how much assistance was needed.

The ultimate objective of the UNFCCC is to achieve "stabilization of greenhouse gas concentrations in the atmosphere at a level that would prevent dangerous anthropogenic interference with the climate system" (Article 2). In addition, the Convention lists several principles, most notably that of **common but differentiated responsibility** (CBDR). This principle was effectuated in the Convention by the introduction of a binary system of obligations for developed (Annex I) and for developing (non-Annex I) countries.

Following the framework-protocol example of the **ozone regime**, the 1997 Kyoto Protocol elaborated on the UNFCCC's provisions, by introducing legally binding emission targets for developed countries, which agreed to reduce their emissions by five percent compared to 1990 levels between 2008 and 2012. To assist developed countries in achieving these targets, it also introduced three flexibility mechanisms: Joint Implementation, the Clean Development Mechanism (CDM), and international emissions trading. The two first mentioned mechanisms are project-based emission crediting schemes, with Joint Implementation providing for trade in credits among industrialized countries, and the CDM for trading between industrialized and developing countries. International emissions trading, by contrast, is a "cap-and-trade" system, where an emission cap is set, and a fixed number of emission allowances are distributed among developed countries.

Although the Kyoto Protocol was a major step forward in terms of specifying targets and timetables for developed countries, it left many important details for future negotiations. These details included rules on the flexibility mechanisms, the **compliance and implementation** system, land use, land-use change and forestry, and the treaty's funding mechanisms (including funds for **adaptation** to climate change). Disagreements over these contentious issues led to a breakdown of the Conference of the Parties in 2001, which was compounded by the rejection of the Protocol by the George W. Bush Administration that same year. The United States' departure jeopardized the future of the agreement, as the entry into force of the Protocol required ratification by at least fifty-five states representing at least 55 percent of $CO_2$ emissions of Annex I countries in 1990. However, compromises brokered by the European Union to secure the crucial participation of other developed countries such as Canada and Russia ensured that the Protocol could enter into force in 2005.

With the Protocol's rulebook largely in place, and implementation having begun in most countries, the shape of international climate policy beyond 2012 became a key issue in international discussions. The design and **effectiveness** of the climate regime, and in particular the Kyoto

27

Protocol, had increasingly come under attack, with critics (e.g. Victor 2004; Prins and Rayner 2007) pointing to: the incongruence between the Kyoto targets and the level of mitigation required to avoid dangerous climate change; the absence of targets for developing countries; problems with the flexibility mechanisms (particularly the CDM); and weaknesses in the compliance mechanism (which arguably did not prevent Canada from withdrawing from the Protocol in 2011).

The post-2012 negotiations, which were formally launched by the Bali Action Plan in 2007, displayed fault lines among parties to the Convention related to these issues, but in particular with respect to the Annex I/non-Annex I "firewall." Concerned by the growing emissions of **emerging countries** such as Brazil, South Africa, India, and China (the "BASIC" countries), developed countries such as the United States argued that developing countries should step up their mitigation efforts. Developing countries, on the other hand, were disappointed by the lack of progress of developed countries, in particular with respect to the provision of climate finance and the transfer of clean technologies. Faced with the fact that most other major economies had no binding constraints on their emissions under international law, the European Union—also coping with domestic concerns about competitiveness and a recession—became an increasingly reluctant leader, even though it was on track toward meeting its Kyoto targets (e.g. Jordan et al. 2010).

Parties in Bali agreed to negotiate a new climate agreement two years later, but notoriously failed to do so in Copenhagen in 2009. The Copenhagen Accord—which was negotiated among a very small group of countries—nevertheless provided the basis for subsequent agreements that arguably have led the climate regime in a new direction (Rajamani 2011). The path indicated by the Copenhagen Accord and subsequent agreements in Cancún (2010) and Durban (2011) is one that shifts from the "targets-and-timetables" approach introduced by the Kyoto Protocol, toward a system of self-selected mitigation commitments and actions accompanied by international monitoring, **reporting**, and verification procedures. Under this new approach, differentiation between groups of developed and developing countries is becoming increasingly less important.

The future of the climate regime remains uncertain. While parties in Durban in 2011 agreed to negotiate "a protocol, another legal instrument or an agreed outcome with legal force under the Convention" by 2015, it is unclear to what extent this agreement will build on the Kyoto Protocol, or whether it will rather reflect the new direction headed into after Copenhagen. In addition, the global response to the climate problem is likely to be influenced by **institutional interactions** between the climate regime and a plethora of initiatives outside of the UNFCCC by public and private actors across multiple scales, in areas such as carbon **markets**, clean energy technology and REDD+ (Biermann et al. 2009).

### References

Biermann, Frank, Philipp Pattberg, Harro van Asselt, and Fariborz Zelli. 2009. "The Fragmentation of Global Governance Architectures: A Framework for Analysis." *Global Environmental Politics* 9(4): 14–40.

Bodansky, Daniel M. 1993. "The United Nations Framework Convention on Climate Change: A Commentary." *Yale Journal of International Law* 18(2): 451–558.

Jordan, Andrew, Dave Huitema, Harro van Asselt, Tim Rayner, and Frans Berkhout (Eds.). 2010. *Climate Change Policy in the European Union: Confronting the Dilemmas of Mitigation and Adaptation?*. Cambridge, Cambridge University Press.

Prins, Gwyn and Steve Rayner. 2007. "Time to Ditch Kyoto." *Nature* 449(7165): 973–975.

Rajamani, Lavanya. 2011. "The Cancun Climate Change Agreements: Reading the Text, Subtext and Tealeaves." *International and Comparative Law Quarterly* 60(2): 499–519.

Victor, David G. 2004. *The Collapse of the Kyoto Protocol and the Struggle to Slow Global Warming*. Princeton, NJ, Princeton University Press.

# COMMISSION ON SUSTAINABLE DEVELOPMENT

**Lynn M. Wagner**

*International Institute for Sustainable Development, Canada*

An examination of the Commission on Sustainable Development (CSD) offers a window on the intergovernmental **sustainable development** policy-making process between the 1992 United Nations Conference on Environment and Development (UNCED, also called Earth Summit) and the 2012 UN Conference on Sustainable Development (also called Rio+20) (see **Summit diplomacy**). The UNCED action plan, titled "Agenda 21," called for the creation of the CSD to ensure the effective follow-up of the Conference, and the Commission began with much of the euphoria that followed the Earth Summit (Chasek 2000). The CSD comprised fifty-three member states of the United Nations that were elected on a rotating basis, although all UN member states could participate in its annual sessions, which were facilitated by a dedicated

**secretariat**. It was established as a functional commission of the Economic and Social Council (ECOSOC), which meant its decisions were forwarded to the annual ECOSOC session for final approval.

Twenty years later, however, CSD delegates had failed to come to agreement at two annual sessions, and even sessions that had reached negotiated agreements were not deemed to have lived up to the CSD's potential (Doran and Van Alstine 2007; Wagner 2013). Intergovernmental Sustainable Development governance had become crowded with institutionalized processes launched for many issue areas, divisions among developed and developing countries had become more intense, and the CSD had failed to establish "a clear set of 'user groups' or customers" for its outputs (Doran and Van Alstine 2007: 139). Delegates at Rio+20 replaced the CSD with a "high-level political forum," which was to benefit from the "strengths, experiences, resources and inclusive participation modalities" of the CSD. As subsequently established, the high-level political forum will hold annual meetings under the auspices of a revitalized ECOSOC, but every four years it will also convene under the auspices of the UN General Assembly at the level of Heads of State and Government.

The CSD offers a case study in how the placement within the UN system bureaucracy has affected an institution's ability to meet its mandate. Initially, Bigg and Dodds (1997) indicated the CSD had "vertical and horizontal" linkages with other parts of the UN system, and the CSD's efforts were complemented by support from other areas in the UN bureaucracy that were focused on sustainable development. Several years later, however, Wagner (2005) notes that the United Nations system pivoted to focus on achieving the Millennium Development Goals. Wagner (2005) and Kaasa (2007) evaluate the CSD's **effectiveness** subsequent to this change, and identify benefits to the CSD's lower-level status—it provided a forum for intergovernmental discussions on issues not addressed in other fora and it helped to set the intergovernmental agenda on some topics—but neither analysis finds the CSD to be completely effective.

Scholars have also focused on CSD member states' **negotiating coalitions** and the CSD's role in bringing in non-state actors for greater **participation** in the discussion on the requirements of sustainable development with governments: "One of the singular achievements of the CSD is its commitment to a highly participatory approach and a commitment to opportunities for all Agenda 21 stakeholders . . . to take the floor and address their concerns directly to government delegations" (Doran and Van Alstine 2007: 132).

## References

Bigg, T. and Felix Dodds. 1997. "The UN Commission on Sustainable Development." In *The Way Forward: Beyond Agenda 21*, Ed. Felix Dodds, 15–36. London, Earthscan Publications.

Chasek, Pamela. 2000. "The UN Commission on Sustainable Development: The First Five Years." In *The Global Environment in the Twenty-first Century: Prospects for International Cooperation*, Ed. Pamela S. Chasek, 378–398. Tokyo, United Nations University.

Doran, Peter and James Van Alstine. 2007. "The Fourteenth Session of the UN Commission on Sustainable Development: The Energy Session." *Environmental Politics* 16(1): 130–142.

Kaasa, Stine Madland. 2007. "The UN Commission on Sustainable Development: Which Mechanisms Explain Its Accomplishments?" *Global Environmental Politics* 7(3): 107–129.

Wagner, Lynn M. 2005. "A Commission Will Lead Them? The UN Commission on Sustainable Development and UNCED Follow-Up." In *Global Challenges: Furthering the Multilateral Process for Sustainable Development*, Eds. Angela Churie Kallhauge, Gunnar Sjöstedt, and Elisabeth Corell, 103–122. Sheffield, Greenleaf Publishing.

Wagner, Lynn M. 2013. "A Forty-Year Search for a Single-Negotiating Text: Rio+20 as a Post-Agreement Negotiation." *International Negotiation* 18(3): 333–356.

# COMMON BUT DIFFERENTIATED RESPONSIBILITY

## Steve Vanderheiden
*University of Colorado Boulder, United States*

The 1992 Rio Earth Summit yielded two influential formulations of this principle of international law and North–South equity in **sustainable development**. The first, from the Rio Declaration, states that:

> In view of the different contributions to global environmental degradation, states have common but differentiated responsibilities. The developed countries acknowledge the responsibility that they bear in the international pursuit of sustainable development in view of the pressures their societies place on the global environment and of the technologies and financial resources they command (Principle 7).

31

In the second, 192 signatory nations adopted this "common but differentiated responsibility" (or CBDR) framework for assigning national climate change burdens through the **climate change regime**. While the primary manifestation of CBDR in international climate policy development was in the division of parties into Annex I developed countries that were assigned greenhouse gas reduction targets under the 1997 Kyoto Protocol and non-Annex I developing country parties that were not, the principle suggests bases for further differentiation of climate change-related burdens. As a result, scholars look to this treaty language in an effort to apply CBDR principles to the design of post-Kyoto climate policy architecture in seeking fair or just burden-sharing arrangements.

Scholars identify CBDR as a key burden-sharing principle, along with equity and capacity, which appear alongside it in the treaty, but interpret those principles differently and defend them in various combinations in articulating competing environmental **justice** frameworks. Equity has often been taken to entail equal per capita national emissions entitlements, while scholars typically rely upon Growth Domestic Product (GDP) as a measure of "respective capability," with more affluent states being assigned greater burdens and poorer ones lesser ones or categorical exemptions from mandatory action. Some have suggested modifications that account for shares of GDP associated with development interests (Baer et al. 2009), and others use capacity as a proxy for beneficiary-pays principles on the assumption that states benefitting most from past emissions are more affluent as a result (Page 2012).

Neither equity nor capacity has received the attention paid by scholars to CBDR, which has been interpreted in two primary ways with several variants on each. Since it appeals to each party's "differentiated responsibility" for contributing to climate change, this responsibility is widely viewed as a function of national greenhouse gas emissions. However, different approaches focus upon different national emissions data, and propose different modifications to that data in order to arrive at distinct burden-sharing formulae. Historical responsibility approaches rely upon each nation's full historical emissions, going back to early industrialization, resulting in relatively greater responsibility assigned to early industrializers such as Europe and the United States and relatively lesser burdens for later-developing countries, for example **emerging countries** such as China and India (Shue 1999). Others propose baseline years before which national emissions are exempted from responsibility **assessments**, arguing that prior emissions resulted from excusable ignorance, thus constituting causal but not moral responsibility for climate change. 1990 is often proposed as a baseline year, since it marked the release of the first Intergovernmental Panel on Climate Change assessment report, clearly linking human activities with climate change and thus undermining subsequent claims that governments lacked adequate knowledge of such causes.

Apart from differences in national greenhouse gas emissions records used to assess differentiated responsibility, scholars have proposed other modifications to or exemptions from such emissions data. Drawing on analyses similar to those associated with excusable ignorance, in which parties are held liable for that share of their causal contributions to a problem for which they can be faulted or expected to act otherwise (see **Liability**), some have proposed distinctions between those emissions associated with meeting basic needs (or survival emissions) and those associated with further affluence (or luxury emissions), counting the latter but exempting the former from national responsibility assessments (Vanderheiden 2008). If accepted, this exemption would shift burdens away from developing countries with relatively low per capita emissions onto developed countries with relatively high luxury emissions. Similarly, scholars have proposed variations in calculation of survival emissions in order to account for geographical or other differences in the energy or land use budgets needed to satisfy basic needs.

All CBDR formulations share the normative foundation for assigning national burdens for climate change in some version of the **polluter pays principle**, but interpret the demands of that principle differently. Historical responsibility versions follow accounts based on strict **liability**, assigning national burdens in proportion to total historical national emissions, given the long atmospheric life of greenhouse gases and commitment to viewing causation as the basis for responsibility. Those proposing various exemptions to national emissions records invoke fault-based interpretations of the principle, appealing either to legal constructions of fault in liability or accounts of moral responsibility that distinguish between faultless and culpable causation. In addition to offering competing formulations of that principle, scholars defend competing burden-sharing formulae in which versions of CBDR are paired with equity or capacity principles (Caney 2005), combining multiple environmental **justice** principles.

Politically, CBDR remains a core ideal for burden-sharing arrangements associated with international climate policy, and of sustainable development more generally, but one around which agreement has been elusive. Since different formulations entail different assignments of national liability for climate change, national delegations to climate policy conferences tend to endorse formulations that reflect national interests, with India defending historical responsibility approaches combined with exemptions for survival emissions and developed countries generally

33

seeking to avoid official adoption of responsibility-based liability criteria. The United States has expressly rejected any interpretation of CBDR in international law that implies acceptance of "any international obligations or liabilities, or any diminution in the responsibilities of developing countries" (French 2000). Nonetheless, considerations of environmental justice in international efforts to fairly allocate the burdens associated with climate change demand that attention be paid to the development of such principles, acceptable versions of which may be necessary for the world's nations to overcome the **tragedy of the commons** that frustrates cooperative international action on climate change and produce agreement upon effective remedial climate policy architecture.

## References

Baer, Paul, Tom Athanasiou, Sivan Kartha, and Eric Kemp-Benedict. 2009. "Greenhouse Development Rights: A Proposal for a Fair Climate Treaty." *Ethics, Place and Environment* 12(3): 267–281.

Caney, Simon. 2005. "Cosmopolitan Justice, Responsibility, and Global Climate Change." *Leiden Journal of International Law* 18(4): 747–775.

French, Duncan. 2000. "Developing States and International Environmental Law: The Importance of Differentiated Responsibilities." *International and Comparative Law Quarterly* 49(1): 35–60.

Page, Edward. 2012. "Give it Up for Climate Change: A Defense of the Beneficiary Pays Principle." *International Theory* 4(2): 300–330.

Shue, Henry. 1999. "Global Environment and International Inequality." *International Affairs* 75(3): 531–545.

Vanderheiden, Steve. 2008. *Atmospheric Justice: A Political Theory of Climate Change.* New York, Oxford University Press.

# COMMON HERITAGE OF MANKIND

## Scott J. Shackelford

*Indiana University, United States*

In 1968, during the twenty-second session of the UN General Assembly, Arvid Pardo, the Maltese delegate, called for an international **regime** to "govern the deep seabed" under international waters (Viikari 2002: 33). He proposed that the seabed should be declared the Common Heritage of Mankind (CHM), which it eventually became in 1970, leading to Pardo being called the "Father of the Law of the Sea conference." What made the CHM concept so revolutionary is that it was the first codification of a common property rights concept that transcended national **sovereignty**. Instead of countries, the CHM dealt directly with humanity as a whole in a way that "transcends national boundaries and unites all peoples under the flag of universalism," a form of cosmopolitan global governance (Baslar 1998: 25).

The CHM arose from two observations. First, some valuable natural resources, such as the ones managed under the **fisheries governance**, were close to exhaustion, and developing nations wanted to ensure that they had some degree of access before they were depleted. Second, the technological divide between developing and developed nations prohibited developing states from reaping the rewards that the developed nations would enjoy as technological advances enabled access to valuable new resource domains, unless **technology transfer** was enforced. The notion was to create a level playing field or, short of that, to share benefits equitably (Baslar 1998: 301).

Neither scholars nor policymakers have agreed on a common understanding of the CHM, but a working definition would likely comprise five main elements (Frakes 2003: 411–413). First, there can be no appropriation of a common heritage space, though some scholars have argued that this prohibition should not necessarily be viewed as a significant impediment to regulation (Baslar 1998: 90, 235). Second, all nations must work together to manage global common pool resources and **global public goods**. As collective management is impractical, though, a specialized agency must be created to aid in coordination, such as the International Seabed Authority that manages deep seabed mining. Third, all nations must share in the benefits derived from exploiting global common pool resources in common heritage regions. Fourth, these spaces should be used for peaceful purposes. But what constitutes "peaceful" differs depending on the common heritage region in question; the **Antarctic Treaty regime**, for example, equates peaceful use with barring "any measures of a military nature" (Baslar 1998: 106), which differs from the more permissive definition in the 1967 Treaty on Principles Governing the Activities of States in the Exploration and Use of Outer Space, Including the Moon and Other Celestial Bodies. The latter accord, commonly known as the Outer Space Treaty, preserves space "exclusively for peaceful purposes" and even addresses the "harmful contamination" of outer space, but it has not directly led to the sustainable, peaceful use of space, in part because of ambiguity in the treaty language. Finally, common heritage regions must be protected for posterity, highlighting the intergenerational equity considerations at the heart of the CHM (see **Justice**).

The CHM concept has been the subject of debate in disciplines ranging from archaeology and economics to public international law, including space law and international environment law. It is now treaty law in the 1982 **Law of the Sea Convention** of the United Nations, the 1983 International Understanding on Plant Genetic Resources, and has found expression in the controversial 1979 Agreement Governing the Activities of States on the Moon and Other Celestial Bodies. However, the amorphous CHM concept that has in large part governed global commons areas since the 1960s is under stress (Baslar 1998: 372–373). For example, international environmental treaties have avoided CHM terminology to describe the atmosphere (Boyle 1991: 1–3).

What, then, is the future of the CHM concept and its ability to ward off a **tragedy of the commons**? Some legal scholars such as Kemal Baslar have argued for a return to common property regulation through recognizing the CHM in environmental governance as a **human and environmental right** and general principle of international law, which could foster greater acceptance of the concept by the international community (1998: 368–369). Others prefer incorporating the core tenants of the CHM concept into the **sustainable development** movement and its pillars of economic and social development, as well as inter- and intra-generational equity and environmental **conservation and preservation** (Ellis 2008: 644). Although sustainable development suffers from some of the same ambiguities as the CHM concept, by avoiding the controversies surrounding the CHM concept, sustainable development may help carry the core CHM element of the equitable, sustainable use of global common pool resources into the twenty-first century.

## References

Baslar, Kemal. 1998. *The Concept of the Common Heritage of Mankind in International Law*. The Hague, Martinus Nijhoff Publishers.

Boyle, Alan E. 1991. "International Law and the Protection of the Atmosphere: Concepts, Categories and Principles." In *International Law and Global Climate Change*, Eds. Robin R. Churchill and David Freestone, 7–19. London, Kluwer Law International.

Ellis, Jaye. 2008. "Sustainable Development as a Legal Principle: A Rhetorical Analysis". In *Select Proceedings of the European Society of International Law*, Eds. Hélène Ruiz Fabri, Rüdiger Wolfrum, and Jana Gogolin, 641–660. Oxford, Hart Publishing.

Frakes, Jennifer. 2003. "The Common Heritage of Mankind Principle and the Deep Seabed, Outer Space, and Antarctica: Will Developed and Developing Nations Reach a Compromise?" *Wisconsin International Law Journal* 21: 409–434.

Viikari, Lotta. 2002. *From Manganese Nodules to Lunar Regolith: A Comparative Legal Study of the Utilization of Natural Resources in the Deep Seabed and Outer Space.* Lapland, Lapland University Press.

# COMPLIANCE AND IMPLEMENTATION

## Sandrine Maljean-Dubois

*Aix-Marseille Université, France*

Since the 1990s and after two decades of abundant law-making activities, scholars and practitioners are still searching for ways and means to improve the **effectiveness** of international environmental law, in particular that of treaty-based obligations. Indeed, the implementation of international law suffers from longstanding difficulties, implementation being understood as measures—legislative, administrative, or judicial— that parties take so as to make international agreements operative in international and domestic law (Young 1999).

The lack of implementation comes from various factors, including the softness of international obligations in this field (often vague, indeterminate, open-textured, non-quantified, and non-self-executing) or the specificities of environmental harm. It can also come from the fact that states have no or little available capacity to meet the various requirements imposed by international environmental law.

Traditional means of response to violations of international obligations do not fit to the needs in the environmental field, and even though international **dispute resolution mechanisms** are developing, it is still exceptional and in several respects poorly tailored to control compliance to obligations arising from multilateral treaties. Similarly, countermeasures are not particularly suited for environmental protection because states' obligations are non-reciprocal and based on a collective and superior interest.

One of the ways to address these difficulties and enhance the protection of the environment is to improve the monitoring and response mechanisms to non-compliance (Sand 1992). Such monitoring has to be tailored to the numerous peculiarities of this specific field of international cooperation. In the eyes of the common interest pursued by all Contracting Parties, it is more appropriate to financially or technically assist the state in difficulties than to ask for state **liability** (Chayes and Chayes 1995). In most cases, cooperation and assistance will fruitfully replace sanction. With a view to promoting the treaty implementation,

37

some means for remedy are proposed to the states, along with possible legal, technical, and financial assistances if necessary. Some believe it is more important to promote compliance than to punish non-compliance, especially as the use of sanctions would discourage states' participation and thus encourage free riding.

All these factors prompted efforts to find alternative ways of settling disputes with an essentially preventive vocation and to the introduction of innovative international monitoring procedures inspired in part by tried and tested methods in other legal fields (such as disarmament or human rights). Since the 1990s, several environmental agreements have succeeded in reinventing themselves, and completed **reporting** and other monitoring methods (monitoring networks, inquiries) with more specific, ambitious, global, and coherent mechanisms to institutionalize monitoring and response to non-compliance.

In most cases, a compliance committee is established by the Conference of Parties, which specifies its composition, mandate, decision-making powers, rules of procedure, and its relationship to other bodies. Most of these committees are designed to prevent non-compliance and facilitate compliance. When non-compliance is found, they can help non-compliance states to return to compliance, for example using **technology transfer** or capacity building assistance. They can also sanction non-compliance and settle disputes. In such cases, monitoring and control are no longer bilateral and reciprocal but multilateral and centralized, placed in the hands of treaty bodies (Conferences of Parties, subsidiary organs, and **secretariats**) as a response to non-compliance, which includes assistance and incentives in addition to actual sanctions (carrots and sticks). Collective measures appear to be more readily adopted, better tolerated and, in principle, less discretionary. Procedures are implemented with flexibility, using soft enforcement and generally a non-adversarial approach. Although in theory the different stages of the compliance-control cycle can be distinguished, in practice the boundaries between these stages are porous, and a situation can trigger the whole extent of compliance-control procedures and stages, from facilitation to enforcement. Non-compliance mechanisms are alternatives to traditional Dispute Resolution Mechanisms but they leave them untouched. Consequently, dispute resolution mechanisms can—at least in theory—complement non-compliance ones in certain cases. Finally, these procedures are used for assessing the **effectiveness** of states' obligations as well as clarifying and developing these obligations. They also foster collective "learning by doing" and increase **transparency**, which in turn builds confidence and limits free riding (Brown Weiss and Jacobson 1998; Maljean-Dubois and Rajamani 2011).

The first non-compliance procedure of an environmental treaty was drawn up in 1990 in the framework of the Montreal Protocol of the **ozone regime**. This pioneering procedure has already been taken up and adapted by a dozen other environmental conventions, becoming little by little a standard practice. Although inspired by the same model, all these procedures have peculiarities of their own.

The Kyoto Protocol of the **climate change regime** has for instance given rise to the most comprehensive non-compliance procedure to date. The importance of the environmental issues at stake and the specificity of the Protocol, which uses economic tools, explain the step taken and its degree of refinement. The monitoring and control procedure is very coherent and intrusive. Divided into two branches, a facilitative branch and an enforcement one, the Compliance Committee is quasi-judicial. Potential sanctions are essentially intended to be dissuasive. However, this procedure could be replaced within the future international climate regime by a softer one, the so-called MRV system for "Monitoring, Reporting, Verification" that applies to pledges made in the framework of the climate change regime since the 2009 Copenhagen Accord.

The non-compliance mechanism of the Aarhus Convention on Access to Information, Public Participation in Decision-Making and Access to Justice in Environmental Matters (1998) provides another remarkable example because of the powers the public is granted under the Compliance Committee's procedure. It may be triggered by a party making a submission on compliance by another party, a party making a submission concerning its own compliance, a referral by the **secretariat** and, something that remains most unusual in non-compliance mechanisms, by members of the public who can submit communications concerning a party's compliance with the Convention. In practice, this is by far the most used and it greatly improves **participation** (Treves 2009).

## References

Brown Weiss, Edith and Harold K. Jacobson. 1998. *Engaging Countries: Strengthening Compliance with International Environmental Accords*. Cambridge, MA, MIT Press.

Chayes, Abram and Antonia H. Chayes. 1995. *The New Sovereignty: Compliance with Treaties in International Regulatory Regimes*. Cambridge, MA, Harvard University Press.

Maljean-Dubois, Sandrine and Lavanya Rajamani (Eds.). 2011. *Implementation of International Environmental Law*. The Hague Academy of International Law, Martinus Nijhoff.

Sand, Peter. 1992. *The Effectiveness of International Environmental Law: A Survey of Existing Legal Instruments*. Cambridge, Grotius Publications.

Treves, Tullio (Ed.). 2009. *Non-Compliance Procedures and Mechanisms and the Effectiveness of International Environmental Agreements*. The Hague, Asser Press.
Young, Oran. 1999. *The Effectiveness of International Environmental Regimes: Causal Connections and Behavioral Mechanisms*. Cambridge, MA, MIT Press.

# CONSERVATION AND PRESERVATION

## Jean-Frédéric Morin
*Université libre de Bruxelles, Belgium*

## Amandine Orsini
*Université Saint-Louis - Bruxelles, Belgium*

How should the environment be protected? Two opposite stances have addressed this question. Proponents of a conservationist approach argue that humans have to intervene on the environment to actively favor **sustainable development**. They believe for example that **ecosystem services** and goods provided by forests (timber, recreation, landscapes, etc.) can only be enjoyed by several generations over time if forestry techniques (species selection, logging methods etc.) are used to ensure that cover and quality of forests remain constant over time. In contrast, advocates of a preservationist approach consider that humans should shy away as much as possible from nature. They claim that management techniques have harmful consequences, while natural processes, such as wildfires or species extinction, are necessary regenerative episodes that should be neither favored nor prevented by human intervention (Epstein 2006).

Among the first conservationist advocates were hunters, farmers, and fishermen who, at the end of the nineteenth century, called for international cooperation to ensure the sustainable exploitation of natural resources and secure their activity. As a result of their efforts, several agreements were concluded such as the 1881 International Phylloxera Convention, which aimed at protecting European wineries from American pests, or the 1902 Convention for the Protection of Birds Useful to Agriculture, protecting insectivorous birds. Since the 1980s, several developing countries have endorsed this conservationist approach as a way of protecting their economic interests. For example, they actively support the 1992 **biodiversity regime**, which aims at favoring the conservation of biodiversity, its sustainable use, and the sharing of benefits that arise from this use.

Preservationist arguments have also deeply influenced international environmental politics. **Nongovernmental organizations** such as the Sierra Club and the Royal Society for the Protection of Birds have pushed states to create protected areas to preserve wildlife. Several international treaties were concluded to promote the creation of natural parks, including the 1940 Convention on Nature Protection and Wildlife Preservation in the Western Hemisphere, the 1971 **Wetlands Convention** and the 1972 Convention Concerning the Protection of World Cultural and Natural Heritage. In some controversial cases, the creation of protected areas on preservationist grounds led to the eviction of **indigenous peoples and local communities** from their traditional land (Adams and Hutton 2007). Other preservationist agreements aim at preserving specific species irrespective of their location, such as the 1973 **CITES** and the 1979 Bonn Convention on Migratory Species of Wild Animals. These treaties are based on scientific, recreational, esthetic grounds or on **ecocentrism**, not on the desire to conserve natural resources for future exploitation.

In some international **regimes**, conservationist and preservationist views openly clash. It is notoriously the case at the **International Whaling Commission**, where Japan advocates for sustainable hunting practices while the United States and other countries support preservation and are opposed to all whaling activity, even for species that are not endangered. There are also heated debates under the **CITES**, as some African countries, such as Kenya, favor a strict ban on the trade of ivory while others, including Zimbabwe, argue that an unmanaged elephant population can negatively impact the ecosystem while ivory sales can fund conservation (Stiles 2004). In several other regimes, however, conservationist and preservationist views coexist without open normative conflicts.

### References

Adams, William and Jon Hutton. 2007. "People, Parks and Poverty: Political Ecology and Biodiversity Conservation." *Conservation and Society* 5(2): 147–183.

Epstein, Charlotte. 2006. "The Making of Global Environmental Norms: Endangered Species Protection." *Global Environmental Politics* 6(2): 32–54.

Stiles, Daniel. 2004. "The Ivory Trade and Elephant Conservation." *Environmental Conservation* 31(4): 309–321.

# CORPORATE SOCIAL RESPONSIBILITY

## Jennifer Clapp and Ian H. Rowlands

*University of Waterloo, Canada*

Corporate social responsibility (CSR) refers broadly to actions that **business and corporations** voluntarily undertake both to promote social and environmental goals and to minimize any potential social and environmental costs associated with their business activities. The rationale behind CSR is that firms themselves are best placed to ensure **compliance and implementation** and to monitor progress toward their own environmental and social performance targets and will do so because it makes good business sense.

The 1960–70s saw strengthening of environmental regulations in many states, and environmental agencies to uphold those rules were established in most countries by the early 1980s. With the rise of **liberal environmentalism** after the mid 1980s, however, state-driven "command-and-control" type environmental regulations began to lose favor with governments, opening space for more flexible voluntary corporate-driven approaches to governing the environmental impact of business and corporations. Initially there was some concern about whether firms that adopted CSR within their business model would be able to fulfill their fiduciary duty to shareholders to prioritize financial earnings. This concern followed Milton Friedman's belief that firms' primary responsibility was to generate profits and not take social issues into consideration (Fleming et al. 2013).

By the early 1990s business leader Stephan Schmidheiny, then head of the Business Council for Sustainable Development, an organization established in 1990 to represent the voice of business leaders at the 1992 Rio Earth Summit, began to champion CSR. He argued that firms must "change course" to put social and environmental issues at the center of their decision-making because it was in the firm's economic interest to do so. He termed this concept "eco-efficiency." The rationale was simple: CSR would help firms to cut costs through efficiency gains from fewer required inputs and reduced waste, while at the same time the green image of firms would help to create new **markets** (Schmidheiny 1992).

Most global business leaders embraced CSR by the early 2000s and it became widely accepted that business knows best how to design and implement environmental measures more efficiently than one-size-fits-all command-and-control regulations. Today, many see CSR as a *de facto* condition for business success. Most international firms undertake some sort of CSR-type activities, such as **reporting, labeling, and certification**, demonstrating how entrenched CSR has become as a normative frame in global governance (Dashwood 2012).

Individual CSR reporting by firms is perhaps the most widespread type of CSR activity. Most transnational corporations now produce regular CSR reports. Self-reported CSR activities typically range from broad statements about commitment to "doing right" for the environment to details on specific programs or initiatives. One of the drawbacks of individual CSR reporting is that firms can be selective in what they choose to report, shaping their own environmental image without necessarily meeting any externally set standards. For example, in 2000 the transnational oil firm British Petroleum widely trumpeted its green energy activities in a major public relations campaign "Beyond Petroleum," while the vast majority of its investments remained in oil and gas exploration in subsequent years. This type of selective CSR approach led to claims by critics of greenwashing.

The vulnerability of firms to external critique for selective CSR reporting was one of the factors behind the rise of collective approaches to CSR. An early industry-established environmental code of conduct was Responsible Care, a chemical industry environmental and safety initiative that was a direct industry response to the chemical **disaster** in Bhopal, India, in 1984. Some corporate codes of conduct involve non-industry stakeholders, such as **nongovernmental organizations** and/or international organizations. The Global Reporting Initiative, for example, is a multi-stakeholder initiative that establishes standards for CSR reporting (Utting and Clapp 2008).

Other multi-stakeholder initiatives involve standards to which firms could gain certification, such as the Forest Stewardship Council standards for sustainable timber and the International Organization for Standardization's ISO 14000 series of environmental management standards (Auld et al. 2008). ISO 26000 is a new standard (launched in 2010) that guides businesses and organizations on best practices regarding social responsibility. While the growing participation of firms in collective CSR initiatives such as those outlined here does show firms' commitment to a higher level of scrutiny over their practices, they are still voluntary and typically do not apply sanctions for noncompliance. Moreover, they have been critiqued for lacking **transparency** and for being process rather than outcome focused.

Debates that define the literature on CSR today tend to fall into two broad categories. The first focuses on firm-level behavior and examines firms' motivations for undertaking CSR and whether activities are transformational, transitional, or marginal in terms of their impact (Crane et al. 2009). Detailed case studies on the impact of CSR and its variation across sectors and according to firm size and location have begun to shed light on these questions, but as yet the jury is still out on the broader questions of firm motivation and impact.

The second key area under debate with respect to CSR focuses on implications of industry self-regulation for governance more broadly. These debates focus on whether CSR activities are sufficient "replacements" for state-based regulation, such as performance standards or **taxation**. Further, these debates also probe what kinds of influence corporations have in shaping global environmental governance and ask what the implications of their participation in multi-stakeholder initiatives are for broader goals such as legitimacy, accountability, transparency, and **effectiveness** (Scherer and Palazzo 2011). Broader conceptual work on these questions has pointed to a blurring of the public and private realms with respect to governance, but whether the firm level "eco-efficiency" (some business and corporations being "less bad") can lead to a more transformational "eco-effectiveness" (all business and corporations doing "good") (McDonough and Braungart 2010) remains to be seen.

### References

Auld, Graeme, Steven Bernstein, and Benjamin Cashore. 2008. "The New Corporate Social Responsibility." *Annual Review of Environment and Resources* 33: 413–435.

Crane, Andrew, Dirk Matten, Abagail McWilliams, Jeremy Moon, and Donald Siegel (Eds.). 2009. *The Oxford Handbook of Corporate Social Responsibility.* Oxford, Oxford University Press.

Dashwood, Hevina S. 2012. *The Rise of Global Corporate Social Responsibility: Mining and the Spread of Social Norms.* Cambridge, Cambridge University Press.

Fleming, Peter, John Roberts, and Christina Garsten. 2013. "In Search of Corporate Social Responsibility." *Organization* 20: 337–348.

McDonough, William and Michael Braungart. 2010. *Cradle to Cradle: Remaking the Way We Make Things.* New York, Macmillan.

Scherer, Andreas G. and Guido Palazzo. 2011. "The New Political Role of Business in a Globalized World: A Review of a New Perspective on CSR and its Implications for the Firm, Governance, and Democracy." *Journal of Management Studies* 48(4): 899–931.

Schmidheiny, Stephan. 1992. *Changing Course: A Global Business Perspective on Development and the Environment.* Cambridge, MA, MIT Press.

Utting, Peter and Jennifer Clapp (Eds.). 2008. *Corporate Accountability and Sustainable Development.* Oxford, Oxford University Press.

# CRITICAL POLITICAL ECONOMY

## Peter Newell

*University of Sussex, United Kingdom*

Critical political economy approaches to the study and practice of global environmental politics take a range of different forms, but often have as their starting point a set of questions about who governs and how, what is to be governed (and what is not) and on whose behalf (Newell 2008). Though these relate to the classic concerns of political economy: who wins, who loses, how and why, most critical accounts tend to situate global institutional arrangements established to manage the global environment within broader social relations (of class, race, and gender for example) and structures of power. This helps to clarify who is afforded environmental protection by global environmental governance, who is not, how and why. They also place relationships of power between states, **business and corporations** (capital), and international institutions at the heart of their analysis because these affect the nature of global action on the environment and what states are able to do (Paterson 2001). Thus, for many critical perspectives capitalism and its inequities and the organization of the global economy along neoliberal lines offer more clues to the nature and extent of responses to the environment than a narrower focus on specific features of institutions charged with managing the environment and a primary focus on the state in isolation from these social relations.

Many critical accounts developed in the wake of the Earth Summit in 1992 from a political ecology tradition drew attention to the power and influence of **businesses and corporations** in undermining **effective** global responses to environmental threats such as climate change and biodiversity loss (Chatterjee and Finger 1994) and promoting a model of development that was at odds with the stated aim of protecting the environment. Academics then sought to develop theoretical approaches to explain the way in which challenges to capitalism were muted and managed by powerful actors and interests. Some made use of Gramsci's understanding of hegemony to explore the ways in which state and corporate elites accommodate challenges to their power and profits while developing responses to environmental threats that enhance their power, through the creation of **markets** in carbon, water, and forests, for example, rather than altering patterns of production and consumption from which they benefit. They focused on the material, organizational, and discursive strategies employed by powerful corporate actors to secure policy responses that left their control over production, technology, and finance intact (Levy and Newell 2002).

Less concerned with governance per se, other critical political economy approaches from ecological Marxism questioned the premise of **ecological modernization** and other liberal approaches such as **liberal environmentalism**, which argued that capitalist growth could be compatible with responding to the ecological crisis. They suggested instead that a second contradiction of capitalism (O'Connor 1994) was its tendency to destroy its own ability to reproduce the ecological (as well as social) conditions necessary for its own survival.

In sum, what unites an array of accounts that might be described by the label critical political economy is a concern with explaining the existing landscape of power in global environmental politics, which is seen to extend far beyond the peculiarities of particular international **regimes**, and identifying possibilities for change in the prevailing order of global (environmental) governance on the basis that the current system is incapable of delivering either **sustainable development** or environmental **justice**. Many such approaches either look to the possibility of strategic alliances among powerful actors that might break down opposition to environmental action, or to more bottom-up forms of resistance and alternatives that seek to construct green economies along non-capitalist lines.

## References

Chatterjee, Pratap and Matthias Finger.1994. *The Earth Brokers: Power, Politics and World Development*. London, Routledge.

Levy, David and Peter Newell. 2002. "Business Strategy and International Environmental Governance: Toward a Neo-Gramscian Synthesis." *Global Environmental Politics* 2(4): 84–101.

Newell, Peter. 2008. "The Political Economy of Global Environmental Governance." *Review of International Studies* 34(3): 507–529.

O'Connor, Martin (Ed.). 1994. *Is Capitalism Sustainable? Political Economy and the Politics of Ecology*. New York, Guilford Publication.

Paterson, Matthew. 2001. *Understanding Global Environmental Politics: Domination, Accumulation, Resistance*. Basingstoke, Palgrave.

# DEEP ECOLOGY

## Andrew Dobson

*Keele University, United Kingdom*

Deep ecology is generally reckoned to have been founded by the Norwegian philosopher, Arne Næss. In 1972 he gave a lecture in Bucharest in which he distinguished between "deep" and "shallow" ecology (Næss, 1973). He defined shallow ecology in terms of a concern for the environment for the effect that its deterioration could have on the welfare of human beings. This is sometimes called an anthropocentric concern. This contrasts with deep ecology, which involves a concern for the environment for its own sake. From a deep ecology point of view, the environment should be protected whether it is useful for human beings or not.

Deep ecologists' view of what "the environment" is can vary. Some take a "biocentric" view (Taylor 2010), which would involve care for living parts of the environment, while others support **ecocentrism**. Deep ecology shares with animal liberation a concern for non-human beings for their own sake, but goes further both in its "holistic" approach to the protection of non-human nature and in its commitment to protecting a broader range of beings, collections of beings (including species), and the contexts in which those beings exist.

Deep ecologists have three types of argument at their disposal for the protection of non-human nature, one relating to intrinsic value, one to interests, and one to a change in consciousness. The first depends on identifying a feature of the non-human natural world that makes it intrinsically valuable, by analogy with the Kantian notion that it is rationality that confers intrinsic value on human beings. Deep ecologists have identified various such features, ranging from the possession of interests (such as an interest in maintaining the conditions for life (Johnson 1991)) to "autopoesis" (referring to the capacity of a closed system to reproduce itself (Fox 1990)). This analytical approach to intrinsic value is rejected by some deep ecologists in favor of intuitive approaches such as that expressed by the so-called "last person" argument. If we feel it would be wrong for the last person on Earth to set in motion a chain of events leading to the destruction of the planet after their death, then, it is said, this is an intuitive recognition of the intrinsic value of non-human nature.

Given the philosophical difficulties involved in establishing non-human nature's intrinsic value, some deep ecologists adopt a "state of consciousness" approach, arguing for a deep identification with non-human nature. Sometimes this approach takes the form of the idea of an "expanded self," according to which care for one's self implies care for the wider non-human natural world since the latter partly constitutes the former (Fox 1990). If this approach overcomes the problems associated with imputing intrinsic value to nature, its own difficulty lies with persuading people to identify with non-human nature in the required way.

A further underlying difficulty is deep ecology's commitment to "biospherical egalitarianism" or the view that all entities in the human and non-human natural world are in principle of equal moral worth. This is a difficult principle to put into practice, and the qualifications made to it tend to result in the re-establishment of a hierarchy of moral worth of a rather traditional sort.

Some regard deep ecology and its commitment to the protection of the non-human natural world as a founding principle of green politics (Dobson 2007). It is probably true to say, though, that its importance in this respect has declined in recent years as green politics has been "mainstreamed," and anthropocentric arguments have come to the fore.

## References

Dobson, Andrew. 2007. *Green Political Thought* (4th Edition). London, Routledge.

Fox, Warwick. 1990. *Towards a Transpersonal Ecology: Developing New Foundations for Environmentalism*. Boston, MA, Shambhala Press.

Johnson, Lawrence. 1991. *A Morally Deep World: An Essay on Moral Significance and Environmental Ethics*. Cambridge: Cambridge University Press.

Næss, Arne. 1973. "The Shallow and the Deep, Long-Range Ecology Movement". *Inquiry* 16(1): 95–100.

Taylor, Paul. 2010. "Egalitarian Biocentrism." In *Environmental Ethics: the Big Questions*, Ed. David Keller. New Jersey: John Wiley & Sons.

# DESERTIFICATION CONVENTION

## Steffen Bauer

*German Development Institute, Germany*

At the beginning of the twenty-first century, up to 70 percent of the world's drylands were considered to be degraded, severely affecting the livelihoods of roughly one billion people (MEA 2005). International efforts to address dryland degradation and recurring droughts date back to the

1960s. Yet these remained largely ineffectual until **summit diplomacy** resolved to tackle "desertification" by means of an international convention during the 1992 United Nations Conference on Environment and Development. In 1994 the United Nations finally adopted the United Nations Convention to Combat Desertification in Those Countries Seriously Affected by Drought and/or Desertification, particularly in Africa (UNCCD) to deal with this specific environmental problem and to facilitate Sustainable Development for the people affected by it.

In the convention text, desertification is defined as "land degradation in arid, semi-arid and dry sub-humid areas resulting from various factors, including climatic variations and human activities" (Article 1(a)). The convention furthermore declares desertification to be of concern for all humankind as one specific aspect of global ecological interdependence. In this sense, the notion of desertification is itself a product of globalization as it bundles together localized biogeophysical phenomena that can be observed across the globe.

Yet, the concept of desertification is contested. Much like the term sustainability, it is employed to encapsulate a number of causes, effects, symptoms, and interactions that are attributed to a highly complex phenomenon. Consequently, the interpretation of the UNCCD, its specific scope, and its role and relevance in global environmental governance, have been subject to much debate. The framing of desertification as both an environment and a development issue was key to conceptualize the UNCCD as a **sustainable development** convention rather than as yet another multilateral environmental agreement (Bruyninckx 2005). However, this overly ambitious stand-alone quality proved a major obstacle to the effective **compliance and implementation** of the convention.

While developing countries routinely emphasize poverty as both a cause and a consequence of desertification, developed countries remain reluctant to subscribe to the UNCCD as an additional instrument for development assistance. At the same time, the former are generally more concerned with development than environmental protection and the latter remain lukewarm in their acknowledgment of desertification as a global environmental problem, even as dryland degradation dynamically progresses in many developed countries. Yet, the framing of desertification as a global issue has tangible implications for the interpretation and implementation of the convention. For instance, it was instrumental in establishing dryland degradation as eligible for funding through the **Global Environment Facility**. Ultimately, the strategic framing of desertification at the international level provides a strong case in point for the influence of non-state actors—in this case notably

**nongovernmental organizations** and the bureaucrats of the UNCCD **secretariat**—in the realm of intergovernmental politics (Corell and Betsill 2001; Bauer 2009).

This notwithstanding, the UNCCD struggles to mobilize adequate attention and, indeed, resources from member states (Akhtar-Schuster et al. 2011). Its structural weakness is compounded by desertification's interdependence with climate change and the loss of biological diversity as both the **climate change regime** and the **biodiversity regime** rank higher on the agenda of most countries, especially in the global North. Indeed, developed countries' subscription to the UNCCD has widely been interpreted as a concession to developing countries' acceptance of the UNFCCC and the CBD at the 1992 "Earth Summit." As such, it also revealed developing countries' increased bargaining power in view of global ecological interdependence (Najam 2004).

However, once the UNCCD was successfully established its advocates failed to capitalize on the evident importance of drylands and specifically of land and soils as natural resources at the nexus of global food production and the protection of essential **ecosystem services** (Stringer 2009). At least partially, this may be explained by the UNCCD's failure to establish an effective **boundary organization** that could enhance well-informed decision-making at the global level (Bauer and Stringer 2009). More importantly, however, it can be argued that the UNCCD has come to represent an almost ideal typical showcase for a host of structural problems that permeate North–South politics and for that matter global environmental governance at the fault-line of socioeconomic needs and ecological concerns.

### References

Akhtar-Schuster, Mariam, Richard J. Thomas, Lindsay C. Stringer, Pamela Chasek, and Mary K. Seely. 2011. "Improving the Enabling Environment to Combat Land Degradation: Institutional, Financial, Legal and Science-Policy Challenges and Solutions." *Land Degradation and Development* 22(2): 299–312.

Bauer, Steffen. 2009. "The Desertification Secretariat: A Castle Made of Sand." In *Managers of Global Change: The Influence of International Environmental Bureaucracies*, Eds. Frank Biermann and Bernd Siebenhüner, 293–317. Cambridge, MA, MIT Press.

Bauer, Steffen and Lindsay C. Stringer. 2009. "The Role of Science in the Global Governance of Desertification." *Journal of Environment and Development* 18(3): 248–267.

Bruyninckx, Hans. 2005. "Sustainable Development: The Institutionalization of a Contested Concept." In *International Environmental Politics*, Eds. Michele M.

Betsill, Kathryn Hochstetler and Dimitris Stevis, 265–298. Basingstoke, Palgrave Macmillan.

Corell, Elisabeth, and Michele M. Betsill. 2001. "A Comparative Look at NGO Influence in International Environmental Negotiations: Desertification and Climate Change." *Global Environmental Politics* 1(4): 86–107.

MEA (Millennium Ecosystem Assessment). 2005. "Ecosystems and Human Well-Being: Desertification Synthesis." Washington, World Resources Institute.

Najam, Adil. 2004. "Dynamics of the Southern Collective: Developing Countries in Desertification Negotiations." *Global Environmental Politics* 4(3): 128–154.

Stringer, Lindsay C. 2009. "Reviewing the Links between Desertification and Food Insecurity: From Parallel Challenges to Synergetic Solutions." *Food Security* 1: 113–126.

# DISASTERS

## Raymond Murphy

*University of Ottawa, Canada*

In 1964 an earthquake followed by a tsunami struck Alaska, killing people and destroying villages. In 1989 the Exxon Valdez oil supertanker spilled 11 million gallons of crude oil, contaminating 1,000 miles of Alaskan shoreline and killing sea life (Herman 2010). Some researchers define the first as a natural disaster, a disturbance of nature having grave consequences for humans, whereas they define the second as an environmental disaster, human practices having grave consequences for their natural environment. This sharp distinction is an oversimplification. A natural disaster is not all natural. It becomes disastrous because of socially constructed vulnerabilities: the 1964 earthquake and tsunami killed Alaskans and damaged property because there were no tsunami warning alarms and building codes were lax. An environmental disaster also affects humans by degrading the environment they need in the future: the oil destroyed fisheries and tourism for years. Moreover, humans are now unleashing nature's dynamics through fossil-fueled global climate change, habitat destruction, and biodiversity loss that threaten disaster for both the environment and future humans. In the **risk society** of the anthropocene, environmental disasters are best defined as interactions between socio-technological constructions and nature's constructions that result in grave adverse consequences for large numbers of people. This inclusive definition has two subtypes of initiating processes, naturogenic and anthropogenic, which captures both the commonalities and differences of phenomena such as earthquakes and oil spills.

The cost of environmental disasters has increased exponentially as populations grew, became more affluent, and placed expensive constructions in harm's way. Reliance on technologies such as electrical grids can make societies more vulnerable to extreme disturbances of nature (Murphy 2009). Fatalities are highest in poor countries, which raises issues of **justice**. Slow-onset environmental disasters are arguably most destructive in the long run: deforestation, desertification, and anthropogenic global climate change.

Governance of rapid-onset environmental disasters is typically multi-**scale**, from the bottom up: the local community deals with small calamities; when its capacity is exceeded, the provincial level takes charge; when its capacity is surpassed, the national government acts, especially financially; and when there is a particularly destructive catastrophe especially for poor countries lacking resilience, other nations help. Electronic media transmit vivid images of these distant environmental catastrophes immediately. Rudel (2013) argues that rapid-onset disasters result in defensive environmentalism, which has the potential to prompt altruistic environmentalism to deal with slow-onset ones. A panoply of **nongovernmental organizations** (Hannigan 2012) provides disaster relief (Red Cross) or reduces social vulnerability to hazards by alleviating poverty. The United Nations Disaster Relief Office provides **aid** whereas its Development Programme and the **United Nations Environment Programme** attempt to reduce social vulnerability. **Boundary organizations**, such as the Intergovernmental Panel on Climate Change, contribute understanding of dangers. Environmental disasters are often caused by profit-seeking **business and corporations**, but others such as the re-insurance industry fund resilience and promote the **precautionary principle**. The **World Bank** has a disaster risk reduction unit.

## References

Hannigan, John. 2012. *Disasters without Borders*. Cambridge, Polity.
Herman, Robert. 2010. *This Borrowed Earth*. New York, Palgrave Macmillan.
Murphy, Raymond. 2009. *Leadership in Disaster*. Montreal, McGill-Queen's University Press.
Rudel, Thomas. 2013. *Defensive Environmentalists and the Dynamics of Global Reform*. New York, Cambridge University Press.

# DISPUTE RESOLUTION MECHANISMS

## Carrie Menkel-Meadow
*University of California, Irvine, United States*

Perhaps the most important issue in international environmental governance is not the making of new environmental rules, but how such rules can be enforced. Arguably, effective **compliance and implementation** requires appropriate dispute resolution mechanisms from the onset.

The first international environmental dispute to have been legally settled at the international level occurred at the end of the 1930s. At that time, there was no formal international court to resolve the United States' claim that fumes discharged by a Canadian smelting company were causing environmental damage in the US state of Washington. This so-called Trail Smelter Case was thus resolved by an international, voluntarily agreed to, arbitration panel. This famous case not only established the **preventive action principle**, but also that voluntarily constituted bodies, such as an arbitration panel, could order injunctions or desist orders.

This first form of dispute resolution set in motion the development of formal environmental litigation. Many formal dispute mechanisms are now active in global environmental governance, including the International Court of Justice (a rare but important adjudicator of inter-state environmental disputes), the International Tribunal of the Law of the Sea (an adjudicative body that has decided very few cases since its formation in 1982), regional courts, such as the European or Inter-American Courts of Human Rights (where claims are now made for **human and environmental rights**), the **World Trade Organization**'s arbitral panels and appellate body (where environmental litigants now intervene in trade disputes), the International Centre for Settlement of Investment Disputes (since foreign investors increasingly claim to have been indirectly expropriated by domestic environmental measures), national courts (which may resolve both intra- and inter-state disputes), international environmental agreements' implementation committees (which report data, issue reports, and occasionally order sanctions), and more recently a new breed of specialized environmental courts or tribunals (ECTs or "green courts") (Pring and Pring 2012).

It has long been argued that several environment disputes are non-zero-sum games and that environmental disputes can more effectively be settled by dialogic, negotiated, and managerial, rather than adversary, approaches. As a result, many multilateral environmental agreements provide for requirements for mediation, negotiation, and conciliation before binding arbitration (called "tiered dispute resolution"). Other well-established alternative dispute settlement mechanisms include fact-finding bodies. The **World Bank**'s Independent Inspection Panel, for example, investigates and performs fact-finding for environmental disputes for communities and World Bank-funded projects.

Other mechanisms are even less formal and more collaborative. They include consensus building and community planning and dispute resolution processes (Camacho 2005). For example, for the **transboundary water regime**, newer forms of collaborative and consensus-building processes attempt to bring all the stakeholders together to share scientific information, legal claims, and expertise (Menkel-Meadow 2008). With the help of professional facilitators, they craft "community agreements" that provide for more flexible standards and monitoring, with provisions for **adaptation**, revisions, and contingency planning when conditions "on the ground" change. These processes assume more party input (with often hundreds of participants) and a growing group of experts trained in environmental mediation and facilitation. This is often called the "New Governance" model (Karkkainen 2004).

While consensus building and mediative processes are still mostly public processes, there is growing evidence that private environmental dispute resolution can bolster **effectiveness**. Private parties set up **private regimes** to use supply chain contracts, loan agreements, codes of conduct commitments, and tiered dispute resolution to demand environmental standards and to enforce them.

Yet, these less formal and more collaborative processes for resolution of environmental disputes raise a host of as yet unanswered questions: How can key environmental principle issues, such as the **precautionary principle**, be dealt with in collaborative process? Do powerful actors exercise stronger control in less formal settings? How can we ensure access for **participation** and appropriate representation for all interested parties? How much **transparency** should there be when private companies make deals with communities? How do we provide sufficient incentives for institutions to adapt to new information or changed circumstances and learn over time? How do we balance the need to resolve short-term disputes and episodic crises such as **disasters** against the need to focus on long-term and intergenerational issues such as **justice**?

## References

Camacho, Alejandro E. 2005. "Mustering the Missing Voices: A Collaborative Model for Fostering Equality, Community Involvement and Adaptive Planning in Land Use Decisions." *Stanford Environmental Law Journal* 24: 3–341.

Karkkainen, Bradley C. 2004. "'New Governance' in Legal Thought and in the World: Some Splitting as Antidote to Overzealous Lumping." *Minnesota Law Review* 89: 471–496.

Menkel-Meadow, Carrie. 2008. "Getting to Let's Talk: Comments on Collaborative Environmental Dispute Resolution Processes." *Nevada Law Journal* 8: 835–852.

Pring, George Rock and Catherine Kitty Pring. 2012. "The Future of Environmental Dispute Resolution." *Denver Journal of International Law and Policy* 40: 482–491.

# DUMPING

## Josué Mathieu

*Université libre de Bruxelles, Belgium*

Environmental dumping (or eco-dumping) is defined as the use of lax environmental standards or poorly enforced regulations allowing the export of goods at a cost advantage or to attract foreign investments. The concept is used by critics of the effects of trade liberalization who consider the comparative advantage stemming from a low level of environmental protection to be unfair, since industries located in "pollution havens" do not bear the cost of environmental externalities, contrary to high-standards abiding industries (Hamilton 2001). This definition of environmental dumping must be distinguished from dumping as price discrimination—selling "below cost"—and from dumping as the export of hazardous waste (see **Hazardous wastes regime**).

The notion of environmental dumping has gained importance over the years, starting in the early 1990s when negotiations of the North American Free Trade Agreement (NAFTA) and the **World Trade Organization** stirred fears of a race to the bottom in environmental protection. In Western countries, political debates over environmental dumping often include a call for countervailing or anti-dumping duties (labeled "environmental tariffs," "green tariffs," or "eco-tariffs"). These environmental tariffs are necessary, according to their proponents, not only to offset unfair competitive advantages (Janzen 2008) but also to induce responsible behavior in countries with low environmental standards. The imposition of duties against imports from low standards countries—a unilateral trade measure—is usually regarded by economists as inefficient, although debates exist on the definition of efficiency and possible ways to improve it (Kraus 2000).

Debates over environmental dumping also contain demands for harmonization of environmental standards (Hudec 1996). Critics of harmonization, for their part, have long disputed such a need, considering that environmental protection is reflective of the level of economic development of a country and of social choices. It has also been argued that upward harmonization can happen without any direct imposition of standards on foreign countries. This phenomenon has been described as the "California effect" (Vogel 1995), where market access regulations lead to the uplifting of environmental standards because firms find it more efficient to align on one single standard set by a large market, through **policy diffusion**.

International trade law does not recognize environmental dumping as a practice that is prohibited and that may be "countervailed." Nevertheless, trade and investment agreements often provide that parties may not use low environmental protection to gain a competitive edge in trade and investments, requiring **compliance and implementation** of existing standards (see Art. 13.7 of the European Union–Korea free trade agreement).

## References

Hamilton, Clive. 2001. "The Case for Fair Trade." *Journal of Australian Political Economy* 48: 60–72.

Hudec, Robert E. 1996. "Differences in National Environmental Standards: The Level-Playing-Field Dimension." *Minnesota Journal of Global Trade* 5(1): 1–28.

Janzen, Bernd. 2008. "International Trade Law and the 'Carbon Leakage' Problem: Are Unilateral U.S. Import Restrictions the Solution?" *Sustainable Development Law and Policy* 8(2): 22–26, 84–85.

Kraus, Christiane. 2000. *Import Tariffs as Environmental Policy Instruments*. Dordrecht, Kluwer.

Vogel, David. 1995. *Trading up: Consumer and Environmental Regulation in a Global Economy*. Cambridge, MA, Harvard University Press.

# ECOCENTRISM

## Sheryl D. Breen

*University of Minnesota Morris, United States*

Ecocentrism is an ethical worldview based on an interconnected web of dynamic relationships among living entities and systems that include land and climate as well as animate individuals and species. By emphasizing the intrinsic worth of ecological systems, ecocentrism stands in particular opposition to an anthropocentric (human-centered) approach to environmental thought and governance, which calls for protection on the basis of instrumental value to human needs and interests. In contrast, ecocentrism is founded on the notion that all parts of nature—human and nonhuman, living and nonliving—have inherent value and are constituted by and dependent on the all-encompassing interrelatedness of ecological communities.

Ecocentrism is not unique to the contemporary environmental movement; ethical systems that see humanity as enmeshed within the multi-layered realms of the natural world are contained within many indigenous worldviews (Selin 2003). Within industrialized nations, ecocentrism developed in response to **liberal environmentalism** and modern **conservation** management techniques. The approach has drawn particular philosophical inspiration from Aldo Leopold's holistic "land ethic," which argues that we must reposition humans' connection with their biotic world through a new ethic that "changes the role of *Homo sapiens* from conqueror of the land-community to plain member and citizen of it" (Leopold 1968 [1949]: 204). In this way, according to Leopold, we must learn to "think like a mountain" in our understanding of the interrelationships between species and their environments (Leopold 1968 [1949]: 129–133).

A second foundational theorist, Arne Næss, moved ecocentric thought toward an emphasis on cosmological consciousness with his separation between an ecocentric **deep ecology** and "shallow" anthropocentric forms of environmental thought. Deep ecology recognizes the lack of any ontological division between the human and nonhuman spheres, according to Næss, and he calls for "biospherical egalitarianism—in principle," recognizing that the practicalities of life unavoidably require some force to be used against other lives (Næss 1973: 95–96). With further development by George Sessions and Bill Devall, the eight-point deep ecology platform incorporates the principle of intrinsic value, rejects the pursuit of higher living standards in favor of life quality, and calls for a commitment to change, including reduced human interference with the nonhuman world and a decrease in human population (Devall and Sessions 1985: 69–73).

Early proponents and critics of ecocentric theory conversed primarily within the philosophical discipline of environmental ethics. Robyn Eckersley forcefully brought the discussion into the realm of politics with her examination of ecocentric thought as an "emancipatory" phase within the dialogue of environmental crisis (Eckersley 1992). She analyzed ecocentrism's enlarged notions of emancipation and autonomy through its radical repositioning of humans within their biotic communities and highlighted the diverging ecocentric components that can be found within intrinsic value theory, deep ecology, and **ecofeminism**. Arguing that "only a thoroughgoing ecocentric Green political theory" can provide the necessary responses to the contemporary ecological crisis, Eckersley described an ecocentric polity as one that incorporates greater economic and political equality with multilayered democratic decision-making structures and market controls, united by "the flowering of an ecocentric emancipatory culture" (Eckersley 1992: 85).

Commentators have offered a range of criticisms. First, some charge that ecocentrism's holistic egalitarianism is misanthropic and that this worldview promotes eco-authoritarianism rather than **green democracy**. In response, ecocentric theorists argue that ecocentrism's emancipatory and egalitarian elements augment and extend rather than replace the hard-fought advances in **human and environmental rights** and environmental **justice**. Second, critics contend that ecocentrism relies on a false dichotomy based on an erroneously harsh definition of anthropocentrism (Barry 1999). This concern has encouraged more complex analyses of anthropocentrism and inspired approaches that move further from deep ecology and perhaps from ecocentrism itself toward a value-pluralist ethic that avoids the anthropocentric/ecocentric duality (Carter 2011). Third, critics question whether ecocentrism is implementable because nonhumans, species, and ecosystems are unable to represent their interests. In response, ecocentrists are examining ways to incorporate nonhuman interests in political decision-making through designated representation in green state structures (Eckersley 2004).

Concerns consistent with ecocentric theory appear in the "ecosystem approach" incorporated into the **biodiversity regime**, in the **fisheries governance**, or in international agreements and declarations on forests. The ecosystem approach, which argues for holistic management and stresses the interconnections within ecosystems, also has found support within mainstream international **nongovernmental organizations** such as Greenpeace International. However, the increasing presence of the ecosystem approach at the international level does not constitute significant political success for ecocentrism. Unlike ecocentrism's explicitly normative mission, the ecosystem approach is designed as an ecological management tool and does not satisfy ecocentrism's more radical move toward an ethical worldview that calls for ideological change.

## *References*

Barry, John. 1999. *Rethinking Green Politics: Nature, Virtue and Progress*. London, Sage.
Carter, Alan. 2011. "Towards a Multidimensional, Environmentalist Ethic." *Environmental Values* 20(3): 347–374.
Devall, Bill and George Sessions. 1985. *Deep Ecology: Living as if Nature Mattered*. Salt Lake City, UT, Gibbs Smith.
Eckersley, Robyn. 1992. *Environmentalism and Political Theory: Toward an Ecocentric Approach*. Albany, NJ, SUNY Press.
Eckersley, Robyn. 2004. *The Green State: Rethinking Democracy and Sovereignty*. Cambridge, MA, MIT Press.
Leopold, Aldo. 1968 [1949]. *A Sand County Almanac, and Sketches Here and There*. New York, Oxford University Press.
Næss, Arne. 1973. "The Shallow and the Deep, Long-Range Ecology Movement: A Summary." *Inquiry* 16: 95–100.
Selin, Helaine (Ed.). 2003. *Nature across Cultures: Views of Nature and the Environment in Non-Western Cultures*. Boston, MA, Kluwer Academic Publishers.

# ECOFEMINISM

## Charlotte Bretherton

*University of Portsmouth, United Kingdom*

Ecofeminism derives from the feminist and environmental movements of the 1970s, in the context of women's protests against environmental degradation. Thus, from the outset, ecofeminism was "about connectedness and wholeness of theory and practice" (Mies and Shiva 1993: 14). It reflected a realization among some feminists that, in the absence of a fundamental reconceptualization of the relationship between the human and natural worlds, their aim of equality with men could be achieved only at the expense of the natural world.

While there is no overarching definition of ecofeminism, ecofeminists share various themes. Some of these, including a holistic approach to human/nature relations, derive from **deep ecology**. In ecofeminist thought, however, there is the perception of an affinity between women and nature associated with the dominance of post-Enlightenment, "masculinist" (primarily Western) discourses that privilege scientific enquiry and technological intervention over traditional knowledge. This has resulted, not in progress, but in "maldevelopment" (Shiva 1988; Merchant 1995), which marginalizes and undervalues women's work and is destroying the planet. In consequence, ecofeminists also attribute to women a special relationship with the planet.

Beyond these general themes ecofeminist perspectives differ considerably. A broad division can be identified between cultural/spiritual and political ecofeminism (Mies and Shiva 1993: 16–19; Merchant 1995: 10–18).

Spiritual/cultural ecofeminism emphasizes women's role as givers of life and their fundamental identification with, and duty of care for, the Earth as mother. It calls for a radical revalidation of social norms in order to reaffirm the significance of "feminine" qualities of empathy and nurturance and women's traditional (sometimes mystical) understanding of nature. These assumptions have frequently been reflected in women's activism, from the Chipko women of India who struggled to save the forests on which their livelihood depended (Shiva 1988: 71–77) to the EcoMom Alliance of North America, whose aim is to convince American mothers that "saving the planet" should be added to their responsibilities (MacGregor 2010: 134–135).

Political ecofeminism rejects claims of women's "natural" affinity with nature. Furthermore, acceptance of principal responsibility for righting environmental wrongs merely adds to the burdens of women, who have limited access to political power and influence (Bretherton 1998: 87). Structures of power, or "mastery," associated with gender, class, race, and species are central concerns of political ecofeminism (Plumwood 1993: 5). Here, women continue to have particular insights due to their subordination to men, regardless of race or class—a disadvantaged status, which they share (in dominant, Western thought) with non-human species (see **Ecocentrism**). Consequently women (in particular) must recognize, challenge, and change the "master identity in culture, in ourselves and in political and economic structures to ensure the survival of our planet" (Plumwood 1993: 195–196).

## References

Bretherton, Charlotte. 1998. "Global Environmental Politics: Putting Gender on the Agenda?" *Review of International Studies* 24(1): 85–100.

MacGregor, Sherilyn. 2010. "A Stranger Silence Still: The Need for Feminist Social Research on Climate Change." *Sociological Review* 57: 124–140.

Merchant, Carolyn. 1995. *Earthcare: Women and the Environment.* New York, Routledge.
Mies, Maria and Vandana Shiva. 1993. *Ecofeminism.* London, Zed Books.
Plumwood, Val. 1993. *Feminism and the Mastery of Nature.* London, Routledge.
Shiva, Vandana. 1988. *Staying Alive: Women, Ecology and Development.* London, Zed Books.

# ECOLOGICAL MODERNIZATION

## Maarten Hajer

*University of Amsterdam, Netherlands*

Ecological modernization refers to the theory claiming that there are reformist solutions to the environmental problems facing society. With this pragmatist outlook, it distinguishes itself from **critical political economy** that suggests that the "ecological crisis" calls for a complete overhaul of Western (capitalist) societies or radical changes in consumer behavior.

The term "ecological modernization" is attributed to Martin Jänicke and Joseph Huber who started using and promoting it in the early 1980s in Germany. Important theorists of ecological modernization are the environmental scientist Ernst-Ulrich von Weiszäcker (Weiszäcker et al. 2009), sociologists Gert Spaargaren and Arthur Mol (Mol et al. 2009). Public policy scholar Maarten Hajer provided a critical analysis (1995). Although "ecological modernization" is an academic term, it is important to keep in mind that many of its protagonists played a role in the shadow of politics. Ecological modernization is, in that sense, a social theory trying to help change the world. The 1987 Brundtland report *Our Common Future* can be seen as a hallmark policy document based on the principles of ecological modernization. It coins the phrase "**sustainable development**" but is silent on more critical issues such as the future of nuclear power or the need for shifts in (Western) patterns of consumption.

Ecological modernization has five core components: (1) it believes "decoupling" of economic growth from environmental degradation is possible; (2) it regards environmental degradation as a problem of collective action, to be overcome by coordination and better incentive setting; (3) it makes environmental damage calculable hence it seeks to allow for an analysis of costs and benefits of environmental pollution; (4) it seeks to internalize environmental costs into mainstream calculations, whether that is on the level of **business and corporations** or in terms of the analysis of macro-economic performance, thus "greening the economy"; (5) it has a firm belief in the potential of technological and social innovation.

In the twenty-first century the ideas of ecological modernization have spread from Western Europe and the US and can enjoy global attention, especially in Asia (e.g. China, Japan, Korea), Australia and Latin America (Brazil, Argentina). The Organisation for Economic Co-operation and Development (OECD) has been intellectually pushing eco-modernist thinking since the 1980s (for instance by pointing out the "costs of inaction") and, recently, reports from the International Monetary Fund (IMF) and **World Bank** have taken up eco-modernist thinking as well (IMF 2013; World Bank 2013).

The latest manifestations of ecological modernization are discourses such as **"environmental services,"** "green accounting," and the debate on environmentally harmful subsidies. Reflecting on its influence one can see that the ideas have been consistently the same since the 1980s. The problem is not the ideas or finding a common language but remains the "discourse institutionalization" (Hajer 1995): the uptake of the ideas in the regular procedures of public policy. In that sense ecological modernization has not yet delivered on its promise.

### References

Hajer, Maarten A. 1995. *The Politics of Environmental Discourse—Ecological Modernization and the Policy Process.* Oxford, Oxford University Press.
International Monetary Fund. 2013. *Energy Subsidy Reform.* Washington, IMF.
Mol, Arthur J.P., David A. Sonnenfeld, and Gert Spaargaren (Eds.). 2009. *The Ecological Modernization Reader—Environmental Reform in Theory and Practice.* London, Routledge.
Weiszäcker, Ernst Ulrich von, Karlson "Charlie" Hargroves, Michael H. Smith, Cheryl Desha, and Peter Stasinopoulos (Eds.) 2009. *Factor Five: Transforming the Global Economy through 80% Improvements in Resource Productivity.* London, EarthScan.
World Bank. 2013. *Turn Down the Heat.* Washington, World Bank.

# ECOSYSTEM SERVICES (PAYMENTS FOR)

## Stefanie Engel

*ETH Zürich, Switzerland*

Payments for ecosystem services (PES) are an increasingly popular positive economic incentive approach for the provision of ecosystem services (ES).

Conflicting definitions exist, from very broad to very specific (Schomers and Matzdorf 2013). Most agree that a meaningful definition requires that the payment is at least partly conditional on the ES provided or on adoption of an activity thought to provide such services. Payments can be performance or activity based, and can be made for adopting an activity (e.g. afforestation) or refraining from a damaging activity (e.g. deforestation) (Engel et al. 2008).

A first debate relates to the degree to which PES can and should rely on private sector involvement through **business and corporations**. PES examples range from decentralized ("Coasean") negotiation solutions to governmental ("Pigouvian") environmental subsidy-like schemes. A Coasean PES evolves as the outcome of a negotiation process between ES buyers and ES providers. An example is the payment by Vittel to farmers for adopting agricultural practices that improve water quality in France. A Pigouvian PES is a government-run program where the government acts on behalf of ES buyers. An example is Sweden's program of performance payments to local Sami villages for wildlife conservation. Pure Coasean PES are very rare as many ES are local or **global public goods**. Many PES schemes are hybrid **partnerships** involving some private sector ES buyers, but also a substantial role for the government or other third parties.

A second debate relates to the degree to which PES can address environmental objectives and poverty alleviation at the same time (Pagiola et al. 2005). PES implement a "steward rewarded" rather than a **polluter pays principle**, providing an alternative income source to ES providers. The degree to which the providers are poor differs across contexts, and benefits depend on the poor's eligibility, willingness, and ability to participate in PES schemes. Other groups may also be affected, e.g. when a water tariff is levied to finance PES or when forest conservation reduces forest access for customary users.

The relationship between PES and economic valuation is often misunderstood. Payment amounts may lie anywhere between the minimum payment required to compensate ES providers for their incremental cost of providing the service and the maximum payment represented by society's full valuation of the services. It is therefore misleading to interpret payments as "the" value of the ES, nor is economic valuation necessarily required to implement PES.

While many authors see PES as a novel conservation approach, some warn that PES may imply a commodification of nature. Recent studies on the environmental **effectiveness** of PES show mixed results and call for a greater focus on the additionality of the ES paid for and improved targeting of payments to achieve more with scarce budgets (Pattanayak et al. 2010). Ongoing research addresses how to deal with leakage and achieve permanence of the ES provided (see **REDD**), how to best implement payments to **indigenous peoples and local communities**, and how PES may affect intrinsic motivations for providing ES.

### References

Engel, Stefanie, Stefano Pagiola, and Sven Wunder. 2008. "Designing Payments for Environmental Services in Theory and Practice—An Overview of the Issues." *Ecological Economics* 65(4): 663–674.

Pagiola, Stefano, Agustin Arcenas, and Gunars Platais. 2005. "Can Payments for Environmental Services Help Reduce Poverty? An Exploration of the Issue and the Evidence to Date from Latin America." *World Development* 33(2): 237–253.

Pattanayak, Subhrendu K., Sven Wunder, and Paul J. Ferraro. 2010. "Show me the Money: Do Payments Supply Environmental Services in Developing countries?" *Review of Environmental Economics and Policy* 4(2): 254–274.

Schomers, Sarah and Bettina Matzdorf. 2013. "Payments for Ecosystem Services: A Review and Comparison of Developing and Industrialized Countries." *Ecosystem Services* 6: 16–30.

# EFFECTIVENESS

## Detlef F. Sprinz

*Potsdam Institute for Climate Impact Research
and University of Potsdam, Germany*

Effectiveness is defined as the degree of improvement in environmental performance (impact) that can be causally attributed to governance, e.g. by way of international treaties, international **regimes**, domestic policies, or international **nonregimes**. While often confused with **compliance and implementation**, the various concepts point to different aspects. Compliance and implementation refer to obligations taken on by parties to a treaty or unilaterally in view of domestic audience costs—which may or may not have effects on environmental performance. Global environmental politics may even have effects in the absence of an international regime (e.g. if a nonregime induces domestic politics to undertake actions nationally that eschew international cooperation) or when international regimes may have effects on non-members. Effectiveness as the improvement of environmental quality or reduction in pollution loads may occur for reasons, inter alia, of international policies, uncoordinated national policies, the coordination of national and international policies, technological change, or life-style changes.

How can we measure effectiveness? In the absence of any policy, we can only take observations of the environment, using chemical, physical, social, political, or welfare measures to characterize the state of the environment and potential changes over time. Most common among social scientists is the interest in the actual or expected effect of specific policies on environmental quality, such as specific pollution reduction policies at different **scales**—the domestic, regional (e.g. Asian or European) or at the international levels—, changes in land use (e.g. designation of nature protection areas), or **adaptation** measures (e.g. building dams to prevent flooding in coastal areas due to the threat of sea-level rise). In the environmental field, policies often take a considerable amount of time to demonstrate an unequivocal break with the past, thereby demanding a sufficiently long time frame for **assessments**. In addition, the policy must be causally related to the effect to afford appropriate attribution. This is captured by the attention that needs to be placed on counterfactual reasoning, i.e. the environmental performance witnessed in the absence of a particular policy or a range of policies.

A fruitful combination of these aspects can be found in the Oslo-Potsdam Solution to measure international regime effectiveness. Building on Underdal (1992), Sprinz and Helm (1999) and Helm and Sprinz (2000) developed a synoptic approach (Hovi et al. 2003a). At the outset, a dimension (e.g. pollution levels or an environmental quality index) has to be chosen that is causally linked to environmental quality. Subsequently, three components have to be located on this dimension: (1) the non-policy counterfactual in the absence of the policy (lower bound), (2) the pollution level actually associated with a specific policy, and (3) the collective optimum of an ideal (counterfactual) policy performance (upper bound). If the distance traveled from the no-policy counterfactual to the actual policy (2–1) is divided by the potential for improvement of the environment (collective optimum minus non-regime counterfactual, 3–1), a simple effectiveness score can be computed, ranging from zero to one (Helm and Sprinz 2000). The Oslo-Potsdam Solution to measuring regime effectiveness has proven useful in a range of applications in research on environmental policy as well as in other fields of international studies (e.g. Grundig 2006) and has enjoyed a range of extensions.

To date, the Oslo-Potsdam Solution is the only numerical solution to measuring the effect of international treaty regimes, but could easily be used in the context of nonregimes (to elucidate whether these have effects), domestic policies (the Oslo-Potsdam Solution score can be computed for each country), or multiple dimensions (necessitating a procedure of aggregation across dimensions). The Oslo-Potsdam Solution has received fruitful criticism by the scholarly community. A friendly exchange between the proponents of the Oslo-Potsdam Solution and Oran Young (Young 2001; Young 2003; Hovi et al. 2003a; Hovi et al. 2003b) clarified a range of opportunities and shortcomings of the Oslo-Potsdam Solution, yet no visible alternative to the Oslo-Potsdam Solution has emerged so far. Empirically, the early regulations under the **transboundary air pollution regime** have received the strongest attention in terms of effectiveness assessments. Depending on the method chosen, the early sulfur and nitrogen protocols have generated only mild to medium effects on environmental quality, thus leaving substantial scope for improved policy design (e.g. Helm and Sprinz 2000).

Perhaps the most heralded global environmental agreement is the **ozone regime** (Montreal Protocol and amendments) on substances that deplete the stratospheric ozone layer. Over twenty-five years, ozone-depleting substances have been reduced by 98 percent as compared to 1980 (albeit with non-compliance by a range of parties at various points in time), yet the stratospheric ozone layer is not expected to return to pre-1980 levels before the second half of the twenty-first century. Thus, the long-term effects of the ozone regime largely rest with model results.

The future **climate change regime** on greenhouse gas mitigation would share the same fate, yet the effects of adaptation are likely to be visible in the nearer future.

## References

Grundig, Frank. 2006. "Patterns of International Cooperation and the Explanatory Power of Relative Gains: An Analysis of Cooperation on Global Climate Change, Ozone Depletion, and International Trade". *International Studies Quarterly* 50(4): 781–801.

Helm, Carsten and Detlef F. Sprinz. 2000. "Measuring the Effectiveness of International Environmental Regimes". *Journal of Conflict Resolution* 44(5): 630–652.

Hovi, Jon, Detlef F. Sprinz, and Arild Underdal. 2003a. "The Oslo-Potsdam Solution to Measuring Regime Effectiveness: Critique, Response, And Extensions." *Global Environmental Politics* 3(3): 74–96.

Hovi, Jon, Detlef F. Sprinz, and Arild Underdal. 2003b. "Regime Effectiveness and the Oslo-Potsdam Solution: A Rejoinder to Oran Young." *Global Environmental Politics* 3(3): 105–107.

Sprinz, Detlef F. and Carsten Helm. 1999. "The Effect of Global Environmental Regimes: A Measurement Concept." *International Political Science Review* 20(4): 359–369.

Underdal, Arild. 1992. "The Concept of Regime 'Effectiveness'." *Cooperation and Conflict* 27(3): 227–240.

Young, Oran R. 2001. "Inferences and Indices: Evaluating the Effectiveness of International Environmental Regimes." *Global Environmental Politics* 1(1): 99–121.

Young, Oran R. 2003. "Determining Regime Effectiveness: A Commentary on the Oslo-Potsdam Solution." *Global Environmental Politics* 3(3): 97–104.

# EMERGING COUNTRIES

**Ana Flavia Barros-Platiau**
*University of Brasilia, Brazil*

**Amandine Orsini**
*Université Saint-Louis - Bruxelles, Belgium*

In 1981, Antoine van Agtmael coined the term "emerging markets," in contrast to the "third world" concept. His idea was to point at the fact that several developing countries were in a period of transition, performing better economically than the rest of the South. Their increased economic performance led them to struggle for more assertiveness in major multilateral institutions, notably those concerning trade, financing, and development. In spite of that, the question of their increasing bargaining power in global environmental governance remains barely explored. Since the Rio Summit, emerging countries have taken turns to host major events such as the climate convention Conference of the Parties (COP) in Durban, the Rio+20 Summit, or the biodiversity COP in India. They demonstrate diplomatic skills (with a climate deal in Copenhagen or the adoption of the Nagoya Protocol for natural genetic resources thanks, among others, to Brazil) and often manage to bring other players into the game.

Emerging countries are considered rich in terms of environmental resources, or megadiverse—as they host most of the world's biodiversity—and have traditional populations that own important knowledge that biotechnology companies can turn into commercial applications (pharmaceuticals, cosmetics, etc.). But they are also large polluters, the fastest growing greenhouse gas emitters and are vulnerable to natural **disasters** due to serious social problems and lack of **adaptation** policies. One should keep in mind that more Indians and Chinese live under the poverty line than the population of all **least developed countries** put together.

Although there is no clear definition of the category of emerging countries in global environmental governance, two emerging countries' **negotiating coalitions** active in economic governance have embraced environmental issues, namely the BRICS (Brazil, Russia, India, China, and South Africa) and the IBSA (India, Brazil, and South Africa). IBSA, in particular, set up a working group on energy (in 2006) and another on the environment (in 2008). Those initiatives were created to discuss the Southern development agenda, an agenda IBSA countries want to preserve in global environmental politics. This is why most emerging countries support more actively multilateral arenas linking development and environment, such as the **Commission on Sustainable Development** than initiatives more narrowly focused on the environment, such as the project for a **world environment organization**.

Both BRICS and IBSA are loose coalitions, heterogeneous, and composed of potential rivals. As a result, they lack delegation and enforcement mechanisms. It was only in 2009, at the Copenhagen summit of the **climate change regime**, that emerging countries expressed themselves in a coalition specifically dedicated to climate change known as the BASIC group (Brazil, India, China, and South Africa). Since then, the four parties have been shown to make great efforts to build consensus on the multilateral stage, supporting **sustainable development** goals, also known as the post-2015 agenda, after the Millennium Development Goals period.

Emerging countries do not have a common agenda (Papa and Gleason 2012), but they share principles and values that enable them to work together, such as the right to development, and the **common but differentiated responsibility** principle, which are the glue that keeps the coalition of developing countries (G77/China) together. Overall, they agree that high-income countries must take first responsibility for financing global environmental solutions. Still, they are inconsistent on a number of other issues. Sometimes they consider nuclear energy as being compatible with sustainable development, while, at other times, they condemn its use. In addition, disparities between the members can be found in the biosafety regime and the genetic resources regime (Cullet and Raja 2004; Gupta and Falkner 2006). It may also be argued that emerging countries have in common a frequently stark dissonance between national forces and foreign policy discourse. As a result, their international agenda is often limited by their poor environmental regulations at home (Economy 2006).

Finally, in global environmental politics, emerging countries are often inclined to maintain a status quo that plays in their favor (with principles such as **sovereignty** or common but differentiated responsibilities), rather than promoting major reforms (Hurrell and Sengupta 2012). A few aspects are changing—there are some indications that emerging countries are trying to embrace donor roles—but overall emerging countries have failed so far to take on the responsibilities that go with their new development.

## References

Cullet, Philippe and Jawahar Raja. 2004. "Intellectual Property Rights and Biodiversity Management: The Case of India." *Global Environmental Politics* 4(1): 97–114.

Economy, Elizabeth. 2006. "Environmental Governance: The Emerging Economic Dimension." *Environmental Politics* 15(2): 171–189.

Gupta, Aarti and Robert Falkner. 2006. "The Influence of the Cartagena Protocol on Biosafety: Comparing Mexico, China and South Africa." *Global Environmental Politics* 6(4): 23–55.

Hurrell, Andrew and Sandeep Sengupta. 2012. "Emerging Powers, North–South Relations and Global Climate Politics." *International Affairs* 88(3): 463–484.

Papa, Mihaela and Nancy W. Gleason, 2012. "Major Emerging Powers in Sustainable Development Diplomacy: Assessing their Leadership Potential." *Global Environmental Change* 22(4): 915–924.

# EPISTEMIC COMMUNITIES

## Mai'a K. Davis Cross

*ARENA Centre for European Studies, University of Oslo, Norway*

Epistemic communities are networks of experts who persuade others (usually elite decision-makers) of their shared norms and policy goals by virtue of their professional knowledge. Their reliance on shared expertise is what differentiates them from other actors that seek to influence policy. This expertise need not necessarily be derived from hard **science**, as knowledge in environmental law or **disasters** response, for example, is no less expertise-driven than knowledge in environmental science or biology. However, epistemic communities' policy goals must derive from their members' expert knowledge, not some other motivation, otherwise they may lose authority with their target audience. Epistemic communities are recognized as key actors in transnational global governance, especially environmental governance, and they are a major means by which knowledge translates into power, in a less formalized way as **boundary organization**s.

The concept of epistemic communities did not become widely known in the environmental politics literature until Peter Haas's 1990 book on the Mediterranean Action Programme. Later, a 1992 special issue of *International Organization* entitled "Knowledge, Power, and International Policy Coordination" defined epistemic community as "a network of professionals with recognized expertise and competence in a particular domain and an authoritative claim to policy-relevant knowledge within that domain or issue area" (Haas 1992: 3). The various contributors to this special issue operationalized the concept, provided numerous case studies, and laid out a research program for the future, which dozens of scholars in disciplines as varied as Education, Management Science, and History of Science, have since followed. International Relations scholars have used it to explain the setup of several international **regimes** including on the ozone layer, acid rain, whaling, or the Mediterranean Sea (Peterson 1992; Toke 1999).

In recent years, the literature has gone beyond the special issue to rethink and explore the boundaries of the concept, particularly in light of increasing globalization and the emergence of new forms of transnational global governance (Cross 2012), of which cooperation in dealing with climate change is a prime example (Gough and Shackley 2001). Epistemic communities can be located both within governance structures as well as outside of them. Moreover, the reason why these groups of experts come together is not as important as how they behave once they form their network. An epistemic community is evident when its members act together beyond their formal mandate, meet frequently in informal settings, develop shared norms, and at times even push against any governmental instructions they might receive to try to influence policy based on their shared expertise. One innovation to the concept is the argument that epistemic communities do not simply exist or not exist, but have varying degrees of influence, depending on their political opportunities (Zito 2001), alliances with environmental NGOs (Gough and Shackley 2001; Meijerink 2005), types of scientific knowledge communicated (Dimitrov 2006), stages of policymaking (Campbell Keller 2009), and internal cohesion as a group (Cross 2012). For example, in the case of international whaling, Peterson (1992) finds that whalers and NGOs had much more influence on the **International Whaling Commission** than epistemic communities of cetologists, as the latter were not as close to decision-makers in government, and had major scientific disagreements within their group at precisely the time when their influence might have mattered.

In an increasingly globalized world, epistemic communities, along with other transnational and non-state actors, such as advocacy networks, multinational corporations, lobbying groups, interpretive communities, rhetorical communities, and communities of practice are of growing importance (see **Transgovernmental networks, Nongovernmental organizations,** and **Business and corporations**). Epistemic communities not only craft specific government policies, but also shape environmental governance more broadly. Meijerink (2005) examines the case study of Dutch coastal flooding policy from 1945 to 2003, and finds that strong advocacy coalitions of safety experts and environmentalists have worked alongside influential epistemic communities of civil engineers and ecologists to develop coastal engineering projects in the Netherlands for **adaptation**. In the area of climate change, Gough and Shackley (2001) find that members of environmental NGOs sometimes contribute to broader epistemic communities as their expertise grows. Indeed, they find that these NGOs may even be too engaged in the formal policy process, as they are increasingly being invited to the negotiation table and losing touch with the constituents whose opinions they wish to represent in the first place.

The concept of epistemic community has faced some criticism, especially stemming from the tendency to neglect the politics and power dynamics that provide the context for knowledge production. Those in power who stand to lose or gain from policy decisions about the environment may easily politicize expert knowledge to suit their own ends (Litfin 1995; Toke 1999; Lidskog 2002). This type of politicization of environmental knowledge has had a clear impact, such as failure to reach agreement in international environmental negotiations or beliefs in some sectors of the public that climate change is a hoax. Thus, while the concept of epistemic communities is valuable in structuring our understanding of the role of expertise in politics, the power context must be taken into account in each case study. Nonetheless, this significant body of research clearly shows that networks with recognized expertise, shared policy goals, and a willingness to act are often highly influential.

## References

Campbell Keller, Ann. 2009. *Science in Environmental Policy: The Politics of Objective Advice.* Cambridge, MA, MIT Press.

Cross, Mai'a K. Davis. 2012. "Rethinking Epistemic Communities Twenty Years Later." *Review of International Studies* 39(1): 137–160.

Dimitrov, Radoslav. 2006. *Science and International Environmental Policy: Regimes and Nonregimes in Global Governance.* Lanham, MD, Rowman & Littlefield.

Gough, Clair and Simon Shackley. 2001. "The Respectable Politics of Climate Change: The Epistemic Communities and NGOs." *International Affairs* 77(2): 329–345.

Haas, Peter. 1990. *Saving the Mediterranean: The Politics of International Environmental Cooperation.* New York, Columbia University Press.

Haas, Peter. 1992. "Introduction: Epistemic Communities and International Policy Coordination." *International Organization* 46(1): 1–35.

Lidskog, Rolf and Göran Sundqvist. 2002. "The Role of Science in Environmental Regimes: The case of LRTAP." *European Journal of International Relations* 8(1): 77–101.

Litfin, Karen, T. 1995. "Framing Science: Precautionary Discourse and the Ozone Treaties." *Millennium* 24(2): 251–277.

Meijerink, Sander. 2005. "Understanding Policy Stability and Change: The Interplay of Advocacy Coalitions and Epistemic Communities, Windows of Opportunity, and Dutch Coastal Flooding Policy 1945–2003." *Journal of European Public Policy* 12(6): 1060–1077.

Peterson, M.J. 1992. "Whalers, Cetologists, Environmentalists, and the International Management of Whaling." *International Organization* 46(1): 147–186.

Toke, David. 1999. "Epistemic Communities and Environmental Groups." *Politics* 19(2): 97–102.

Zito, Anthony. 2001. "Epistemic Communities, Collective Entrepreneurship and European Integration." *Journal of European Public Policy* 8(4): 585–603.

# FISHERIES GOVERNANCE

## Elizabeth R. DeSombre

*Wellesley College, United States*

Fish are an important resource for human consumption, and play central roles in aquatic ecosystems. But they are frequently overharvested, according to a **tragedy of the commons** scenario, and most ocean fisheries are either overexploited or can withstand no additional harvesting (FAO 2012: 53). Governance of fishing resources on the high seas is provided by **regional governance** through Regional Fishery Management Organizations (RFMOs). These organizations generally have a regional focus, and often a species focus as well, as exemplified by the Indian Ocean Tuna Commission.

Although each RFMO has its own rules of procedure, they have some common elements. Decisions about catch limits or permitted equipment are made through a regulatory process that takes place every year or two. Most RFMOs have scientific committees that either conduct or aggregate research. These committees generally make recommendations on sustainable levels of fish catches or other management approaches (see **Science**). Those recommendations are then voted on by a fisheries

72

commission, in which each state has one vote. Often these commission decisions do not require unanimity, and therefore allow dissenting states to opt out of rules with which they disagree. In addition, the regulations passed by fisheries commissions are rarely as strict as scientific advice advocates (Barkin and DeSombre 2013: 72).

Under the best of circumstances, fisheries governance is a challenge. There is often uncertainty about the health of fish stocks and the level of fishing they can sustain. Those whose livelihoods depend on continuing fishing often have short time horizons, and advocate high catches in the short term (even though they are the ones that would most benefit from successful long-term **conservation and preservation**), creating political pressure for laxer rules. And because of the vastness of the ocean and the difficulty of monitoring, **compliance and implementation** of the rules that are created can be low (Barkin and DeSombre 2013: 21–22).

States can also decline to be bound by international regulations, whether by opting out of rules or by simply remaining outside of the international regulatory system. Fishing vessels can also register in "flags of convenience," adopting the flag of states that keep fees and level of regulation low. Since a ship is bound by the rules its registry state has taken on, registry states lure fishing vessel registration by refraining from joining RFMOs.

Fisheries governance is made more difficult by subsidies that many states give to support their domestic fishing industries, thereby generating greater fishing capacity than can be supported by global fish stocks (Sumaila and Pauly 2006). The regional system of fisheries regulation also does not fit well with the global nature of the fishing industry; when ships are prevented by regulation from fishing for a given species or in a particular region, ships can shift focus to a different species or region. The regulated stock may be well protected, but at the cost of increased fishing pressure elsewhere.

## References

Barkin, J. Samuel and Elizabeth R. DeSombre. 2013. *Saving Global Fisheries.* Cambridge, MA, MIT Press.

Food and Agriculture Organization (FAO). 2012. *State of the World's Fisheries and Aquaculture.* Rome, FAO.

Sumaila, Ussif Rashid and Daniel Pauly (Eds.). 2006. *Catching More Bait: A Bottom-Up Re-Estimation of Global Fisheries Subsidies.* Fisheries Centre Research Reports 14(6). University of British Columbia, Vancouver.

# GAIA THEORY

## Karen Litfin

*University of Washington, United States*

At its simplest, Gaia theory is a falsifiable scientific hypothesis which posits that Earth's biosphere interacts with the atmosphere, lithosphere, and hydrosphere in ways that create planetary conditions conducive to the furtherance of life (Lovelock 1979). In contrast to conventional evolutionary theory, Gaia theory postulates that life (including humans and non-humans following an **ecocentrist** approach), rather than merely adapting to a fixed environment, co-creates its environment. Gaia theory represents a paradigm shift from reductionism to scientific holism, most evident in its contribution to the integrative field of Earth system science.

Yet Gaia theory's sociopolitical impact may be even greater. By endowing the ancient image of *anima mundi* (or living Earth) with scientific credibility, Gaia theory undercuts modernity's mechanistic conception of Earth as a vast storehouse of inert resources for human consumption. Already, Gaia theory is influencing the full panoply of academic disciplines in its depiction of Earth as a complex system constituted by the biosphere, the atmosphere, the hydrosphere, and the lithosphere (Crist and Rinker 2009). The theory emerged just as the double-edged sword of globalization and environmental destruction signaled the urgent need for planetary governance. While Gaia theory's implications for political institutions are necessarily unclear at this early juncture, we can nonetheless discern some broad principles.

At a minimum, the incompatibility of existing human systems with Gaian equilibrium suggests a need for a systemic understanding of Gaia's great biogeochemical subsystems: the global carbon, nitrogen, oxygen, sulfur, and water cycles. The global economy, which drives matter and energy on a linear trajectory from resource extraction to production to consumption, is profoundly at odds with living systems, where one species' "waste" is always another species' food. Living systems, from the cell to Gaia, are constituted through interdependent symbiotic networks that transform waste into food even as they propel Gaia's geophysiology (Litfin 2012). Gaian governance would regulate production and consumption within the homeostatic equilibrium of the Earth system. Unlike today's competitive global economy, the actors in a Gaian economy would operate to the benefit of both themselves and the whole.

A Gaian politics would involve symbiotic networks rather than centralized or authoritarian institutions. A mode of governance informed by Gaia theory would therefore comprise a nested system of participatory democratic polities, applying models such as **global deliberative democracy** at different **scales**. The guiding principle would be subsidiarity, the idea that social and political decisions should be made at the lowest level practicable. Ecologically, the question would be: *what functions are most appropriate to the global scale?* A global Internet might pass the test, but most of today's trade and travel would not. Gaian governance would therefore entail relocalization, but this alone would leave the primary levers of power in the hands of the powers that be. The need, therefore, is to "think *and* act globally *and* locally." In a profoundly unequal world, this raises the enormous distributive question: how should economic development proceed in an ecologically full world? (Litfin 2010). Likewise, Gaian governance highlights the perennial procedural question—*who gets to decide and how?*—on a planetary scale. Natural and social scientists are collaborating on all of these questions in the emerging field of Earth-system governance (Biermann et al. 2012).

In a time when anxiety and despair threaten our capacity for positive action, Gaia reminds us that we are an integral part—and an astonishing result—of an evolutionary process that has been unfolding on our home planet for over four billion years. We are neither separate from nor masters of nature; rather, we are the means by which Gaia is growing into self-awareness. The ramifications of this insight will no doubt suffuse human culture and institutions for generations to come.

## *References*

Biermann, Frank, K. Abbott, S. Andresen, K. Bäckstrand, S. Bernstein, M.M. Betsill, H. Bulkeley, B. Cashore, J. Clapp, C. Folke, A. Gupta, J. Gupta, P.M. Haas, A. Jordan, N. Kanie, T. Kluvánková-Oravská, L. Lebel, D. Liverman, J. Meadowcroft, R.B. Mitchell, P. Newell, S. Oberthür, L. Olsson, P. Pattberg, R. Sánchez-Rodríguez, H. Schroeder, A. Underdal, S. Camargo Vieira, C. Vogel, O.R. Young, A. Brock, R. Zondervan. 2012. "Earth System Governance: Navigating the Anthropocene." *Science* 335: 1306–1307.

Crist, E. and Rinker, B. (Eds.). 2009. *Gaia in Turmoil: Climate Change, Biodepletion, and Earth Ethics in an Age of Crisis*. Cambridge, MA: MIT Press.

Litfin, Karen. 2010. "Principles of Gaian Governance: A Rough Sketch." In *Gaia in Turmoil: Climate Change, Biodepletion, and Earth Ethics in an Age of Crisi*s, Eds. Eileen Crist and H. Bruce Rinker, 195–219. Cambridge, MA, MIT Press.

Litfin, Karen. 2012. "Thinking Like a Planet: Integrating the World Food System into the Earth System." In *International Handbook of Environmental Politics*, 2nd Edition, Ed. Peter Dauvergne, 419–430. Cheltenham, Edward Elgar.

Lovelock, J. 1979. *Gaia: A New Look at Life on Earth*. Oxford, Oxford University Press.

# GLOBAL DELIBERATIVE DEMOCRACY

## John Dryzek

*Australian National University, Australia*

Global deliberative democracy as developed by (among others) Bohman (2007) and Dryzek (2006), then applied to environmental affairs by Baber and Bartlett (2009), involves application of ideas drawn from the theory and practice of deliberative democracy to global governance. As such it seeks to redeem the promise of **green democracy** at the global level. Deliberative democracy rests on the idea that democratic legitimacy depends on the right, capacity, and opportunity of those subject to a collective decision (or their representatives) to participate in consequential deliberation about the content of that decision. Deliberation in turn is a particular form of communication that involves mutual justification of and reflection upon the reasons for collective actions, though it is also open to a range of communications such as rhetoric and testimony, not just argument. Participants should strive to make sense to those who do not share their conceptual framework. So, for example, supporters of **deep ecology** should endeavor to reach those who subscribe to business-friendly versions of **sustainable development** such as **liberal environmentalism** or **ecological modernization**. Deliberative democratic ideas are more applicable to global politics than conventional approaches to democracy that emphasize elections, which are currently hard to envisage being organized at the global level. The principles of deliberative democracy can be used to both evaluate existing practices such as **treaty negotiations** (normally a long way from the ideal) and inform prescriptions for institutional arrangements such as citizen forums and more informal practices such as the engagement of environmental **nongovernmental organizations** with each other and with established centers of power.

In an environmental context (at any level) many authors claim that deliberative democracy can produce more **effective** collective decisions, not just more legitimate ones (Smith 2003; Baber and Bartlett 2005). The specifically environmental case for deliberative democracy rests on several theoretical claims. The first is that deliberation provides an effective mechanism for integrating the perspectives of those concerned with different aspects of complex problems, be they experts, ordinary people, political activists, or public officials. The second is that deliberation brings collective as opposed to partial interests to the fore, because points made through reference to **global public goods** or generalizable interests are

76

more powerful than those based on partial interests. Environmental conservation and the condition of commons resources therefore stand to benefit. The third is that **participation** in deliberation brings to mind the interests of those who are not present in a particular forum—and this can extend to future generations and nonhumans (see **Ecocentrism** and **Justice**). The fourth is that deliberation is a particularly good way of incorporating feedback on the condition of social-ecological systems into collective decision processes. The fifth is that participation in deliberative forums helps make people better environmental citizens. Findings from micro-level studies of citizen forums offer empirical support to these claims, though more important is whether they can be redeemed in macro-level systems. Here the evidence is less compelling, because such systems have rarely been organized along deliberative lines.

From the point of view of deliberative democracy, global environmental governance currently looks problematic for several reasons (Stevenson and Dryzek 2014). The first is that communication often occurs among actors organized within enclaves of like-minded actors. Such enclaves might include various World Business Summits, and radical civil society forums such as Klimaforum09 organized in parallel with the UNFCCC Conference of the Parties in Copenhagen in 2009. The second is that the vitality of deliberative activity in the broader public sphere does not extend into the forums where global agreements are negotiated by the representatives of states. The third is that new forms of transnational networked environmental governance (such as the International Council for Local Environmental Initiatives, cities network, or the Clean Technology Fund; see **transgovernmental networks** and **partnerships**) often feature representation only from a limited range of governmental and market actors. In practicing, seemingly deliberative forums can fall short on inclusiveness and consequentiality, as Schouten et al. (2012) demonstrate for the cases of multi-stakeholder roundtables on responsible soy production and sustainable palm oil production. On the other hand, global environmental governance is not irredeemable in deliberative terms. Litfin's (1994) account of the force of the "ozone hole" idea in spurring agreement on the **ozone regime** 1987 Montreal Protocol suggests rhetoric can make a difference; and rhetoric is just one of the forms of persuasion that can be (conditionally) accepted in deliberative democracy.

In light of the current obvious deliberative deficiencies, a number of reforms have been proposed by deliberative democrats. Many have been implemented in environmental governance at different **scales** (local, regional, and national), but relatively few at the global level. One reform would be to introduce moments of citizen deliberation directly into the system. The most ambitious of such global attempts to date have been the World Wide Views processes conducted on the **climate change regime** in 2009 and on **biodiversity regime** in 2012 (Rask et al. 2012). In both cases a forum of 100 ordinary citizens using an identical design was conducted on the same day in thirty-eight countries (on climate change) or twenty-five countries (biodiversity). In almost all countries citizens supported stronger action than their governments were prepared to contemplate. The results were presented at subsequent international negotiations but had no obvious impact on the content of the negotiations. Baber and Bartlett (2009) suggest instead using citizen juries to deliberate hypothetical environmental issues in order to generate principles that could be added to a body of international common law; they have conducted pilots in several countries.

Other reform proposals target the system of global governance as a whole. They include promoting deliberation across as well as within enclaves in the broader public sphere. So, for example, we might seek engagement across gatherings in parallel to **summit diplomacy**, for instance organized by the World Business Council for Sustainable Development and radical forums such as the Peoples Summit for Social and Environmental Justice during the United Nations Conference on Sustainable Development (Rio+20) in 2012. International treaty negotiations could be made more like deliberation than bargaining by reforming process—for example, putting them under the auspices of a facilitator rather than a chair, following procedural guidelines of deliberation as opposed to rules of debate. Negotiators could be encouraged to make themselves accountable to civil society representatives in deliberative (two-way) as opposed to the more common narrative (one-way) style that characterizes government delegation briefings for their national media and NGOs at multilateral negotiations. Governance networks such as the Climate Technology Initiative's Private Financing Advisory Network could benefit from more contestatory activity involving activists and not just low-visibility communication among like-minded state and market actors. The role of expertise (such as that claimed by the Intergovernmental Platform on Biodiversity and Ecosystem Services) could be re-thought in ways that would involve validation by competent citizens— not just assertion of the authority of science as is the case for most **boundary organization**s. The deliberative qualities of the system as a whole might benefit from moments of disruption that force reflection and establish or drive home the seriousness of particular concerns. So, for example, the **shaming** strategy of the Climate Action Network's Fossil of the Day ceremony at UNFCCC negotiations can sometimes induce reflection and more considered justification of positions on the part of its recipients.

In global environmental governance no less than elsewhere, democratic legitimacy matters, and so does policy **effectiveness**. Global deliberative democracy is an attempt to realize these twin aims by seeking authentic, inclusive, and consequential deliberation.

### References

Baber, Walter F. and Robert V. Bartlett. 2005. *Deliberative Environmental Politics: Democracy and Ecological Rationality*. Cambridge, MA, MIT Press.

Baber, Walter F. and Robert V. Bartlett. 2009. *Global Democracy and Sustainable Jurisprudence: Deliberative Environmental Law*. Cambridge, MA, MIT Press.

Bohman, James. 2007. *Democracy Across Borders: From Demos to Demoi*. Cambridge, MA, MIT Press.

Dryzek, John S. 2006. *Deliberative Global Politics: Discourse and Democracy in a Divided World*. Cambridge, Polity Press.

Litfin, Karen T. 1994. *Ozone Discourses: Science and Politics in Global Environmental Cooperation*. New York, Columbia University Press.

Rask, Mikko, Richard Worthington, and Minna Lammi. 2011. *Citizen Participation in Global Environmental Governance*. London, Earthscan.

Schouten, Greetje, Pieter Leroy, and Pieter Glasbergen. 2012. "On the Deliberative Capacity of Private Multi-Stakeholder Governance: The Roundtables on Responsible Soy and Sustainable Palm Oil." *Ecological Economics* 83: 42–50.

Smith, Graham. 2003. *Deliberative Democracy and the Environment*. London, Routledge.

Stevenson, Hayley and John S. Dryzek. 2014. *Democratizing Global Climate Governance*. Cambridge, Cambridge University Press.

# GLOBAL ENVIRONMENTAL FACILITY

**Benjamin Denis**

*Université Saint-Louis - Bruxelles, Belgium*

The Global Environment Facility (GEF) is an international organization dedicated to the protection of the global environment through the financing of projects in developing countries and countries in transition, including **emerging countries**.

Initially launched in 1991 as a temporary three-year co-financing program managed by the **World Bank**, this initiative—jointly supported by UNDP and the **United Nations Environment Programme**—was a political compromise reflecting power relations at that time (Young and Boehmer-Christiansen 1998). Creating the GEF fostered the preparatory work of the 1992 Rio **Summit** by demonstrating the goodwill of developed countries regarding one of the developing countries' demands and it also pre-empted "other proposals for the creation of financial mechanisms" (Boisson de Chazournes 2005: 193). The creation of a stand-alone organization would have been more costly and developed countries preferred at that stage to launch a pilot before contemplating either the creation of a new structure or the integration of environmental issues into the World Bank portfolio as the US would have liked.

Occasionally portrayed as being dominated by the World Bank (Gupta 1995), the GEF became an independent and permanent organization in 1994. Since then, as a fully fledged organization, it has had its own structure and decision-making procedures that reflect a subtle balance between two major preoccupations: equitable and balanced representation on the one hand and, on the other hand, the need to take into account the financial contributions made by donor countries (Boisson de Chazournes 2005: 196–197). For instance, the Council, which is the GEF's main governing body, is made up of thirty-two members, eighteen from beneficiary countries (sixteen developing countries and two from countries in transition) and fourteen from developed countries. Replicating the Bretton-Woods model of constituencies, most members represent groups of states. This complex system ensures a broad and balanced representation of the various categories of states within the entity, which adopts and evaluates GEF's policies and programs. The decision-making procedure also seeks to strike a complex balance: it is based on consensus but also foresees a double-weighted system, which requires 60 percent of the total amount of contributions and 60 percent of participating states. It responds to the universality principle—"one state, one vote"—but, at the same time, accords the right of veto to the main donor countries. However, the voting procedure has never been invoked.

The funds administered by the GEF are made up of voluntary grants provided by states. Every four years, countries that want to participate pledge financial resources and discuss the GEF activities through negotiations called "GEF replenishment." The fifth replenishment of the GEF Trust Fund mobilized $4.34 billion for the period 2011–2014.

One of the GEF's main features is to cover different issue areas. The initial four so-called "focal areas"—**climate change**, international waters, **biodiversity**, and the **ozone** layer—have been progressively complemented by additional issues, notably land degradation and persistent organic pollutants. The cross-cutting nature was strengthened by the formal appointment of the GEF as an "operating entity" of various environmental treaties such as the **Persistent Organic Pollutants Convention** and the **Desertification Convention**. Its multi-area, multi-convention nature is a source of synergies and provides for economies of scale but can also lead to **institutional interactions** and coordination challenges given the proliferation of guidance and entities the GEF has to work with (Boisson de Chazournes 2005: 200–201).

With regard to its funded projects, the GEF cooperates with agencies that are responsible for project development and management. Initially, UNDP, UNEP, and the World Bank were the only three implementing entities working with the GEF. This list has been extended to include development banks and other UN agencies so that there are currently ten international entities operating as GEF implementing agencies. The GEF is currently launching a pilot project aimed at working with partner agencies that can also be national entities.

Despite limited financial resources (Clémençon 2007), the GEF can be seen as an essential element of global environment governance. This autonomous but embedded institution, steered by entities made up of states' representatives, works through a network of actors with different profiles, and thus epitomizes what governance beyond the state could concretely mean (Streck 2001).

## References

Boisson de Chazournes, Laurence. 2005. "The Global Environment Facility (GEF): A Unique and Crucial Institution." *Review of European and International Environmental Law* 14(3): 193–201.

Clémençon, Raymond. 2007. "Funding for the GEF Continues to Decline." *The Journal of Environment and Development* 16(1): 3–7.

Gupta, Joyeeta. 1995. "The Global Environment Facility in a North–South Context". *Environmental Politics* 4(1): 19–43.

Streck, Charlotte. 2001. "The Global Environment Facility: A Role Model for International Governance." *Global Environmental Politics* 1(2): 71–94.

Young, Zoe and Sonja Boehmer-Christiansen. 1998. "Green Energy Facilitated? The Uncertain Function of the GEF." *Energy and Environment* 9(1): 35–59.

# GLOBAL ENVIRONMENTAL GOVERNANCE STUDIES

## Oran R. Young

*University of California, Santa Barbara, United States*

The need for environmental governance beyond the level of the state arises in situations where (1) human users exploit common pool resources (e.g. fish, marine mammals, genetic resources) that are located outside the jurisdiction of individual states or move across boundaries of national **sovereignty**, (2) human activities involve the use of other resources located in international spaces (e.g. deep seabed minerals, the geomagnetic spectrum), (3) environmental externalities have transboundary impacts (e.g. long-range air pollution), and (4) there is a need to protect or enhance ecosystems of international importance (e.g. the stratospheric ozone layer, the climate system). In municipal or domestic systems, we ordinarily turn to governments to fulfill needs for environmental governance. But the anarchic character of international society rules out this approach to the supply of environmental governance beyond the level of the state. This has given rise to a sustained interest in the conditions under which it is possible to meet needs for governance in the absence of a government. Research on "governance without government" is well developed with regard to small-scale settings where face-to-face interaction is common and social norms and culturally embedded practices often provide a basis for addressing needs for governance (Ostrom et al. 2002). As the success of the effort to phase out the production and consumption of ozone-depleting substances demonstrates in the case of the **ozone regime**, meeting needs for governance at the international or global level in the absence of a government is also possible. This realization has triggered a stream of research concerned with needs for governance involving environmental issues and with possible solutions that do not require fundamental changes in the character of international society through, for instance, **regional governance** systems.

The resultant body of global environmental governance studies, reflected prominently in journals such as *Global Environmental Politics* and *International Environmental Agreements*, directs attention to several interrelated but distinct substantive themes (Young et al. 2008). Initially, the research community focused on the determinants of success or failure in efforts to form governance systems or **regimes** as they are often called. A natural corollary deals with the **effectiveness** of international environmental regimes. Why do some regimes (e.g. the ozone regime) succeed in meeting the need for governance, while other regimes (e.g. the **climate change regime**) fail? From these core concerns, the field has branched out in several directions. Some analysts have directed attention to change in environmental governance systems, looking for patterns in the responses of regimes to combinations of internal and external pressures. Others have studied **institutional interactions**, including the consequences of interplay between environmental regimes and similar governance systems operating in other issues areas (e.g. the international trade regime). Still others, struck by the developments we now characterize as the onset of the anthropocene, ask whether the requirements for success in this new era differ from earlier requirements (Biermann 2012). Cross-cutting these substantive concerns is an interest in the design of successful governance systems. Can we extract lessons from the study of environmental governance systems that will make it possible to design and implement more effective arrangements to address emerging needs for environmental governance in international society?

The field of global environmental governance studies is eclectic with regard to methodology. The mainstream consists of theoretically grounded but qualitative case studies (Andresen et al. 2012). Hundreds of such case studies are now available. There is also a small but growing body of quantitative studies that deal with relatively large universes of cases and make use of statistical procedures to develop empirical generalizations about environmental governance systems (Breitmeier et al. 2011). A notable feature of recent research in this field is a search for methods that make it possible to analyze sizable numbers of cases, while probing the complex patterns of causality that are common in this field. An example is Qualitative Comparative Analysis, which employs Boolean algebra to search for sets of conditions that are necessary or sufficient to explain outcomes of interest (e.g. the success or failure of environmental governance systems) (Stokke 2012). Convergence in the findings emanating from several modes of analysis reinforces confidence in the validity of the conclusions; divergence leads to the framing of new puzzles energizing the next phase of research. Today, this field remains a vibrant source of insights regarding environmental governance.

## References

Andresen, Steinar, Elin Lerun Boasson, and Geir Hønneland (Eds.). 2012. *International Environmental Agreements.* New York, Routledge.
Biermann, Frank. 2012. "Greening the United Nations Charter: World Politics in the Anthropocene." *Environment: Science and Policy for Sustainable Development* 54(3): 6–17.

Breitmeier, Helmut, Arild Underdal, and Oran Young. 2011. "The Effectiveness of International Environmental Regimes." *International Studies Review* 13(4): 579–605.

Ostrom, Elinor, Thomas Dietz, Nives Dolsak, Paul C. Stern, Susan Stonich, and Elke U. Weber (Eds.). 2002. *The Drama of the Commons*. Washington, National Academy Press.

Stokke, Olav S. 2012. *Disaggregating International Regimes*. Cambridge, MA, MIT Press.

Young, Oran R., Leslie A. King, and Heike Schroeder (Eds.). 2008. *Institutions and Environmental Change*. Cambridge, MA, MIT Press.

# GLOBAL PUBLIC GOOD

## Sélim Louafi

*Cirad, France*

The concept of global public good (GPG) draws from at least two theoretical backgrounds. The first one relates to the extension to the global level of the public good theory developed in the 1950s by the economist and Nobel laureate Paul Samuelson. It builds on the two attributes of publicness (as opposed to private goods): non-rivalry (no one is affected by the consumption of these goods by others) and non-excludability (no one can be excluded from their consumption). In the case of GPG, these two attributes span across national boundaries: the public good has benefits that extend across national **sovereignty**, substantial cross-border externalities and is consumed by all. Sunlight or climate stability are two classic illustrations of non-rival and non-excludable goods at the global level (for a discussion on non-excludable but rival goods, see **Tragedy of the commons**). With globalization and increased interdependence between countries, public goods increasingly acquire such global scope.

The second theory comes from the field of **critical political economy**. It focuses on the limitations of the current international architecture to address global challenges. Three gaps in global policy-making lead to the underprovision of GPGs (Kaul et al. 1999: 450): (1) a jurisdictional gap due to the discrepancy between the global scope of challenges and the territorial competencies of nation states; (2) a **participation** gap due to the under-representation of many stakeholders contributing to GPGs in international policymaking; and (3) an incentive gap due to the lack of sufficient inducement at the international level to cooperate for GPGs.

In the absence of one unique international government on global environmental governance, being one individual **regime** or one **world environment organization**, collective actions between state and non-state actors at the global level are essential for the provision of GPGs. Transnational problems and international coordination to deal with them existed long before the GPG concept emerged (e.g. cholera epidemic containment in the nineteenth century). The concept however provided an analytical framework to address in a systematic manner issues with similar characteristics and previously only considered in a discrete or sectoral way, such as access to medicines and access to food (Segasti and Bezanson 2001: 1).

While some global issues have public characteristics by nature, many GPGs are constructed. In these cases, the distinction between privateness and publicness results from a political decision with regard to the allocation of property rights—and thus of rivalry and excludability. Plant genetic resources are not inherently global public goods but it was a decision of the member states to the International Treaty on Plant Genetic Resources for Food and Agriculture (ITPGRFA) to construct them this way. This raises many questions: How are collective preferences aggregated at the international level? How are GPGs to be financed? What is the role of international organizations in their provision?

This concept has raised extensive debates in the literature about its fuzziness and usefulness (Carbone 2007: 185). Despite these weaknesses, it cannot be contested that this concept has raised real issues faced by the international community that were formalized in the Millennium Development Goals. Although the longevity of this concept could be questioned (the bulk of the literature about GPGs is from the 2000s), it has indisputably led to some major innovations that continue to shape current international discussions—for example in terms of new international agreements, such as the ITPGRFA, and of new multi-scale governance approaches for development assistance, such as the funding of international agronomic research.

## *References*

Carbone, Maurizio. 2007. "Supporting or Resisting Global Public Goods? The Policy Dimension of a Contested Concept." *Global Governance* 13(2): 179–198.

Kaul, Inge, Isabelle Grunberg, and Marc Stern (Eds.). 1999. *Global Public Goods: International Cooperation in the 21st Century*. New York, Oxford University Press.

Segasti, Francisco and Keith Bezanson. 2001. *Financing and Providing Global Public Goods: Expectations and Prospects*. Stockholm, The Swedish Ministry of Foreign Affairs.

# GRASSROOTS MOVEMENTS

## Brian Doherty

*Keele University, United Kingdom*

Although the meaning of "grassroots" is debatable, there is broad agreement that grassroots movements share certain characteristics: they exist outside political institutions, that is they are not the creation of governments or political parties; they have informal organizations, without professional staff (which distinguishes them from **nongovernmental organizations**); participants are not for the most part powerful or well resourced; and their scope is mainly local, in that they pursue issues within a specific locality.

Beyond these broad tendencies, there is a lack of systematic data on grassroots movements, in part because they are so numerous. For instance, thousands of grassroots campaigns on environmental issues are being pursued globally at any one time, so that it would be impossible for scholars to analyze or even record all of them. Thus academic knowledge is based on case studies of particular grassroots campaigns, which are not necessarily scientifically comparable (Rootes 2007). Empirically, grassroots environmental movements can be divided into three types: (1) the resistance of "affected communities" in the global South; (2) environmental **justice** campaigns in the global North and (3) direct action anarchistic green networks (mainly in the global North) inspired by **ecocentrism** or **deep ecology**.

The first two of these types of grassroots movement typically emerge in reaction to a new threat or suddenly imposed grievance affecting a locality. In the past two decades the commodification of common resources has led to an upsurge of local resistance groups in the global South against mines, dams, and land grabbing. This can be connected to the neoliberal restructuring of global political economy in which development is closely linked to dismantling environmental and planning regulations and reducing state and social spending. In Latin America in particular the struggles of **indigenous peoples and local communities** and the rural poor against a new extractivism, in the form of mining for minerals, oil, and gas has generated frequent clashes and a strong discourse of resistance organized around **critical political economy**.

The discourses, forms of mobilization and action repertoires of grassroots groups are contingent on the context. For example, Doyle (2004) contrasts militant traditions of non-engagement with opponents by anti-mining activists in the Philippines with the lobby-based strategies and dialogue with mining companies or symbolic direct action favored by Australian activists. Discursively, grassroots movements engaged in conflicts over environmental issues more often define their identity as a defense of community rather than in the name of a global environmentalism. This also means that how they mobilize is shaped by a socially constructed sense of community. In an analysis of environmental **justice** campaigns in the United States, Lichterman (1996) contrasted more hierarchical organizations in communities of color, where support for the campaign was a taken for granted assumption, with the flatter structures of mainly white "green" groups, where becoming activists marked them out as different and in which, as a consequence, they needed to feel they were valued individually. Nor is it necessarily the case that grassroots groups are democratic; they often reproduce forms of inequality that exist in their locality (Hickey and Mohan 2004).

The lack of resources of grassroots groups relative to their opponents means that their impact is often dependent on external factors—economic and political decisions that can make a project unviable (Rootes 2007), or successful alliances with NGOs or other grassroots groups. There is some evidence that reduced communication costs through the Internet have enabled more transnational networking between grassroots groups (Bandy and Smith 2005). Evidence of this is the new transitional NGOs that have developed such as La Via Campesina and the **participation** of grassroots networks in international spaces such as the World Social Forum (Reitan 2007).

Place-based grassroots environmental movements are rarely bound wholly by their location and are linked to national politics and international political actors through network ties (Dwivedi 2001; Doherty et al. 2007; Featherstone 2008). As a result, their discourses are more often pluri-vocal rather than being a simple defense of local autonomy and traditional knowledge against development or Western **science**. However, it can also be argued that such alliances with external actors, including environmental NGOs, run the risk that local agendas are recast to fit with the interests of national or international groups.

## *References*

Bandy, Joe and Jackie Smith (Eds.). 2005. *Coalitions across Borders, Transnational Protest and the Neoliberal Order.* Oxford, Rowman & Littlefield.

Doherty Brian, Alexandra Plows, and Derek Wall. 2007. "Environmental Direct Action in Manchester, Oxford and North Wales: A Protest Event Analysis." *Environmental Politics* 16(5): 805–825.

Doyle, Timothy J. 2004. *Environmental Movements in Majority and Minority Worlds: A Global Perspective.* New Brunswick, NJ, Rutgers University Press.

Dwivedi, Ranjit. 2001. "Environmental Movements in the Global South: Issues of Livelihood and Beyond." *International Sociology* 16(1): 11–31.
Featherstone, David. 2008. *Resistance, Space and Political Identities: The Making of Counter-Global Networks.* Oxford, Wiley-Blackwell.
Hickey, Samuel and Gilles Mohan (Eds.). 2004. *Participation: From Tyranny to Transformation?* London, Zed Books.
Lichterman, Paul. 1996. *The Search for Political Community: American Activists Reinventing Tradition.* Cambridge, Cambridge University Press.
Reitan, Ruth. 2007. *Global Activism.* London, Routledge.
Rootes, Christopher. 2007. "Acting Locally: The Character, Contexts and Significance of Local Environmental Mobilisations." *Environmental Politics* 16(5): 722–741.

# GREEN DEMOCRACY

## Robyn Eckersley

*University of Melbourne, Australia*

The idea of green democracy was developed by environmental political theorists in the 1990s out of a critique of the ecological failings of liberal democracy in the wake of the exponential growth in ecological problems in the post-World War II period. Whereas the "limits-to-growth" debate of the early 1970s (see **Carrying capacities paradigm**) had generated calls for an eco-authoritarian state as the only means of preventing ecological overshoot and collapse, advocates of green (or ecological) democracy argue that more, rather than less, democracy is needed to tackle the ecological crisis. Green democrats also highlight the many ways in which the modern environmental movement and green political parties have enriched liberal democracy.

Green democrats join liberal democrats in arguing that civil and political rights and free elections generally lead to better environmental protection compared to centrally planned economies managed by a one-party state. However, they do not treat this as an ecological vindication of liberal democracy. Rather, they argue that meeting the sustainability challenge requires a stronger and more ecologically informed democracy across all **scales** of governance, but especially at the national level.

According to the green critique, liberal democracy is beset with a range of democratic deficits that favor short-term, well-organized private interests at the expense of the long-term, **global public good** of environmental protection. These problems include the short-term horizons of election cycles, a distorted public sphere and inequalities of political **participation** and bargaining power in the policymaking process. More fundamentally, liberal democracies are criticized for being ill-suited to an ecologically interdependent world because elected representatives have a limited view on accountability and do not have to answer to the constituencies affected by the transboundary and transtemporal ecological consequences of their decisions. Nor do they provide any systematic representation of the interests of the nonhuman world. These arguments for widening democratic representation draw from **ecocentrism.**

The primary goal of green democrats has been to defend and/or develop a range of supplementary rights, norms, laws, administrative procedures, institutions and practices of political participation, deliberation, representation, and accountability that would enable more systematic consideration of long-range, transboundary, ecological concerns. These include new constitutional **human and environmental rights**, new forms of proxy representation for future generations and nonhuman species, new legal principles such as the **precautionary principle**, and new treaties that promote transboundary environmental procedural rights, such as the Aarhus Convention 1998 (Eckersley 2004).

Green democrats also defend **global deliberative democracy** and **reflexive governance** over strategic bargaining, cost–benefit analysis or the aggregation of unreflective preferences because the critical, public exchange of reasons that is the essence of deliberation helps to weed out uninformed and purely self-interested arguments in favor of generalizable interests such as environmental protection. Green democrats have defended "mini-publics," such as citizen juries, consensus conferences, and deliberative polls, as one means of institutionalizing deliberative democracy (e.g. Smith 2003).

Critics have argued that "proxy representation" for future generations and nonhuman species gives rise to new problems of accountability because the environmental representatives do not have to answer to their constituency. Others have pointed out that those who seek to represent future generations and nonhuman others would have their claims tested in the public sphere (O'Neill 2001).

## *References*

Eckersley, Robyn. 2004. "From Liberal to Ecological Democracy." In *The Green State: Rethinking Democracy and Sovereignty*, Ed. Robyn Eckersley, 111–138. Cambridge, MA, MIT Press.

O'Neill, John. 2001. "Representing People, Representing Nature, Representing the World." *Environment and Planning C: Government and Policy* 19(4): 483–500.

Smith, Graham. 2003. *Deliberative Democracy and the Environment*. London, Routledge.

# HAZARDOUS CHEMICALS CONVENTION

## Peter Hough

*Middlesex University London, United Kingdom*

The 1998 Rotterdam Convention on the Prior Informed Consent Procedure for Certain Hazardous Chemicals and Pesticides in International Trade, which came into force in 2004, commits exporters of chemicals banned in their own countries because of their human or environmental toxicity to notify importers of this through a prior informed consent procedure (PIC). Under PIC exporters are obliged to provide Decision Guidance Documents detailing the pollution and health grounds for the domestic restriction of chemicals such as dichloro-diphenyl-trichloroethane and parathion. The Convention was meant to give a legally binding character to Article 9 of the voluntary Food and Agriculture Organization's (FAO) 1986 International Code of Conduct on the Distribution and Use of Pesticides, inspired by the tragedy of the 1984 Bhopal chemical plant **disaster** in India. Thousands of people have died as a consequence of the disaster, resulting from the leak of the chemical methyl-isocyanate, a substance completely unknown to the Indian government hosting the plant owned by the US multinational corporation Union Carbide. The establishment of PIC as a binding international rule was sealed by eventually gaining the support of the chemical industry in the early 1990s, after they had opposed its inclusion even in the voluntary code, after a civil society campaign led by the Pesticides Action Network, an alliance of **non-governmental organizations** set up in 1982 through concern at the polluting effects of increased pesticide use in the Global South. The reason for this "U-turn" by the industry was a fear of the alternatives, such as an outright prohibition of the export of certain pesticides, a bill of which was debated in the United States during 1991–1992 (Hough 1998).

The Rotterdam Convention features a Chemical Review Committee, which considers proposals from Parties or NGOs for including new chemicals to the automatically triggered PIC list (Annex III). By 2013, this contained forty-three chemical formulations. Inclusion on the list requires the unanimous agreement of the Parties. Progress in adding chemicals to Annex III has been slow as **business and corporations** have often persuaded national delegations to block this. Most notoriously the listing of chrysotile (white) asbestos, a known carcinogen responsible for over 100,000 deaths a year worldwide, has been resisted by delegations of major exporters led by Canada, to the horror of that country's prominent environmental movement. Governance hence has inched forward, in line with Rotterdam's "sister" regimes, the **persistent organic pollutants** regime, and the **hazardous wastes regime** (Selin 2010; Hough 2011). The sheer existence of these regimes has created a discourse on global chemical safety and helped expose displays of blatant vested interest. Thus in 2012, in the face of pressure from NGOs and evidence generated by the regime's **epistemic communities**, the Canadians announced that they would no longer oppose this listing of chrysotile asbestos, opening the door for the further evolution of global chemical safety governance.

### References

Hough, Peter. 1998. *The Global Politics of Pesticides: Forging Consensus from Conflicting Interests*. London, Earthscan.

Hough, Peter. 2011. "Persistent Organic Pollutants and Pesticides." In *Global Environmental Politics: Concepts, Theories and Case Studies*, Ed. Gabriela Kutting, 179–191. London, Routledge.

Selin, Henrik. 2010. *Global Governance of Hazardous Chemicals: Challenges of Multilateral Governance*. Cambridge, MA, MIT Press.

# HAZARDOUS WASTES REGIME

## Henrik Selin

*Boston University, United States*

The 1989 Basel Convention on the Control of Transboundary Movements of Hazardous Wastes and Their Disposal is the main global agreement governing the trade and management of wastes hazardous to human health and the environment. Examples of hazardous wastes range from discarded chemicals and household electronic goods to obsolete ships. Most trade in hazardous waste takes place between industrialized countries, but it was mainly movements from industrialized to developing countries and related environmental and human health risks that led to **treaty negotiations** (Clapp 2001).

The Basel Convention is one of the first environmental agreements to mandate "prior informed consent" where an exporting party must receive approval from the importing party before a shipment can proceed. A party can also only trade with non-parties if movements are subject to an agreement that is at least as stringent as the requirements under the Basel Convention. Exports are prohibited to Antarctica and to parties that

91

have adopted domestic import bans. The parties have also developed technical guidelines for the environmentally safe storage and disposal of hazardous wastes.

After the Basel Convention entered into force in 1992, some countries and **nongovernmental organizations** including Greenpeace and the Basel Action Network argued for stricter trade regulations to protect developing countries from unwanted imports (Kummer 1995). The 1995 Ban Amendment prohibits the export of hazardous wastes for final disposal and recycling from countries that are members of the Organisation for Economic Co-operation and Development (OECD) and the EU as well as Liechtenstein to all other parties. A lack of ratifications has prevented the Ban Amendment from taking effect, but the EU has adopted a ban on hazardous waste exports to developing countries.

In addition, developing countries invested in **regional governance** and negotiated regional agreements to supplement the Basel Convention (Selin 2010). The 1991 Convention on the Ban of the Import into Africa and the Control of Transboundary Movements and Management of Hazardous Wastes within Africa (the Bamako Convention) prohibits imports of hazardous wastes from non-African countries. The 1991 Lomé IV Convention bans the trade in hazardous wastes between members of the EU and former colonies in Asia, the Caribbean, and the Pacific. The 1995 Waigani Convention bans the import of hazardous and radioactive wastes to Island countries in the South Pacific region.

The 1999 Basel Convention Protocol on Liability and Compensation identifies who is financially responsible in case of an incident during the transport of hazardous wastes (see **Liability**). The protocol, however, has not yet become legally binding. The parties have also created a **compliance and implementation** mechanism to monitor the generation and transnational transport of hazardous wastes. In addition, the parties have established regional centers assisting parties on capacity building and **technology transfer** for improved waste handling (Selin 2012).

To strengthen governance, the parties in 2011 adopted a strategic framework on implementation outlining goals and performance indicators to better measure progress on waste management. The growing trade in electronic goods for reuse and/or recycling draws increased attention to hazardous wastes. Many people mainly in developing countries involved in the recovery business are exposed to a large number of toxic substances, involving important environmental **justice** issues (Pellow 2007).

## References

Clapp, Jennifer. 2001. *Toxic Exports: The Transfer of Hazardous Wastes from Rich to Poor Countries*. Ithaca, NY, Cornell University Press.

Kummer, Katharina. 1995. *International Management of Hazardous Wastes: The Basel Convention and Related Legal Rules.* Oxford, Clarendon Press.

Pellow, David Naguib. 2007. *Resisting Global Toxics: Transnational Movements for Environmental Justice.* Cambridge, MA, MIT Press.

Selin, Henrik. 2010. *Global Governance of Hazardous Chemicals: Challenges of Multilevel Management.* Cambridge, MA, MIT Press.

Selin, Henrik. 2012. "Global Environmental Governance and Regional Centers." *Global Environmental Politics* 12(3): 18–37.

# HUMAN AND ENVIRONMENTAL RIGHTS

## Sophie Lavallée

*Université Laval, Canada*

In 1972, the Stockholm Declaration stated that a healthy environment is essential if humans are to enjoy their other rights. Since then, the right to a clean environment has been recognized in various instruments. This right, which underpins the same major objective as environmental law, namely the protection of humans through a sound living environment, is not, however, applied by public authorities. The right to environment is a fundamental human right, which humans are responsible for enforcing against states that do not uphold it.

Although the first two generations of human rights, whether civil and political rights or economic, social, and cultural rights, are acknowledged in all universal human rights instruments, the new right to a clean environment is not. Despite the indivisibility of human rights, there are only two universal international conventions that recognize this right in specific circumstances. In the first of these, the Convention on the Rights of the Child of 1989, Article 24 protects the right to the environment in order to further the right of children to enjoy the best possible state of health. The Convention 169 concerning Indigenous and Tribal Peoples in Independent Countries of 1989 also refers to the right to a clean environment in Article 4, which requires states to take special steps to protect the environment of their indigenous peoples (see **Indigenous peoples and local communities**).

It is in terms of **regional governance** that progress in this direction has been made. The 1981 African Charter on Human and Peoples' Rights states that "All peoples shall have the right to a general satisfactory environment favorable to their development." This collective reference to the right of "peoples" is not found in the Additional Protocol to the

93

American Convention on Human Rights in the Area of Economic, Social and Cultural Rights (San Salvador). Despite this, some decisions made under the inter-American human rights system appear to be moving toward recognition for a collective approach to human rights (Francioni 2010: 51).

Neither the European Convention for the Protection of Human Rights, adopted in the 1950s, nor its protocols, recognize a right to a clean environment. In the European system, individual environmental rights are regarded as an extension, by way of interpretation, of other expressly recognized human rights, such as the rights to life, health, private and family life, information, and consultation.

For many authors, despite the anthropocentrism of human rights, the recognition of an autonomous right to a clean environment is necessary (Anderson 1996; Attapatu 2002; Shelton 2007). First, because only a human right is universal enough to allow all individuals to benefit, however inactive their government in terms of protecting the environment. By approaching environmental protection through rights, the right to a clean environment obtains a preferential place in the hierarchy of legal norms, and moves out of the area of preferences that can be changed through policy, into the area of rights that must be compared and balanced among themselves. Second, a right is never fully guaranteed if victims have only an indirect recourse via other human rights. Even though the courts can interpret first—and second—generation rights in a way that punishes environmental violations, they will never be able to ensure optimum protection for the environment using this approach. Proving a causal link between environmental degradation and the undermining of a guaranteed right creates a major hurdle in terms of evidence (Shelton 2007).

A collective fundamental right to a clean environment should therefore be considered, inspired by the example of the African Charter. Indeed, if only the individual aspect of human rights is protected, this may be a factor for social regression. Individual human rights can only prevent the worst from happening, and do not allow for any kind of social progress. More work is needed in this direction to give the right a more collective dimension (Francioni 2010: 54–55).

## References

Anderson, Michael R. 1996. "Human Rights Approaches to Environmental Protection: An Overview." In *Human Rights Approaches to Environmental Protection*, Eds. Alan Boyle and Michael Anderson, 1–24. Oxford, Clarendon Press.

Atapattu, Sumudu A. 2002. "The Right to a Healthy Life or the Right to Die Polluted?: The Emergence of a Human Right to a Healthy Environment under

International Law." *Tulane Environmental Law Journal* 16(1): 65–126; and also in *Human Rights and the Environment*, Ed. Dinah Shelton, 57–118. Cheltenham, Edward Elgar.

Francioni, Francesco. 2010. "International Human Rights in an Environmental Horizon." *European Journal of International Law* 21(1): 41–55.

Shelton Dinah. 2007. "Human Rights and the Environment: What Specific Environmental Rights Have Been Recognised?" *Denver Journal of International Law and Policy* 35: 129–171.

# INDIGENOUS PEOPLES AND LOCAL COMMUNITIES

## Marc Hufty

*Graduate Institute of International and Development Studies, Switzerland*

Indigenous peoples and local communities represent a major but neglected category of actors in global environmental governance. In a nutshell, indigenous peoples were defined by the United Nations in the 1980s as those human groups who have a historical continuity in a territory, a distinct culture and who recognize themselves as indigenous. This comprises up to 350 million people worldwide, 70 percent of them living in Asia. They occupy 22 percent of the world's land area. Local communities is a broader term sometimes used as a way to avoid the controversy over who is or is not indigenous. It commonly refers to communities embodying traditional lifestyles in close contact with their natural environment.

Not long ago, indigenous peoples and local communities were still considered as an impediment to progress towards the rational use of natural resources in a modern world led by nation-states. They were thought to damage the environment by ignorance. Swidden agriculture (slash-and-burn) in particular was emphasized as a major factor in deforestation. Therefore, the incorporation of indigenous and local communities into modern societies was seen as positive, necessary, and unavoidable.

A radical shift in the perception and attitude towards them has occurred through a series of historical developments, namely indigenous peoples' political emergence, an increasing importance accorded to the local level, and the recognition that traditional knowledge may bring key contributions to environmental governance.

Indigenous peoples gradually emerged as a major international category of actors in the twentieth century, first in defense against state pressures, then in a more comprehensive way. The first interventions of indigenous representatives in the international arena date back to the early 1920s when the Iroquois (Haudenosaunee) Confederacy applied for membership in the League of Nations and appealed to it in its dispute with Canada over its **sovereignty** (Ayana 1996). Perceived at that time as a domestic affair involving an ethnic minority, the initiative failed. Yet, indigenous representatives relentlessly addressed the international community until they acquired an international legal status and the issues they raised were considered.

A major development was the adoption of the International Labor Organization (ILO) Convention No. 107 in 1957, in response to reports of labor discrimination against indigenous peoples in Latin America. Later criticized for its paternalism, the Convention had nevertheless situated the question within the context of colonialism and asserted, among other rights, the right of indigenous populations to ownership over the land they occupied, and to compensation if dispossessed. This was followed in 1989 by ILO Convention No. 169, today's major binding international instrument on indigenous peoples, ratified by twenty-two countries, fifteen of them Latin American. Based on the principle of non-discrimination, it recognizes the cultural specificities of indigenous peoples, while requiring that they be allowed to participate in a free, prior, and informed way in matters that affect them, and be consulted in good faith.

Within the UN System, the debate took place in the Sub-Commission on Human Rights. It led to the authoritative "Martinez Cobo Report" (UN 1983) that concluded there is a generally low respect of human rights standards for the indigenous and called for new legal international instruments, paving the way to the landmark 2007 UN Declaration on the Rights of Indigenous Peoples, which asserts, among other rights, their right to self-determination.

These developments occurred in parallel with the political awakening of indigenous peoples at the national level in many countries, especially in Latin America, where it coincided with the 1980s wave of democratization. Despite their many differences, indigenous peoples created political networks at the national and international levels, as well as alliances with environmental and human rights **nongovernmental organizations**, demanding the recognition of their rights. Among these, territorial rights and autonomy were the most sensitive issues for republican states accustomed to seeing their territories as indivisible. States responded to the land issue in diverse ways, from outright rejection to new constitutional models in which land rights were entrusted to communities. Indigenous peoples now legally manage as much as 11 percent of the world's forests (Sobrevila 2008).

The rediscovery of traditional local institutions in the governance of resources provided a theoretical legitimacy for these rights. Studies demonstrated that besides the market and the state, some local institutions had enabled a sustainable management of natural resources, sometimes over very long periods of time (Ostrom 1990). Suddenly, the local had become fashionable. An entire body of studies emerged, calling attention to experiments, especially in nature conservation (see **Conservation and protection**), such as the CAMPFIRE Program in Zimbabwe.

It had become obvious that indigenous and local communities play a crucial role in environmental governance. There is for example a strong coincidence between the world's most biodiverse ecoregions and the presence and diversity of indigenous peoples. And while protected areas are admittedly the main effective mechanism to preserve biological diversity, it has been demonstrated time and again that natural areas managed by local communities are especially well preserved. They have gradually become key partners in the mechanisms aimed at nature conservation, as well as water and forest management (Brosius et al. 2005; Kothari et al. 2012).

Finally, as the technical solutions based on modern **science** have reached their limits in some areas, traditional knowledge and practices are increasingly taken seriously in domains such as agriculture, pharmacology, and the management of ecosystems. This role has been formally recognized in the 1993 **biodiversity regime** Convention Article 8J. It is now understood that indigenous and local communities often have a deep understanding of the complex interactions of environmental cycles (see **Gaia theory**). This expertise could prove critical for example in agroecology, recognized by the Food and Agriculture Organization (FAO) as having a role to play in future food security, or **adaptation** to climate change.

Yet, in spite of this hard-earned recognition, indigenous and local communities are still vulnerable. The confrontation with the modern world is often at their expense. They continue to be expelled from their traditionally inhabited lands for the creation of parks or for dams, soy and oil palm plantations. Their **participation** in environmental governance is also too often reduced to mere attendance at informational meetings in top-down projects. Their potential contribution to global environmental governance has yet to be fully developed.

### References

Ayana, James. 1996. *Indigenous Peoples in International Law*. Oxford, Oxford University Press.

Brosius, J. Peter, Anna L. Tsing and Charles Zerner (Eds.). 2005. *Communities and Conservation*. Lanham, MD, Altamira Press.

Kothari, Ashish with Colleen Corrigan, Harry Jonas, Aurélie Neumann, and Holly Shrumm (Eds.). 2012. *Recognising and Supporting Territories and Areas Conserved by Indigenous Peoples and Local Communities: Global Overview and National Case Studies*, Technical Series no. 64. Montreal, Secretariat of the Convention on Biological Diversity.

Ostrom, Elinor. 1990. *Governing the Commons: The Evolution of Institutions for Collective Action*. Cambridge, Cambridge University Press.

Sobrevila, Claudia. 2008. *The Role of Indigenous Peoples in Biodiversity Conservation*. Washington, World Bank.

United Nations. 1983. *Study of the Problem of Discrimination against Indigenous Populations: Final Report*. New York, Ecosoc, Commission on Human Rights. E/CN.4/sub.2/1983/21.

# INFLUENTIAL INDIVIDUALS

## Bob Reinalda

*Radboud University Nijmegen, Netherlands*

In social history individuals may matter because of their critical ideas, but they need movements and organizations to become influential. Some people make a difference in world history because they become aware of certain dangers very early. Modern technology has often raised expectations, but it took people longer to notice, and think through, the negative consequences, such as the formation of smog in cities and the effects of the pesticide DDT (dichloro-diphenyl-trichloroethane) on wildlife in water. Physicist Harrison Brown warned of such dangers in his book *The Challenge of Man's Future* (1954) and biologist Rachel Carson did so in her *Silent Spring* (1962). However, when most people ignore their warnings, early awareness does not mean that these individuals are taken seriously. To become influential, critical ideas should be elaborated further and attract support. During the 1960s larger groups of young people and critical scientists began to question the assumption that nature could bear any burden human beings might place on it and set up organizations with identifiable spokespersons. Canadian journalist Robert Hunter changed from being a reporter to becoming an activist after his adventurous journey to the Gulf of Alaska, where the US was planning nuclear tests in 1971, and founded the activist **nongovernmental organization** Greenpeace International, which set off for locations where large-scale, but low-visibility, environmental abuses were taking place, to bring them to the world's attention through publicity stunts. In 1972 Donella and Dennis Meadows and their colleagues from the Massachusetts Institute of Technology modeled for the Club of Rome the use of natural resources and announced that the "limits to growth" would be reached within a century.

The increasing environmental consciousness affected the UN too, with a conference on the human environment in Stockholm and the creation of the **United Nations Environment Programme** (UNEP) in 1972. The conference became a stepping stone for private environmental organizations and encouraged multilateral diplomacy in various international organizations. Unlike in the previous phase of consciousness-raising by individuals and NGOs, an intergovernmental organization makes possible the creation, spread and implementation of international standards (e.g. the 1972 **polluter pays principle** of the Organization for Economic Cooperation and Development) and programs. Among UNEP's leading executives two different leadership styles emerged. Canadian Maurice Strong, Secretary-General of the Stockholm conference, UNEP's first Executive Director (1973–1975) and Secretary-General of the 1992 Rio Conference on the Environment, as a leader proved an "initiator," someone with the competence and ability to set up operations, leaving their further development to others. He launched UNEP's Regional Seas Programme (with the 1975 Mediterranean Action Programme, in force in 1978), which later developed into a program for oceans and coastal areas. Strong's successor, Egyptian microbiologist Mostafa Tolba, UNEP's Executive Director between 1976 and 1992, is known for his scientific arguments, persistent consultations with political leaders, and intergovernmental negotiating skills. His organizational leadership and ability to deliver results are shown by the adoption of the 1987 Montreal protocol to the 1985 Vienna convention for the protection of the ozone layer that is part of the **ozone regime**, the creation of the Intergovernmental Panel on Climate Change (IPCC; 1988, together with the World Meteorological Organization) and the permanent Ozone Secretariat (1989), and the adoption of the Basel convention on the transboundary movement of hazardous wastes and their disposal (1989) that is part of the **hazardous wastes regime**) (Tolba 1998). In 1992 in Rio Tolba helped successfully negotiate the framework conventions of the **biodiversity regime** and the **climate change regime** by his mastery of the subjects and diplomatic skills. Oran Young (1991) developed his concept of "entrepreneurial leadership" for his tripartite typology of political leadership (also structural and intellectual) on the basis of Tolba's role. Entrepreneurial leaders frame issues, devise mutually acceptable formulas, and broker the interests of key players in building support for these formulas. Norwegian Gro Harlem Brundtland embodies the "intellectual leader" who generates new ideas. As chair of the World Commission on Environment and Development, established by the UN General Assembly in 1983, she combined political experience, environmental expertise, and intellectual leadership to develop a new political concept that helped overcome several deadlocks and opened up new venues for international political action. The Commission's 1987 report *Our Common Future*, also known as the "Brundtland report," called for a strategy that combined development with the environment, with the term **sustainable development** linking the needs of present and future generations.

Successful individual leadership is discussed more abstractly in the context of bureaucracies. Biermann and Siebenhüner argue in their *Managers of Global Change* (2009) that the **secretariats** (bureaucracies) of international environmental organizations are concerned with their potential to contribute to problem solving in international relations. The bureaucracies of major international organizations with far-reaching mandates and extensive resources are more influential than the small secretariats of environmental agreements with their narrow mandates and limited resources. However, both act as knowledge brokers, negotiation facilitators, and capacity builders. Knowledge brokers influence the behavior of political actors by changing their knowledge and belief systems and have a significant effect on the creation and **effectiveness** of **regimes**. Strong leadership by secretaries-general or senior staff is not automatic, but depends on factors such as the staff's ability to generate and process knowledge and the set of commonly shared basic assumptions that result from previous organizational learning processes. Secretaries-general bring different types of leadership and combine specific qualities and capabilities, as is shown by personalities such as Strong, Tolba, and Brundtland. Strong leadership includes the "ability to rapidly gain acceptance and acknowledgement by employees and externals, to develop, communicate, and implement vision, and to learn and change routines." It correlates positively with organizational performance and will thus increase the influence of international secretariats and their representatives in the development and implementation of international policies (Biermann and Siebenhüner 2009: 58).

Influence through the media is shown by activists, who work as journalists and documentary makers and use their media exposure to promote environmental awareness, such as marine conservationist and filmmaker Jacques Cousteau and documentary maker Nicolas Hulot in France, zoologist and science broadcaster David Suzuki in Canada, "crocodile hunter" Steve Irwin in Australia, and maker of natural history programs for the BBC David Attenborough. Former US Vice-President Al Gore made the film *An Inconvenient Truth* (2006) and, jointly with the IPCC, was awarded the 2007 Nobel Peace Prize. The first environmentalist to win the Nobel Peace Prize was Kenyan political activist Wangari Maathai for her contribution to sustainable development, democracy, and peace (2004).

## References

Biermann, Frank and Bernd Siebenhüner (Eds.). 2009. *Managers of Global Change: The Influence of International Environmental Bureaucracies.* Cambridge, MA, MIT Press.

Tolba, Mostafa K. 1998. *Global Environmental Diplomacy: Negotiating Environmental Agreements for the World, 1973–1992.* Cambridge, MA, MIT Press.

Young, Oran. 1991. "Political Leadership and Regime Formation: On the Development of Institutions in International Society." *International Organization* 45(3): 281–308.

# INSTITUTIONAL INTERACTIONS

## Sebastian Oberthür

*Vrije Universiteit Brussel, Belgium*

## Thijs Van de Graaf

*Ghent University, Belgium*

The number of international **regimes**, **private regimes**, and organizations has grown exponentially over the past decades, both in the sphere of the environment and beyond. Consequently, most environmental issue areas are now co-governed by multiple institutions. This institutional proliferation has led to the emergence in the 2000s of a new field of research within **global environmental governance studies** dealing with "institutional interactions," situations in which one institution affects the development or performance of another institution (Oberthür and Stokke 2011). We address here so-called "horizontal interactions" (Young 2002) between international institutions (and do not cover vertical interplay across different **scales**).

Early research on institutional interaction focused heavily on developing conceptual taxonomies. Young (1996), for example, introduced a

101

distinction between four types of what he terms regime interplay: "embeddedness" within overarching principles (such as **sovereignty**); "nesting" within broader institutional frameworks (such as the nesting of various **regional governance** regimes such as the regional seas regimes within the UN **Law of the Sea Convention**); "clustering" in institutional packages (as is the case with the linked but differentiable components of the **Antarctic Treaty regime**); and "overlap" between regimes in substantial but often unexpected ways (for instance, the phase-out of chlorofluorocarbons under the **ozone regime** prompted states to turn to substitutes, some of which are potent greenhouse gases that are to be curbed under the **climate change regime**).

Building on these conceptual foundations, several scholars have set out to identify the driving forces and effects of institutional interaction. Their research can be mapped along two dimensions (Oberthür and Stokke 2011). First, a basic distinction can be drawn between systemic and actor-centered research strategies. Systemic approaches focus on the relationship among institutions, so that the key variables of interest are located at the macro-level of institutions. Studies of the interaction between the global trade regime and multilateral environmental agreements provide an example of this approach. Actor-centered approaches, by contrast, see actors as either the independent variable or the dependent variable, locating other variables at the macro-level of institutions. Raustiala and Victor (2004), for instance, describe how states have purposefully created inconsistency across the different institutions that govern plant genetic resources as they sought to jolt the international rules in one or another direction.

Second, scholars can focus on different kinds of interaction settings as units of analysis. At one end of the spectrum, research can explore dyadic relationships between two institutions examining the causal pathway through which influence runs from one to the other (Oberthür and Gehring 2006). One may, for example, study the mutual influence of the **biodiversity regime** (CBD) and the **World Trade Organization** (WTO). At the other end, more integrationist approaches explore broader interaction settings involving several dyadic cases of interaction and/or several institutions (e.g. the WTO and several or all multilateral environmental agreements). Such settings have been termed "governance architectures" (Biermann et al. 2009) or "regime complexes," defined as an "array of partially overlapping and non-hierarchical institutions governing a particular issue area" (Raustiala and Victor 2004). Studying sets of institutions may allow us to identify new properties that are not inherent in the individual components but emerge from their interrelationship. Keohane and Victor (2011), for example, study the range of institutions involved in global climate governance and argue that the climate change regime complex has greater flexibility and adaptability than a comprehensive regime could possibly have. Their view contrasts with others who see the fragmentation of institutional structures as at least potentially problematic.

Such research on broader interaction settings has become particularly prominent in recent years, covering both more systemic and actor-centered approaches. Exemplifying a more systemic approach, Johnson and Urpelainen (2012) argue that negative spill-overs encourage regime integration, whereas positive spill-overs foster regime separation. Negative spill-overs exist when cooperation in one issue area undermines the pursuit of objectives in another issue area. Adopting a more actor-centric approach, Van de Graaf (2013) argues that the institutional capture of the International Energy Agency (IEA) by fossil and nuclear energy interests spurred the creation of the International Renewable Energy Agency (IRENA). In turn, IRENA's creation has opened up opportunities for forum-shopping that may make the IEA more responsive to the views and interests of renewables stakeholders.

An important dimension of institutional interaction and complexes concerns their governance effects. While institutional interactions may in principle produce synergistic, cooperative/neutral or conflictive/disruptive outcomes (Oberthür and Gehring 2006; Biermann et al. 2009), most attention has been devoted to instances of conflict. A popular hypothesis has been that the WTO undermines the **effectiveness** of multilateral environmental agreements by "chilling" the negotiation of environmentally motivated trade-related obligations (Eckersley 2004). Nonetheless, a large-*n* study of institutional interaction found that a clear majority of cases of interaction creates synergy, whereas about one-quarter resulted in disruption (Oberthür and Gehring 2006: 12). While a focus of attention on socially problematic interaction may be comprehensible, the significance of synergistic effects deserves particular consideration when thinking about options for improved governance of institutional complexes and fragmentation.

Such thinking about governance options has been further advanced under the heading of "interplay management" that refers to conscious efforts to address and improve institutional interaction and its effects (Oberthür and Stokke 2011). The plea for the establishment of a **World Environment Organization** has in part been justified with problems of institutional interaction and can thus be considered part of related debates. Nevertheless, the governance of institutional interaction and complexes, including its potential and conditions, remains a prominent and promising research area.

## References

Biermann, Frank, Philipp Pattberg, Harro van Asselt, and Fariborz Zelli. 2009. "The Fragmentation of Global Governance Architectures: A Framework for Analysis." *Global Environmental Politics* 9(4): 14–40.

Eckersley, Robyn. 2004. "The Big Chill: The WTO and Multilateral Environmental Agreements." *Global Environmental Politics* 4(2): 24–50.

Johnson, Tana and Johannes Urpelainen. 2012. "A Strategic Theory of Regime Integration and Separation." *International Organization* 66(4): 645–677.

Keohane, Robert O. and David G. Victor. 2011. "The Regime Complex for Climate Change." *Perspectives on Politics* 9(1): 7–23.

Oberthür, Sebastian and Thomas Gehring (Eds.). 2006. *Institutional Interaction in Global Environmental Governance: Synergy and Conflict among International and EU Policies.* Cambridge, MA, MIT Press.

Oberthür, Sebastian and Olav Schram Stokke (Eds.). 2011. *Managing Institutional Complexity: Regime Interplay and Global Environmental Change.* Cambridge, MA, MIT Press.

Raustiala, Kal and David G. Victor. 2004. "The Regime Complex for Plant Genetic Resources." *International Organization* 58(2): 277–309.

Van de Graaf, Thijs. 2013. "Fragmentation in Global Energy Governance: Explaining the Creation of IRENA." *Global Environmental Politics* 13(3): 14–33.

Young, Oran R. 1996. "Institutional Linkages in International Society: Polar Perspectives." *Global Governance* 2(1): 1–23.

Young, Oran R. 2002. *The Institutional Dimensions of Environmental Change: Fit, Interplay, and Scale.* Cambridge, MA, MIT Press.

# INTERNATIONAL WHALING COMMISSION

## Steinar Andresen

*Fridtjof Nansen Institute, Norway*

The objective of the International Convention for the Regulation of Whaling (ICRW) is to establish regulations for purposes of conservation and utilization of whale resources (see **Conservation and preservation**). The Schedule to the Convention is an integral part of the Convention and its purpose is to set the specific conservation regulations applicable. Amendments to the Schedule require a three-quarter majority vote.

The Convention was adopted in 1946 and came into force in 1948 and the first meeting of the International Whaling Commission (IWC) was held in 1949. The IWC has undergone sharp changes over time and three rather distinct phases have been pointed out (Andresen 2008). In the first stage, until the mid 1960s, the IWC was for all practical purposes a "whalers club." It was marked by the depletion of most large whale species due to the predominance of short-term economic interests of the pelagic whaling nations. Advice from the Scientific Committee was disputed (see **Science**), and the scientists were not able to quantify the necessary reductions in the total quota. In the second stage, a more conservation-oriented approach is adopted, due in part to more consensual and advanced scientific advice, but primarily to the fact that depletion had made it impossible for whalers to fulfill their quotas. Most Antarctic whaling nations therefore closed down their pelagic whaling operations and towards the end of this period pelagic whaling was only conducted by the Soviet Union and Japan. The more conservation-oriented approach was also due to a gradual increase in non-whaling members as the IWC was open to all states (Andresen 2000).The last stage of the IWC is characterized by a protectionist-oriented approach.

Why did the IWC turn from a conservation organization to a protectionist body? The main reason was probably the rapid spread of a strong anti-whaling norm in major Western countries (Friedheim 2001). As a result of active environmental **nongovernmental organizations** campaigning, it was now seen as morally wrong to kill whales and **shaming** and blaming towards the few remaining whaling nations was strong (Epstein 2006). New anti-whaling nations became members, actively recruited by NGOs such as Greenpeace as well as the United States (DeSombre 2001). The anti-whaling majority was so strong that a moratorium against commercial whaling was adopted in 1982 and entered into force in 1985 for coastal whaling and for the 1986 pelagic season. By 1988 all commercial whaling had ended, due not least to threats of economic sanctions and political pressure from the United States. However, aboriginal whaling was still allowed, although this type of whaling was not much different from small-scale commercial whaling. The United States is a major aboriginal whaling nation.

How, then, can we account for the recent recovery of the pro-whaling forces? The anti-whalers have a simple explanation: active recruitment by Japan, believed to link its bilateral aid to recruitment and subsequent voting. That is, economic assistance was given to new IWC members voting for the pro-whaling stance (Miller and Dolsak 2007). Links to other international forums can also explain the relative decline in anti-whaling sentiment (see **Institutional interactions**). Important here are developments in the **CITES**, especially over "charismatic megafauna" such as the elephant and large whales (Friedheim 2001). Sustainable use rather than protection is gaining ground, especially among developing countries. Furthermore, the anti-whaling norm has been undermined by a number of factors more recently (Bailey 2008). Despite the fact that the moratorium is still in place, and is likely to be upheld in the foreseeable future, catches have been increasing since Norway and Iceland decided to resume commercial whaling. They did so primarily because limited commercial whaling of certain species is sustainable and this has been endorsed by the IWC Scientific Committee, but not by the Commission. Presently there is most controversy over Japanese large catch for scientific purposes not least due to strong opposition from Australia and activism by NGOs such as the Sea Shepherds.

## *References*

Andresen, Steinar. 2000. "The International Whaling Regime." In *Science and Politics in International Environmental Regimes: Between Integrity and Involvement*, Eds. Steinar Andersen, Tora Skodvin, Arild Underdal, and Jørgen Wettestad, 35–68. Manchester, Manchester University Press.

Andresen, Steinar. 2008. "The Volatile Nature of the International Whaling Commission: Power, Institutions and Norms." In *International Governance of Fisheries Ecosytems: Learning from the Past, Finding Solutions for the Future*, Eds. Michael G. Schechter, Nancy J. Leonard, and William W. Taylor, 173–189. Bethesda, American Fisheries Society.

Bailey, Jennifer. 2008. "Arrested Development: The Prohibition of Commercial Whaling as a Case of Failed Norm Change." *European Journal of International Relations* 14(2): 289–318.

DeSombre, Elisabeth. 2001. "Distorting Global Governance: Membership, Voting and the IWC." In *Toward a Sustainable Whaling Regime*, Ed. Robert Friedheim, 183–200. Seattle, WA, University of Washington Press.

Epstein, Charlotte. 2006. "The Making of Global Environmental Norms: Endangered Species Protection." *Global Environmental Politics* 6(2): 32–54.

Friedheim, Robert (Ed.) 2001. *Toward a Sustainable Whaling Regime*. Seattle, WA, University of Washington Press.

Miller, Andrew and Nives Dolšak. 2007. "Issue Linkage in International Environmental Policy: The International Whaling Commission and Japanese Development Aid." *Global Environmental Politics* 7(1): 69–96.

# JUSTICE

## Katia Vladimirova

*Libera Università Internazionale degli Studi Sociali Guido Carli, Italy*
*and Université libre de Bruxelles, Belgium*

Environmental justice can refer to (1) a social movement concerned with issues of uneven distribution of environmental risks and burdens generated by industrial societies and to (2) a theory of justice that focuses on environmental concerns (Dryzek 1977). This entry looks at the second interpretation of environmental justice and at various justice issues related to the global environment.

Degrading the environment creates multiple problems that, in turn, pose major ethical questions: conflicts over scarce natural resources and changes in the natural environments give rise to violence and discrimination, and create large numbers of environmental **migrants**. Global environmental justice is closely interlinked with global justice, poverty eradication, **sustainable development**, and North–South debates and, in a way, embraces some of their key ethical concerns. For example, since the emergence of the sustainable development concept in the 1980s, questions of equal rights for development have gained more prominence. Use of local natural resources for "unsustainable" development by the **least developed countries** were put into question by the new paradigm, limiting options available to these states for growth. Imposing restrictions on the global South, while maintaining or even increasing consumption in the global North, is one of many moral dilemmas behind the idea of sustainable development. Other examples include, but are not limited to, various trade-offs between the preservation or depletion of natural resources, between economic efficiency or traditional livelihoods of **indigenous peoples and local communities**. Global environmental justice can be interpreted not only in terms of states' actions and responsibilities but also at the level of individuals and organizations.

Rather particular and complicated from the moral perspective is the case of climate change. Climate justice, as part of a broader concept of environmental justice, is often interpreted in spatial terms and refers to the moral obligations of rich countries responsible for the current atmospheric levels of greenhouse gases towards the poor countries that are most vulnerable to the negative consequences of climate change caused by the first group. These ethical concerns were reflected in the principle of **common but differentiated responsibility** and in the **climate change regime**. These obligations are deeply rooted in past emissions, and consistent proponents of climate justice could question whether developed countries should be held responsible for the greenhouse gas levels emitted before the harmful consequences of these actions were recognized (historical emissions). While ignorance could be a strong moral argument with regard to actions taken before the first Intergovernmental Panel Climate Change (IPCC) reports, it can no longer be used as an excuse since the harmful impacts of these actions were confirmed by the world's most authoritative scientific report on climate change in 1990.

There is another important dimension of environmental justice related to its intergenerational, or temporal, reading (Gardiner 2011). Actions of the present generation will have significant impact on the lives of people in the future: biodiversity loss, deforestation and desertification, ocean dumping, nuclear waste dumping, and climate change will all leave the planet a different place for future generations to inhabit compared to how we've inherited it from our ancestors. How much should we provide for the future people and what would be the guiding principles of justice in this case are logical questions to follow. Economists attempt to answer by employing discount rates; however, these seemingly neutral indicators are, in fact, based on value judgments (Stern 2012), a fact that challenges the reliability of economic projections with regard to environmental problems (see **Critical political economy**). Our moral theories, on the other hand, require further development in order to guide our actions towards future people, especially in cases when those actions require sacrifices from the present generation. Some trade-offs between the present and the future are chimerical though. For instance, there is a broad consensus among philosophers, lawyers, economists, and practitioners working on the topic that the needs of the present poor and vulnerable groups should have priority over the interests of the future and that sustainable development should in fact meet the needs of both present and future people.

Environmental justice, in the minds of many, is an anthropocentric concept, which mostly concerns relations among humans. As Jamieson (1994) rightly points out, however, environmental justice should also include moral obligations that humans have towards the global environment, including wild animals, plants, species, populations, or ecosystems (see **Ecocentrism**).

## *References*

Dryzek, John. 1977. *The Politics of the Earth*. Oxford, Oxford University Press.
Gardiner, Stephen. 2011. *A Perfect Moral Storm: The Ethical Tragedy of Climate Change*. Oxford, Oxford University Press.

Jamieson, Dale. 1994. "Global Environmental Justice." In *Philosophy and the Natural Environment*, Eds. Robin Attfield and Andrew Belsey, 199–210. Cambridge: Cambridge University Press.

Stern, Nicholas. 2012. *Ethics, Equity and the Economics of Climate Change*. Center for Climate Change Economics and Policy, Working Paper No. 97; Grantham Research Institute on Climate Change and the Environment, Working Paper No. 84.

# KUZNETS CURVE (ENVIRONMENTAL)

## David I. Stern

*Australian National University, Australia*

The environmental Kuznets curve (EKC) is a hypothesized inverted U-shape relationship between various environmental impact indicators and income per capita. In the early stages of economic growth environmental impacts and pollution increase, but beyond some level of income per capita economic growth leads to environmental improvement. The name comes from the similar relationship between income inequality and economic development called the Kuznets curve. Grossman and Krueger (1991) introduced the EKC concept in an analysis of the potential environmental effects of the North American Free Trade Agreement. The EKC also featured prominently in the 1992 **World Bank** *World Development Report* and has since become very popular in policy and academic circles. The EKC is seen as empirical confirmation of the interpretation of **sustainable development** as the idea that developing countries need to get richer in order to reduce environmental degradation.

However, the EKC is a controversial idea and the econometric evidence that is claimed to support it is not very robust (Stern 2004). It is undoubtedly true that some dimensions of environmental quality have improved in developed countries as they have become richer. City air and rivers have become cleaner since the mid twentieth century and in some countries forests have expanded. But the overall human burden on the global environment has continued to increase and the contribution of developed countries to global problems such as climate change has not been reduced. Carbon dioxide emissions have declined over recent decades in only a few European countries. Therefore, it does not seem to be generally true that economic growth eventually reduces environmental degradation. There is also evidence that **emerging countries** take action to reduce severe pollution (Stern 2004). Japan cut sulfur dioxide emissions in the early 1970s following a rapid increase in pollution when its income was still below that of the developed countries (Stern 2005) and China has also acted to reduce sulfur emissions in recent years (Lu et al. 2010).

Alternatively, while the **scale** of economic activity increases environmental impacts, improvements in technology can reduce these impacts both locally and globally according to the famous IPAT identity (*Impact = Population × Affluence × Technology*). If improvements in technology occur across countries irrespective of their level of income, in developed countries, where economic growth is slow, impacts would decrease over time (Brock and Taylor 2010) while rapid economic growth in emerging countries would overwhelm the rate at which technology improved resulting in increasing impacts. Thus the apparent EKC for some pollutants might be a result of slower economic growth at higher income levels rather than due to the increased income itself. Further research is needed to determine the separate roles of growth rates and income levels.

## References

Brock, William A. and M. Scott Taylor. 2010. "The Green Solow Model." *Journal of Economic Growth* 15: 127–153.

Grossman, Gene M. and Alan B. Krueger. 1991. *Environmental Impacts of a North American Free Trade Agreement*, National Bureau of Economic Research Working Paper 3914. Cambridge, NBER.

Lu, Zifeng, David G. Streets, Qiang Zhang, Siwen Wang, Gregory R. Carmichael, Yafang F. Cheng, Chao Wei, Mian Chin, Thomas Diehl, and Qian Tan. 2010. "Sulfur Dioxide Emissions in China and Sulfur Trends in East Asia Since 2000." *Atmospheric Chemistry and Physics* 10: 6311–6331.

Stern, David I. 2004. "The Rise and Fall of the Environmental Kuznets Curve." *World Development* 32(8): 1419–1439.

Stern, David I. 2005. "Beyond the Environmental Kuznets Curve: Diffusion of Sulfur-Emissions-Abating Technology." *Journal of Environment and Development* 14(1): 101–124.

# LABELING AND CERTIFICATION

**Benjamin Cashore**
*Yale University, United States*

**Graeme Auld**
*Carleton University, Canada*

**Stefan Renckens**
*Yale University, United States*

Labeling and certification programs are a form of **private regime** and **corporate social responsibility** (CSR) instrument that aim to address environmental and social issues in global supply chains by developing standards for responsible **business and corporate** practices and offering market benefits, such as increased prices, to participating operators. **Nongovernmental organizations**, firms, and business associations, or **partnerships** of these actors, develop these programs. Organic farming and fair trade certification emerged in the 1970s and 80s (Raynolds et al. 2007); since the establishment of the Forest Stewardship Council in 1993, this form of governance has proliferated to many sectors, including fisheries, tourism, and the garment industry.

Two main features distinguish these programs from other CSR initiatives: (1) state actors usually do not direct the standard setting process and do not impose their sovereign authority to require adherence to the standards; (2) their survival and authority depends on support from market actors along the supply chain (Cashore 2002). Most programs rely on third-party verification to ensure compliance, and provide an on-product label to identify certified products.

Scholars explain the emergence of certification programs in two main ways. Some refer to the need to overcome information asymmetries between producers and customers and consider certification programs a means to increase responsible businesses' reputation (Potoski and Prakash 2009). Others focus on their emergence in areas of (inter)governmental regulatory failure and the power struggles between and among public and private actors surrounding these new sources of global rules (Bartley 2007; see also **Critical political economy**).

Fitting within the overall norm of **liberal environmentalism,** some see these programs as a potential means to overcome the negative externalities of neoliberal globalization and the underprovision of **global**

**public goods**, such as environmental sustainability (Ruggie 2004); others consider them as instruments perpetuating unsustainable capitalist production and consumption (Lipschutz 2005). Critiques also focus on the distributional consequences of certification, including that certification is costly, can act as a non-tariff trade barrier, and favors larger producers and vertically integrated firms (Pattberg 2006). A major dilemma for certification programs is thus to ensure broad **participation** while maximizing their impact on sustainability. Setting high standards might address the latter; however, it makes **compliance and implementation** difficult, thereby limiting a program's overall impact.

Recognizing these limits, recent research focuses on the interactions among private and public rules to understand how they shape processes of governance, and what these interactions then mean for **effectiveness**. For each process, effects may be positive, neutral, or negative, and can change over time. Beyond bilateral interactions, certification is increasingly examined within larger complexes of institutions where the **institutional interactions** of public and private rules may require orchestration for global governance to operate more effectively (Abbott and Snidal 2009).

## References

Abbott, Kenneth W. and Duncan Snidal. 2009. "Strengthening International Regulation through Transnational New Governance: Overcoming the Orchestration Deficit." *Vanderbilt Journal of Transnational Law* 42, 501–578.

Bartley, Tim. 2007. "Institutional Emergence in an Era of Globalization: The Rise of Transnational Private Regulation of Labor and Environmental Conditions." *American Journal of Sociology* 113(2): 297–351.

Cashore, Benjamin. 2002. "Legitimacy and the Privatization of Environmental Governance: How Non-State Market-Driven (NSMD) Governance Systems Gain Rule-Making Authority." *Governance* 15(4): 503–529.

Lipschutz, Ronnie. 2005. "Environmental Regulation, Certification and Corporate Standards: A Critique." In *Handbook of Global Environmental Politics*, Ed. Peter Dauvergne, 218–232. Cheltenham/Northampton, Edward Elgar.

Pattberg, Philipp. 2006. "Private Governance and the South: Lessons from Global Forest Politics." *Third World Quarterly* 27(4): 579–593.

Potoski, Matthew and Aseem Prakash. 2009. "A Club Theory Approach to Voluntary Programs." In *Voluntary Programs: A Club Theory Perspective*, Eds. Matthew Potoski and Aseem Prakash, 17–39. Cambridge, MA, MIT Press.

Raynolds, Laura T., Douglas Murray, and Andrew Heller. 2007. "Regulating Sustainability in the Coffee Sector: A Comparative Analysis of Third-Party

Environmental and Social Certification Initiatives." *Agriculture and Human Values* 24(2): 147–163.

Ruggie, John Gerard. 2004. "Reconstituting the Global Public Domain—Issues, Actors, and Practices." *European Journal of International Relations* 10(4): 499–531.

# LAW OF THE SEA CONVENTION

## Jaye Ellis
*McGill University, Canada*

The Law of the Sea Convention (UNCLOS), concluded in 1982 and entered into force in 1994, is a quasi-constitutional treaty, addressing the division of ocean spaces into distinct zones, and identifying the rights, competencies, and responsibilities of states and other actors in those spaces. Its substantive environmental provisions are very general; for more specific rules and standards, one must turn to a network of legal and policy texts, customary law, and international organizations.

One of the most important issues in this field is the matter of jurisdiction to adopt and enforce law. Particularly challenging are the high seas, which are res nullius and can be considered as **global public goods** (Rothwell and Stephens 2010). Freedom of the high seas, meaning not subject to the jurisdiction of any state, and the near exclusive jurisdiction of the flag state over vessel activity on the high seas are fundamental characteristics of the law (Warner 2009).

The environmental issues that receive the greatest attention in the UNCLOS are pollution, including vessel-source, land-based and atmospheric (Basedow and Magnus 2007; de la Rue and Anderson 2009), environmental impacts from deep seabed mining, and fisheries (see **Fisheries governance**). Two other important issues are noise pollution and marine protected areas.

The overarching structure of the UNCLOS does not prevent fragmentation in ocean law and governance, which is affected by jurisdictional, sectoral, and regional boundaries, creating potential **institutional interaction** problems. This engenders difficulties for marine environmental protection: the interactions of different ocean spaces and various drivers of environmental degradation are not adequately addressed. Ecosystem management of large marine spaces is an approach to ocean governance that seeks to address this weakness (Wang 2004). The term does not appear in the UNCLOS, but the approach is compatible with the structure and objectives of that convention. Its impact has been felt in the area of fisheries conservation and management (see **Conservation and preservation**), notably in the 1995 Fish Stocks Agreement, which elaborates on provisions in the UNCLOS that straddle the boundary between the high seas and waters over which states have **sovereignty**, and the Antarctic convention on marine living resources. Further progress on implementing this approach is moving forward through collaboration between the **Law of the Sea Convention** and the **biodiversity regime** (Drankier 2012).

### References

Basedow, Jürgen and Ulrich Magnus. 2007. *Pollution of the Sea: Prevention and Compensation.* Berlin, Springer.

de la Rue, Colin and Charles B. Anderson. 2009. *Shipping and the Environment: Law and Practice.* London, Informa.

Drankier, Petra. 2012. "Marine Protected Areas in Areas beyond National Jurisdiction." *International Journal of Marine and Coastal Law* 27(2): 291–350.

Rothwell, Donald and Tim Stephens. 2010. *The International Law of the Sea.* Oxford, Hart Publishing.

Wang, Hanling. 2004. "Ecosystem Management and its Application to Large Marine Ecosystems: Science, Law, and Politics." *Ocean Development and International Law* 35(1): 41–74.

Warner, Robin. 2009. *Protecting the Oceans beyond National Jurisdiction: Strengthening the International Framework.* Leiden and Boston, Martinus Nijhoff.

# LEAST DEVELOPED COUNTRIES

**Alexandra Hofer**

*Université libre de Bruxelles, Belgium*

The term least "developed countries "(LDCs) is a category created by the United Nations General Assembly in 1971 in order to bring support to what the UN describes as the "poorest and weakest segment of the international community" (2001: 3). This grouping of countries currently comprises thirty-four states from Africa, fourteen from Asia, as well as Haiti in the Americas. The UN uses thirteen criteria to identify LDCs, all related to poor income, weak human assets or economic vulnerability. Three of these criteria are linked to the environment and natural resources: agricultural production, undernourishment, and natural **disasters**.

When it comes to LDCs, environmental issues are typically considered through the impact they have on these countries' economies. Because their livelihood depends on agriculture and the consequences of natural disasters hit their economies hard, LDCs are considered to be economically vulnerable to environmental degradation. One only needs to think of the earthquake that devastated Haiti in 2010, or the severe 2011 droughts and resulting famine in East Africa as examples. The vulnerability of LDCs has been recognized in several environmental treaties. The climate convention to the **climate change regime** takes LDCs seriously, stressing the "specific needs and special situations of the least developed with regards to funding and transfer of technology" (Article 4.9). The **biodiversity regime**, the **Persistent Organic Pollutants Convention**, and the **Desertification Convention** adopted similar provisions (for instance in Article 20.5, Article 12.5, and Article 3(d) respectively).

To implement the climate change convention's Article 4.9, the Conference of the Parties adopted in 2001 a LDC working program, establishing a LDC Fund and a LDC expert group in order to implement and finance effective national **adaptation** programs (Williams 2005: 65). Other environmental institutions use similar expert groups in order to take proper measures for LDCs. Occasionally, LDCs benefit from specific sponsored projects that seek to enhance their negotiating capacity and help promote their interests. For instance, LDC negotiators receive assistance from the European Capacity Building Initiative, which aims at helping them overcome structural obstacles and improve their skills within the UNFCCC negotiations. Another well-known support received by LDCs in climate negotiations has been the inclusion of renowned and powerful **nongovernmental organizations** in their delegations, such as FIELD and Greenpeace for small island LDCs (Newell 2006: 13).

Because successful negotiations call for significant financial and human resources, which most LDCs lack (Kasa et al. 2008), LDCs coordinate their actions through the LDC Group, a **negotiating coalition**. This group organizes bilateral meetings with other negotiating blocs, especially the African Group and the Alliance of Small Island States (AOSIS) in climate negotiations over adaptation, in order to coordinate interests and strategies. On a country basis, a LDC will join different negotiating coalitions depending on the issue at stake (Betzold et al. 2011: 3). This is so because significant disparities appear within the LDC category. For example, small island states, such as Tuvalu and Vanuatu, do not always share the same environmental interests as inland African countries. Consequently, small islands LDCs often operate in climate negotiations through the AOSIS, while African LDCs are part of the African Group of negotiators.

The impacts LDCs have on negotiations are usually low. One exception has been the AOSIS, which enabled small island LDCs to have an influential voice in climate change negotiations despite their geographical disparity and limited power. By working as a bloc, using a discourse of vulnerability and working with stronger states, small island states were granted a special seat during the negotiation of the framework convention of the **climate change regime**. As Betzold notes, "This was the first time a seat was specifically reserved for a group other than a UN regional group, and it helped AOSIS to affect the overall coordination of the negotiations" (2010: 139).

African LDCs suffering from land degradation also achieved some relative success through their broader coalitions in the process leading to the **Desertification Convention**. This convention is viewed as an interesting case study because it was "called for by the developing countries" (Najam 2004: 130). Nevertheless, the convention also revealed LDCs coalitions' vulnerability. Indeed, European countries decided, together with the G77, to negotiate an agreement on desertification (the EU was initially opposed to this) in exchange for an international agreement on forests (the G77 was initially opposed to this). The proposal created a wedge between LDCs with rainforests (many of which were opposed to a forests' agreement) and those without. Yet, the first category of LDCs had to accept the G77 proposal (Najam 2004).

## *References*

Betzold, Carola. 2010. "'Borrowing Power' to Influence International Negotiations: AOSIS in the Climate Change Regime, 1990–1997." *Politics* 30(3): 131–148.

Betzold Carola, Paula Castro, and Florian Weiler. 2011. "AOSIS in the UNFCCC Negotiation: From Unity to Fragmentation." *CIS Working Paper* 72: 1–32.

Kasa Sjur, Anne T. Gullberg, and Gørild Heggelund. 2008. "The Group of 77 in the International Climate Negotiations: Recent Developments and Future Directions." *International Environmental Agreements* 8(2): 113–127.

Najam, Adil. 2004. "Dynamics of the Southern Collective: Developing Countries in Desertification Negotiations." *Global Environmental Politics* 4(3): 128–154.

Newell, Peter. 2006. *Climate for Change*. Cambridge, Cambridge University Press

United Nations General Assembly. 2001. "Programme of Action for the Least Developed Countries for the Decade 2001–2010." *Conference on the Least Developed Countries*, A/CONF.191/11.

Williams, Marc. 2005. "The Third World and Global Environmental Negotiations: Interests, Institutions and Ideas." *Global Environmental Politics* 5(3): 48–69.

# LIABILITY

## Cymie R. Payne

*Rutgers University, United States*

Environmental liability is the legal responsibility to provide a remedy for damaging the environment. Activities that can give rise to environmental liability range from pollution of air, land, and water to the effects of **military conflicts**; to the release of genetically modified organisms; to climate-changing actions. States, individuals, and other entities have mutual duties to prevent harm to the environment from their activities and activities under their responsibility or control, based in international **regimes**, customary international law, and domestic law (see for instance the **Preventive action principle**). These obligations may also be owed to the international community as a whole (such obligations are called *"erga omnes"*), **indigenous peoples and local communities**, or future generations. To incur environmental liability there must be an obligation to prevent or avoid harm, a causal link between the responsible party's activity and the harm, and a remedy for the harm. Sanctions include financial compensation, in-kind restoration, and criminal penalties (see International Law Commission 2001). Environmental liability incentivizes prevention of harm, provides accountability, allocates costs of damage, and ensures environmental restoration. Where natural incentives risk depleting or destroying a natural resource (see **Tragedy of the commons**), legal liability and privatization of the resources are alternative management strategies (Sands and Peel 2012.

Examples of liability regimes in international law include the Trail Smelter Arbitration awards for air pollution damage to fruit trees in the US from a smelter in the town of Trail, Canada (see also **Transboundary air pollution regime**; and the International Oil Pollution Compensation Funds (IOPC Funds), an environmental liability regime for oil spills that fall within the scope of the Civil Liability conventions. Both of these examples represent the **polluter pays principle** (Fitzmaurice 2007).

Criticisms of liability as an approach to environmental governance observe that procedural obstacles in proving causation and attribution are often insurmountable and that there are gaps in liability regimes. Some legal regimes control the economic consequences of an incident to a favored industry through insurance or limits on financial compensation; this reduces the preventive and restorative roles of liability. Sanctioning multinational **business and corporations** can be constrained for many reasons, including the terms of initial foreign investment agreements, which are protected by foreign investment treaties (Wolfrum, et al. 2005; Faure and Ying 2008).

The scope of harm subject to environmental liability can include the cost of monitoring the injury, the value of lost use of resources from the time of injury to recovery, and the cost of response measures to mitigate the harm. The subjects of environmental liability have expanded from market-valued resources such as timber and tourism to "pure" environmental (or ecological) resources that are not traded in **markets**, such as wildlife, ecosystems or other public environmental resources, and cultural heritage (Bowman and Boyle 2002). The UN Compensation Commission's environmental claims category based substantial awards on these theories and valuation approaches for the first time in a large-scale international proceeding (Payne and Sand 20011).

This concept is particularly relevant to the protection of **global public goods**, such as the high seas, ecological function, and biodiversity. In such cases, the public interest is protected by public trustees, a concept that is well accepted in US law and becoming more common in other jurisdictions. The role of trustee is assumed by the government, which is legally obligated to use financial compensation provided as a remedy for the benefit of the public interests that were harmed; the UN Compensation Commission created a follow-up program for this purpose (Payne and Sand 2011).

These issues pose challenges to new theories of liability. Climate change liability claims present causation problems and would strain the legal system because the activities that cause climate change are so pervasive in modern life. Damage from commercial GMOs may take a long time to appear, remedies may be inadequate, and attribution is likely to be difficult. Indigenous peoples and local communities continue to face judicial rejection of their cultural damage claims based on subsistence lifestyle. Claims on behalf of future generations and of nature itself have been largely symbolic, so far (see **Ecocentrism** and **Justice**) (Anton and Shelton 2011).

### References

Anton, Donald K. and Dinah L. Shelton. 2011. *Environmental Protection and Human Rights*. New York, Cambridge University Press.

Bowman, Michael and Alan Boyle. 2002. *Environmental Damage in International and Comparative Law: Problems of Definition and Valuation*. New York, Oxford University Press.

Faure, Michael and Song Ying (Eds.). 2008. *China and International Environmental Liability*. Cheltenham, Edward Elgar.

Fitzmaurice, Malgosia. 2007. "International Responsibility and Liability." In *The Oxford Handbook of International Environmental Law*, Eds. Daniel Bodansky, Jutt Brunnée, and Ellen Hey, 1010–1035. New York, Oxford University Press.

International Law Commission. 2001. "Report of the International Law Commission on the Work of its 53rd Session." *Yearbook of the International Law Commission*, 2001, vol. II, Part Two, as corrected, UN Doc A/56/10.

Payne, Cymie R. and Peter H. Sand. 2011. *Gulf War Reparations and the UN Compensation Commission: Environmental Liability*. New York, Oxford University Press.

Sands, Philippe and Jacqueline Peel. 2012. *Principles of International Environmental Law*. Cambridge, Cambridge University Press.

Wolfrum, Rüdiger, Christine Langenfeld, and Petra Minnerop. 2005. *Environmental Liability in International Law—Towards a Coherent Conception*. Berlin, Erich Schmidt Verlag GmbH and Co.

# LIBERAL ENVIRONMENTALISM

## Steven Bernstein

*University of Toronto, Canada*

Liberal environmentalism describes the normative compromise in global governance that has predicated international environmental protection on the promotion and maintenance of a liberal economic order (Bernstein 2001). Environmental governance norms define how policy actors and political communities understand the appropriate purposes and means to which political action should be directed, with important implications for how they address the world's most serious environmental problems.

Liberal environmentalism reflects an historical North–South bargain generated from the interaction of policy ideas and evolving structural features in the wider international political economy. This formulation differs somewhat from Newell and Paterson's argument based on **critical political economy** that economic actors and interests (e.g. finance capital in the contemporary period) empowered by the structure of economic relations have driven practices of global environmental politics in a neoliberal direction. While both literatures point to some similar consequences, "liberal environmentalism" directs attention to the enabling and constraining norms that generate and circumscribe the acceptable range of policy practices and the politics of their resiliency, contestation, and evolution.

Liberal environmentalism differs from the first wide-scale global responses to environmental problems in the late 1960s and early 1970s, which focused on the negative environmental consequences of unregulated industrial development, suspicions of economic growth, and planetary consciousness. The popularization of **sustainable development** by the 1987 Brundtland Commission as a way to link environment and development marked a key turning point. Its articulation promised to integrate the environment, the economy and societal needs under a single rubric, in part to address longstanding worries among developing country elites that environmental concerns would trump economic growth, poverty eradication and access to the markets of wealthy countries. However, Brundtland's focus on intergenerational equity and human needs in its definition of sustainable development—"development that meets the needs of the present without compromising the ability of future generations to meet their own needs" (WCED 1987: 43)—proved, in hindsight, less influential than its proposition that action on the global environment rested on a foundation of liberal economic growth.

Meanwhile, policymakers in the North had increasingly examined their own environmental policies through economic lenses and sought ways to address environmental problems without disrupting economic priorities. This policy trend, characterized by some as **ecological modernization**, focused especially on ways to internalize environmental costs through the **polluter pays principle** and to develop market mechanisms, such as tradable emissions permits (see **Markets**), to address environmental problems. The 1992 UN Conference on Environment and Development in Rio de Janeiro brought these lines of thinking together (see **Summit diplomacy**). It institutionalized the view that liberalization in trade and finance is consistent with, and even necessary for, international environmental protection. It thus embraced and helped legitimize the new economic orthodoxy then sweeping North and South alike, which promoted open markets, deregulation, and working with the private sector to achieve policy goals.

While the 1992 Rio Declaration on Environment and Development includes a range of norms (see Bernstein 2001), liberal environmentalism characterizes its overall interpretation of sustainable development, which Rio Principle 12 articulates most clearly: "States should cooperate to promote a supportive and open international economic system that would lead to economic growth and sustainable development in all countries, to better address the problems of environmental degradation." This interpretation legitimated this understanding of sustainable development across the UN system, the Bretton Woods Institutions and the **World Trade Organization**. For example, the 1994 WTO Ministerial Declaration on Trade and Environment approvingly cites Rio Principle 12, stating, "there should not be . . . any policy contradiction between upholding and safeguarding an open, non-discriminatory and equitable multilateral trading system . . . and acting for the protection of the environment, and the promotion of sustainable development . . . ."

The 2002 World Summit on Sustainable Development further reinforced liberal environmentalism when it promoted public–private **partnerships** to implement sustainable development, a practice the UN **Commission on Sustainable Development** then institutionalized. Partnerships are set to continue their prominent role in the post-2015 development agenda and the work of the new UN High-Level Political Forum on Sustainable Development, which will replace the Commission in 2013 (Bernstein 2013).

Policies and practices continue to reflect norms of liberal environmentalism in a wide range of issue areas, including climate change generally (Newell and Paterson 2010) and specifically transnational and experimental forms of climate change governance—especially the proliferation of carbon markets—largely outside of the formal multilateral **climate change regime** (Hoffmann 2011); forestry (Humphreys 2006); and water governance (Conca 2005).

While liberal environmentalism created the necessary political space for the mainstreaming of environmental protection in global policy, over the longer term it has contributed to fragmentation of institutions and authority, and the subordination of environmental goals to economic principles. Meanwhile, it remains resilient despite ongoing contestation in the governance of particular environmental issues. The latest round of global negotiations on sustainable development leading to the 2012 Rio+20 Conference reaffirmed the 1992 Rio Declaration, reflecting the universal consensus not to reopen negotiations on norms.

That consensus, however, masked ongoing contestation over the meanings of norms and how to implement them (see **Compliance and implementation**). Debate persists, for example, on the meaning of **common but differentiated responsibility** of developed and developing countries (Rio Principle 7), one of the few norms that suggests limits to liberal environmentalism, but also the **polluter pays principle**, which implies internalizing costs for some, but responsibility of industrialized countries "to pay" for their historical pollution for others. Moreover, the attempt to introduce the concept of the "green economy" at Rio+20—which negotiations reframed as "green economy in the context of sustainable development and poverty eradication"—highlights still-sharp disagreements about what sustainable development means in practice. It also renewed suspicions among some developing country governments and stakeholders that the concept tilts policy too far toward the environment, "green" jobs, and investment at the expense of poverty eradication, broader employment goals and **technology transfer**, or development priorities. This contestation signals stress on liberal environmentalism, though the compromise remains resilient in lieu of a clearly articulated alternative. Its spotty implementation also suggests liberal environmentalism's weakness in generating effective policy may be endemic to its underlying political consensus that masks differences rather than confronts or resolves them.

## References

Bernstein, Steven. 2001. *The Compromise of Liberal Environmentalism*. New York, Columbia University Press.

Bernstein, Steven. 2013. "The Role and Place of a High-Level Political Forum in Strengthening the Global Institutional Framework for Sustainable Development." Consultant's report for the UN Department of Economic and Social Affairs. Available at http://sustainabledevelopment.un.org.

Conca, Ken. 2005. *Governing Water: Contentious Transnational Politics and Global Institution Building*. Cambridge, MA, MIT Press.

Hoffmann, Matthew J. 2011. *Climate Governance at the Crossroads: Experimenting with a Global Response after Kyoto*. New York, Oxford University Press.

Humphreys, David. 2006. *Logjam: Deforestation and the Crisis of Global Governance*. London and Sterling, VA, Earthscan.

Newell, Peter and Matthew Paterson. 2010. "The Politics of the Carbon Economy." In *The Politics of Climate Change: A Survey*, Ed. Maxwell T. Boykoff, 80–99. New York: Routledge.

# MARKETS

## Matthew Paterson

*University of Ottawa, Canada*

Environmental policy and governance has seen innovation in recent decades with the creation of markets as policy instruments. These markets operate by creating rights or credits to do with the environmental problem concerned that can be traded among actors within that particular domain. These markets started in the US in the 1970s, but expanded in particular from the 1990s onwards, notably within the **climate change regime**.

The conceptualization of environmental markets started from the 1960s onwards, when environmental economists argued that pollution control could be achieved at lower cost than with traditional regulatory approaches. The role of government would be reduced to one of setting overall goals for environmental policy, and conceptualized as a task of "internalizing environmental externalities"—those impacts of a particular activity that are not contained in its market price.

Achieving this goal can be done either by a direct internalization of those costs, via a **taxation** mechanism, or by creating a scarcity in the rights to cause environmental damage. Environmental markets arise from the latter strategy. Ronald Coase (1960) was the first to argue that externality problems were best understood as a problem of imperfect property rights, and that assigning such rights was the best means to internalize external costs. Dales (1968) extended this argument to argue for the establishment of emissions trading systems to manage environmental problems (for a fuller history see Gormon and Solomon 2002).

In an emissions trading system, an authority allocates rights to emit pollution or use a specific environmental resource, and then enables the rights holders to trade those rights with all the other players. Within a specific time frame each permit holder would have to hold an amount of permits equivalent to the environmental damage (s)he causes. The logic is that while all economic actors thus have an incentive to reduce their damage, those polluters that find it relatively cheap to do so will engage in more aggressive abatement in order to realize profits from the sale of surplus permits, while those that find it relatively expensive will be able to purchase those extra permits rather than reduce their own pollution. The system overall therefore is intended to create incentives both for reduced consumption of particular pollution-producing goods, but also for research and development and investments in alternative technologies.

During the 1970s and 1980s there were a number of experiments, notably in programs to phase out leaded gasoline and chlorofluorocarbons (Gormon and Solomon 2002: 294). The most prominent experiment came in the US Clean Air Act amendments of 1990. These established an emissions trading system in the US for sulfur dioxide emissions. More recently, environmental markets have been established in wetlands (Robertson 2004; Swyngedouw 2007) and in the emergence of payment for **ecosystem services**. Also important were key conceptual innovations, notably the idea of offsets. With offsets, instead of allocating emissions rights, polluters are enabled (or forced) to invest elsewhere in projects to compensate for their polluting activity.

However, by far the largest environmental marketization project has been in the development of carbon markets. These were mooted early on in the debates about climate change (e.g. Grubb 1989). But they became institutionalized only in the later part of the 1990s.

The Kyoto Protocol, agreed in 1997, established three market mechanisms. One is an emissions trading system, whereby industrialized states' obligations to reduce their emissions were transformed into a series of tradable permits, known as Assigned Amount Units. The other two are offset markets, where investment by country A in country B in emissions reductions can be used against the obligations of country A to reduce its own emissions. Joint Implementation involves investments among industrialized countries, while the Clean Development Mechanism (CDM) involves investments by industrialized countries in developing countries.

The Kyoto Protocol was then followed by a number of emissions trading systems at national, or in the case of the EU, **regional governance** levels, as well as some private sector internal schemes (see Betsill and Hoffmann 2011 for the fullest survey). Such systems are at different stages of development in a number of other places.

The EU Emissions Trading System (EU ETS) remains the largest market. Its impact on emissions is disputed, with some crediting it for contributing to emissions reductions and others regarding it as a dangerous distraction. The EU ETS has also been the principal driver for the main offset market, the CDM. The EU allowed companies regulated under the EU ETS to purchase credits from the CDM and turn them in against their ETS obligations. This has driven demand for credits from the CDM and thus from projects. Most of this investment has gone to **emerging Countries** such as China and India.

Environmental markets, in particular carbon markets have come under sustained criticism. They are variously criticized for the basic idea of commodifying the atmospheric **global public goods**, for being "climate fraud," "carbon colonialism," as well as other problems (see for example Lohmann 2006).

Carbon markets have arguably gained traction in policy worlds precisely because of their economic attractiveness to a range of **business and corporations** actors, irrespective of their **effectiveness** in resolving climate change or other environmental problems (Newell and Paterson 2010), or of the various problems they produce as highlighted powerfully by their critics. Nevertheless, despite these criticisms, carbon markets continue to expand around the world, and there are also pushes to extend the market logic to other areas of environmental governance.

### References

Betsill, Michele and Matthew J. Hoffmann. 2011. "The Contours of 'Cap and Trade': The Evolution of Emissions Trading Systems for Greenhouse Gases." *Review of Policy Research* 28(1): 83–106.

Coase, Ronald. 1960. "The Problem of Social Cost." *Journal of Law and Economics* 3(1): 1–44.

Dales, John H. 1968. *Pollution, Property and Prices*. Toronto, University of Toronto Press.

Gorman, Hugh S. and Barry D. Solomon. 2002. "The Origins and Practice of Emissions Trading." *Journal of Policy History* 14(3): 293–320.

Grubb, Michael. 1989. *The Greenhouse Effect: Negotiating Targets*. London, Royal Institute of International Affairs.

Lohmann, Larry. 2006. "Carbon Trading: A Critical Conversation on Climate Change, Privatization and Power." *Development Dialogue* (48): 1–356.

Newell, Peter and Matthew Paterson. 2010. *Climate Capitalism: Global Warming and the Transformation of the Global Economy*. Cambridge, Cambridge University Press.

Robertson, Morgan M. 2004. "The Neoliberalization of Ecosystem Services: Wetland Mitigation Banking and Problems in Environmental Governance." *Geoforum* 35(3): 361–373.

Swyngedouw, Erik. 2007. "Dispossessing $H_2O$: The Contested Terrain of Water Privatization." In *Neoliberal Environments: False Promises and Unnatural Consequences*, Eds. Nik Heynen, James McCarthy, Scott Prudham, and P. Robbins, 51–62. London, Routledge.

# MIGRANTS

## François Gemenne

*Université de Liège, Belgium and Université de Versailles Saint-Quentin-Yvelines, France*

Throughout history, environmental changes have always been key drivers of human migration. Both environmental **disasters** and more gradual changes such as climate change have led to massive population movements, shaping the distribution of the population on the planet as we know it today. Yet, until the mid 2000s, both scholars and policy-makers had overlooked this important driver of human migration, focusing mostly on economic and political drivers. However, in the past decade, massive population displacements have often been described among the most dramatic consequences of climate change, and environmental disruptions have been increasingly recognized as a major driver of migration. Over time, migration has become instrumental in the discourses and representations of climate change, and migrants have often been portrayed as the "human faces of climate change," the first witnesses and victims of the impacts of global warming (Gemenne 2011a). This perception, however, often contradicts the empirical realities of environmental migration.

The definition of environmental migration remains disputed in the literature. The concept was coined by environmental scholars in the late 1970s: along with many **nongovernmental organizations** and think tanks such as the WorldWatch Institute, they initially described environmental migration as a new and distinct category of migration, an unavoidable byproduct of climate change. Migration scholars, however, first insisted on the multi-causality of migration, and on the impossibility of isolating environmental factors from other migration drivers (Kibreab 1997). It is, however, now usually acknowledged that environmental migrants are:

> persons or groups of persons, who, for compelling reasons of sudden or progressive changes in the environment that adversely affect their lives or living conditions, are obliged to leave their habitual homes, or choose to do so, either temporarily or permanently, and who move either within their country or abroad.
>
> (International Organization for Migration 2007)

The number of environmental migrants remains extremely difficult to estimate, partly because most do not cross an international border and are therefore not accounted for in statistical databases. Between 2008 and 2012, about 142 million people were displaced as a result of natural **disasters** (IDMC 2013). This figure, however, does not include those who migrate as a result of slow-onset changes, and whose number is almost impossible to estimate today (Gemenne 2011b). The importance of environmental disruptions in migration dynamics is likely to increase dramatically in the future as a result of climate change.

The concept of "environmental migrants" encompasses a wide array of diverse environmental changes, but also of migration patterns. Key environmental disruptions that can induce migration include flash floods, earthquakes, droughts, storms, and hurricanes, but also slow-onset changes such as sea-level rise, desertification, or deforestation. Large development or conservation projects, such as dams and natural reserves, are sometimes included as well. These disruptions lead to diverse forms of migration, requiring different policy responses. Empirical research shows that most of these migration movements occur over short distances, often within national boundaries (Foresight 2011). Contrary to a frequent assumption, those who migrate are usually not the most vulnerable populations. These are often trapped and immobile when faced with environmental changes, as they do not have access to the resources, networks, and information that would enable them to relocate to safer areas (Foresight 2011). Though most of these migrations occur in the

**least developed countries,** and particularly in South Asia, Southeast Asia and Sub-Saharan Africa, developed countries can also experience them, as evidenced by the massive population displacements resulting from hurricane Katrina in the south of the US, or by the Fukushima disaster in Japan. Environmental migration remains inadequately addressed by international law. The 1951 Geneva Convention, which defines refugee status, does not take into account environmental factors: "environmental refugees" is therefore a misnomer. Though some scholars had initially favored a new treaty that would have created a refugee status for environmental migrants, many have deemed this solution inadequate or unrealistic, and other policy responses are now preferred (McAdam 2011), such as the Nansen Initiative, a process of intergovernmental consultations that seeks to promote a global protection agenda for those displaced across borders by **disasters.** This protection agenda would not be a binding treaty, but rather a series of good principles and recommendations elaborated on the basis of consultations with different governments. **Regional governance** solutions have also been promoted, especially in Asia-Pacific, the region most affected by environmental migration (Asian Development Bank 2012). These gaps in international law also mean that no UN agency is specifically mandated to assist those displaced by environmental changes, though different organizations and agencies, such as the UN High Commissioner for Refugees (UNHCR), the International Organization for Migration (IOM) or the Red Cross, conduct humanitarian interventions and/or policy projects on a regular basis.

Many have also turned to the negotiations related to the **climate change regime** as a suitable forum to design policy responses. Whereas environmental migration was initially viewed as a solution of last resort, a failure to adapt to environmental changes, it is now increasingly recognized as a possible **adaptation** strategy (Black et al. 2011). Finally, debates on the security implications of climate change have also resulted in migration being presented as a **security** threat, a view that has been refuted by scholars (Gemenne 2011a).

### References

Asian Development Bank. 2012. *Addressing Climate Change and Migration in Asia and the Pacific.* Manila, ADB.

Black, Richard, Stephen R.G. Bennett, Sandy M. Thomas, and John R. Beddington. 2011. "Climate Change: Migration as Adaptation." *Nature* (478): 447–449.

Foresight. 2011. *Migration and Global Environmental Change*. Final Project Report. London, Government Office for Science.

Gemenne, François. 2011a. "How They Became the Human Face of Climate Change: Research and Policy Interactions in the Birth of the 'Environmental Migration' Concept." In *Migration and Climate Change*, Eds. Etienne Piguet, Antoine Pécoud, and Paul de Guchteneire, 225–259. Cambridge and Paris, Cambridge University Press/UNESCO.

Gemenne, François. 2011b. "Why the Numbers don't Add up: A Review of Estimates and Predictions of People Displaced by Environmental Changes." *Global Environmental Change* 21(S1): 41–49.

International Displacement Monitoring Centre (IDMC). 2013. *Global Estimates 2012: People Displaced by Natural Hazard-Induced Disasters*. Geneva, Internal Displacement Monitoring Centre.

International Organization for Migration (IOM). 2007. *Discussion Note: Migration and the Environment*. Geneva, International Organization for Migration, MC/INF/288.

Kibreab, Gaim. 1997. "Environmental Causes and Impact of Refugee Movements: A Critique of the Current Debate." *Disasters* 21(1): 20–38.

McAdam, Jane. 2011. "Swimming against the Tide: Why a Climate Change Displacement Treaty is Not the Answer." *International Journal of Refugee Law* 23(1): 2–27.

# MILITARY CONFLICTS

## Maya Jegen

*Université du Québec à Montréal, Canada*

The history of war is replete with examples of environmental degradation. To fight off Napoleon and Hitler, Russian and Soviet armies adopted the "scorched earth" policy, destroying all of their resources that could be used by the enemy, including food, land, and people. During World War I, European forces used mustard gas to poison the air around trenches. In Vietnam, the US sprayed the herbicide "Agent Orange" to defoliate forests, thus exposing and starving guerillas (Zierler 2011). In 1991, Iraq released oil into the Persian Gulf to prevent a landing of US ground forces, severely damaging the marine ecosystem, curtailing fishery, threatening a desalinization plant and thus potable water sources (Caggiano 1993).

The impact of military conflicts on the environment can be intentional or unintentional. We speak of intentional damage, or environmental warfare, when the environment is manipulated for hostile military purposes; in other words, when the environment is used as a strategic instrument. Arthur H. Westing (2013: 84), one of the main thinkers on the environmental impact of war, points out that already "The ancient Greeks envied Zeus his ability to hurl thunderbolts. Moses was said to have been able to control the Red Sea in such a way as to drown the Egyptian forces that were pursuing the Israelites." One of the most devastating examples of environmental warfare occurred during the Second Sino-Japanese War, when the Chinese army destroyed the Huayuankow dike on the Yellow River in an attempt to stop the Japanese invasion. Several thousand Japanese soldiers drowned, as did 750,000 Chinese civilians. Millions of Chinese were left homeless, and millions of hectares of arable land were destroyed by the flood (Schwabach 2000: 134).

Although hypothetical, the most radical scenario of environmental warfare would be the "nuclear winter." According to Sagan and Turco (1993), a global nuclear conflict would not only destroy our physical environment through its blast, fire, and radioactive fallout; it would also have an adverse effect on the earth's climate, reducing temperatures and destroying human activity (Gleditsch 1998). From an **ecocentric** perspective, some authors would then speak of "ecocide" (Drumbl 1998).

Yet armed forces will often cause environmental damage unintentionally. The environment is then the victim of collateral damage: for instance, NATO's air bombing of a petrochemical factory in 1999, ostensibly to deny fuel to Serbian forces, released highly toxic chemicals into the air and the waterways, causing one of the biggest **disasters** in volume and toxicity in recent history (Schwabach 2000: 119).

Two trends can be observed that mitigate the impact of military conflicts on the environment. First, there is the timid rise of normative consciousness as indicated by, for instance, the United Nations' 1976 Environmental Modification Convention that limits the use of environmental modification as a method of warfare, or the inclusion of two provisions in the 1977 Additional Protocol I to the Geneva Convention of 1949 that limit the environmental damage permitted during international armed conflict (Schmitt 2000: 88). Likewise, Principle 5 of the 1982 World Charter for Nature holds that "Nature shall be secured against degradation caused by warfare or other hostile activities." Second, some armed forces such as NATO's are beginning to incorporate environmental **assessment** in their management practices (safeguarding hazardous materials, treating waste water, or reducing energy consumption).

While the causal relations between environmental **scarcity and conflicts** remain contested, there is no doubt that wars cause major environmental degradation. Intentional damage is most visible, but collateral damage is more difficult to assess and mitigate.

## References

Caggiano, Mark J.T. 1993. "Legitimacy of Environmental Destructions in Modern Warfare: Customary Substance over Conventional Form." *Boston College Environmental Affairs Law Review* 20(3): 479–506.

Drumbl, Mark A. 1998. "Waging War against the World: The Need to Move from War Crimes to Environmental Crimes." *Fordham International Law Journal* 22(1): 122–153.

Gleditsch, Nils Petter. 1998. "Armed Conflict and the Environment: A Critique of the Literature." *Journal of Peace Research* 35(3): 381–400.

Sagan, Carl, and Richard P. Turco. 1993. "Nuclear Winter in the Post-Cold War Era." *Journal of Peace Research* 30(4): 369–373.

Schmitt, Michael N. 2000. "War and the Environment: Fault Lines in the Prescriptive Landscapes." In *The Environmental Consequences of War*, Eds. Jay E. Austin and Carl E. Bruch, 87–136. Cambridge, Cambridge University Press.

Schwabach, Aaron. 2000. "Environmental Damage Resulting from the NATO Military Action against Yugoslavia." *Columbia Journal Environmental Law* 25(1): 117–140.

Westing, Arthur H. 2013. *Arthur H. Westing: Pioneer on the Environmental Impact of War*. Heidelberg, Springer.

Zierler, David. 2011. *The Invention of Ecocide: Agent Orange, Vietnam, and the Scientists Who Changed the Way We Think about the Environment*. Athens, University of Georgia Press.

# NEGOTIATING COALITIONS

## Pamela Chasek

*Manhattan College, United States*

A coalition is an ad hoc grouping of nations united for a specific purpose. Coalitions offer countries a way to increase their relative strength—a position presented on behalf of multiple countries is given more weight than a position presented by a single country (Wagner et al. 2012). Coalitions also create the necessary structure to simplify **treaty negotiations** by reducing the number of speakers. A country's ability to contribute constructively relies on size of delegation, negotiator skill, and influence, which can be enhanced when countries enter into coalitions (Gupta 2000).

When forming a coalition, negotiators must first perceive an issue or issues that require attention. The degree of success or effectiveness of a coalition depends largely on its type (majority versus minority coalitions, general versus issue-specific) and on the nature and precision of its objectives. Coalitions may strive for an optimal or merely satisfactory agreement or they may seek to deprive the outcome of certain clauses, conditions, or rules that their members do not want (Dupont 1996). There can be shifts in positions and membership depending on the issues under negotiation. Goals may be general (e.g. a satisfactory worded resolution or decision coming out of an international conference) or very specific in terms of the contents of the agreement (e.g. agreement to ban a chemical). Assessments of the effectiveness of a coalition are influenced by bargaining strength and its evolution over time, role of the coalition in the negotiations, size of the coalition, leadership, cohesion, organization, and strategies (Dupont 1996).

In environmental negotiations, coalitions are often based on level of development, or shared geopolitical or socioeconomic interests. The Group of 77 (G77), which was formed in 1964 by seventy-seven countries at the end of the first session of the UN Conference on Trade and Development, is the largest coalition, now including more than 130 developing countries. The G77 usually coordinates with China, for example, in arguing that environmental rules should not hinder economic development. Thus, since the early 1990s, developing countries have called for environmental **aid, technology transfer**, and capacity building to help them implement multilateral environmental agreements (MEAs) (Chasek and Rajamani 2002). In addition, the G77 and China maintain that the historical responsibility for climate change lies with industrial countries, which should bear the main responsibility for correcting the problem according to **common but differentiated responsibilities**.

However, differences between developing countries are often pronounced. Defining countries' common interests is increasingly difficult, resulting in the formation of smaller coalitions. In the climate change negotiations, the G77 has been fractured by radically different national interests and priorities (Barnett 2008). At one end of the spectrum lie the members of the Alliance of Small Island States (AOSIS), which are particularly vulnerable to climate change because sea level rise will destroy or render uninhabitable all or part of their territory. At the other end lie the members of the Organization of Petroleum Exporting Countries (OPEC), which stand to lose substantial revenue from measures to avert climate change (Chasek and Rajamani 2002).

131

In recent years many sub-coalitions of developing countries have emerged. Some are general coalitions that focus on many issues. For example, the **least developed countries** are concerned with ensuring their development needs are taken into consideration. Members of **regional governance** groups also often speak as a coalition on many issues, especially the African Group, the Arab Group, the Latin American and Caribbean Group. Some are more issue specific, such as the Like-Minded Megadiverse Countries (Brazil, China, Colombia, Costa Rica, India, Indonesia, Kenya, Philippines, Mexico, Peru, South Africa, and Venezuela), which was established to promote interests and priorities related to **conservation and preservation**.

Numerous coalitions have developed in the **climate change regime** negotiations, in addition to AOSIS and OPEC. For example, the Association of Independent Latin American and Caribbean states (Colombia, Costa Rica, Chile, Peru, Guatemala, and Panama—with the support of the Dominican Republic), has decided to stop waiting for emissions reductions or financial support from wealthy countries, and launch an ambitious case for low-carbon development (Roberts and Edwards 2012). The BASIC Group (Brazil, South Africa, India, and China), formed in November 2009 (Olsson et al. 2010), was instrumental in brokering the Copenhagen Accord. The Bolivarian Alliance for the Peoples of Our America (ALBA: Bolivia, Venezuela, Ecuador, Nicaragua, and Cuba) takes a hard line on many issues, including opposition to the use of **market** mechanisms to control carbon emissions and calling for 7 percent of developed countries' gross domestic product to be designated for climate change finance (Wagner et al. 2012). The Group of Mountain Landlocked Developing Countries (Armenia, Kyrgyzstan, and Tajikistan) focuses on issues faced by landlocked mountain developing countries vulnerable to transportation costs and food insecurity.

Moreover, there are two issue-specific developed country coalitions that operate in the climate change negotiations. One is a loose coalition of non-EU developed countries called the Umbrella Group, which is usually made up of Australia, Canada, Japan, New Zealand, Norway, Russian Federation, Ukraine, and the United States. This coalition works to ensure that climate agreements do not contain language that is antithetical to their energy and economic interests and often shares an insistence that developing countries should undertake quantified emission reduction commitments along with the developed countries. The other is the Environmental Integrity Group, comprising Mexico, Liechtenstein, Monaco, the Republic of Korea, and Switzerland. This coalition of non-EU developed countries shares a desire to uphold the integrity of the climate change negotiations and seeks a more progressive approach than that advocated by the Umbrella Group. There exist many developed countries coalitions. The largest developed country coalition is regional: the European Union (EU). Unlike most coalitions, the EU as a regional economic integration organization is a party in its own right to many MEAs and its members are legally bound together. The twenty-eight members usually speak with a single voice at environmental negotiations.

A second general developed country coalition was formed when Japan and the United States began consulting with the CANZ group (Canada, Australia, and New Zealand) in 1995, creating JUSCANZ (Newell 1997). Switzerland, Norway, and several other non-EU OECD countries (Iceland, Andorra, Republic of Korea, Liechtenstein, Mexico, San Marino, Turkey, and Israel) also occasionally consult with this group, often referred to as JUSSCANNZ to reflect participation beyond the original five countries. This coalition usually seeks to balance the power of the EU in various environmental negotiations.

Another general coalition consists of the Russian Federation, former Soviet republics that are not G77 members, and non-EU Eastern European countries. These countries work together in a coalition referred to as "countries with economies in transition" (Wagner et al. 2012). Their goal is to ensure that their interests are not lost in **treaty negotiations** that are often dominated by the EU, JUSSCANNZ, and the G77.

Multiple memberships in both broad coalitions and small ones appear to confer greater leverage: while the small, issue focused groups help define, voice, and protect the shared interests of its members, such as the specific needs of the Group of Mountain Landlocked Developing Countries, the broad coalitions, such as the G77, may offer more general support and more power through a larger coalition across negotiations. On the other hand, sometimes multiple coalition memberships can lead to a conflict of interest, such as AOSIS's concern with climate change when the G77 (to which all AOSIS members belong) is dominated by its more powerful members who are defending their fossil-fuel dominated economies.

## References

Barnett, Jon. 2008. "The Worst of Friends: OPEC and G-77 in the Climate Regime." *Global Environmental Politics* 8(4): 1–8.
Chasek, Pamela and Lavanya Rajamani. 2002. "Steps toward Enhanced Parity: Negotiating Capacity and Strategies of Developing Countries." In *Providing Global Public Goods: Managing Globalization*, Ed. Inge Kaul, 245–262. New York, Oxford University Press.

Dupont, Christoph. *1996*. "Negotiation as Coalition Building." *International Negotiation* 1(1): 47–64.

Gupta, Joyeeta. 2000. *On Behalf of My Delegation, . . . A Survival Guide for Developing Country Climate Negotiators.* Washington, Center for Sustainable Development in the Americas.

Newell, Peter. 1997. "A Changing Landscape of Diplomatic Conflict: The Politics of Climate Change Post-Rio." In *The Way Forward: Beyond Agenda 21,* Ed. Felix Dodds, 37–46. London, Earthscan.

Olsson, Marie, Aaron Atteridge, Karl Hallding, and Joakim Hellberg. 2010. *Together Alone? Brazil, South Africa, India, China (BASIC) and the Climate Change Conundrum.* Stockholm, Stockholm Environment Institute Policy Brief.

Roberts, Timmons and Guy Edwards. 2012. "A New Latin American Climate Negotiating Group: The Greenest Shoots in the Doha Desert." *UpFront* www.brookings.edu/blogs/up-front/posts/2012/12/12-latin-america-climate-roberts.

Wagner, Lynn M., Reem Hajjar, and Asheline Appleton. 2012. "Global Alliances to Strange Bedfellows: The Ebb and Flow of Negotiating Coalitions." In *The Roads from Rio: Lessons Learned from Twenty Years of Multilateral Environmental Negotiations,* Eds. Pamela Chasek and Lynn Wagner, 85–105. New York, RFF Press.

# NONGOVERNMENTAL ORGANIZATIONS

## Michele M. Betsill

*Colorado State University, United States*

Nongovernmental organizations (NGOs) are a prominent force in global environmental politics. For example, in the realm of **summit diplomacy**, more than 900 NGOs participated in the 2012 United Nations Conference on Sustainable Development. Scholars of global environmental governance use the term "NGO" in reference to a broad spectrum of formal non-profit organizations that are independent of governments and are committed to the provision of **global public goods** (Betsill and Corell 2008). While this clearly excludes political parties, organizations that advocate violence, as well as **business and corporations**, non-profit associations representing particular industrial sectors occupy a gray area. They operate in distinction to the state, do not (formally) represent governmental interests, and are active participants in debates over public issues, but they often are seen to pursue private rather than public goals. NGOs are a diverse population (Alcock 2008); they work at and across different levels of social and political organization (often in coalitions or networks with other NGOs), focus on a broad set of issues, and engage in a variety of activities from research to lobbying to project development. Global environmental governance scholars often differentiate between NGOs' role as advocates for particular policies and their role as global governors.

NGOs became a focus of global environmental governance research in the 1990s, prompted in part by their visibility at the 1992 United Nations Conference on Environment and Development, and by broader debates on the role of non-state actors in world politics, the changing nature of state–society relations, and the importance of norms and ideas (e.g. Wapner, 1996; Raustiala, 1997). Global governance scholars contend that non-state actors (including NGOs) represent a new form of authority whose interactions constitute alternative public spaces for confronting global issues. Today, NGOs are seen as valuable partners in addressing global environmental problems, especially in light of globalization processes that challenge the ability of nation-states to deal with these problems themselves.

Many NGOs advocate for particular policies and practices (Betsill and Corell 2008; Newell 2008). They frequently target states, either in multilateral fora such as environmental **treaty negotiations** or international economic institutions, or through domestic channels. At the international level, NGOs often interact directly with state decision-makers by serving on national delegations or participating as observers to negotiation processes. Where such direct access is blocked (or as a complement to these activities), NGOs engage in public protests or **shaming** public awareness campaigns to put pressure on states via the public and the media. NGOs also target multinational corporations through consumer boycotts and shareholder activism (Wapner 1996; Newell 2008). Specialized knowledge and expertise along with appeals to moral arguments are key sources of leverage in NGO advocacy work (see **Science**). Whether they achieve their goals depends on several factors related to both the nature of NGO strategies and resources as well as the institutional context in which the advocacy takes place (Betsill and Corell 2008). Even when they fail to achieve their specific goals, NGO advocacy may contribute to changes in norms and ideas about global environmental governance (Wapner 1996).

NGOs increasingly are recognized as global environmental governors. States routinely delegate specific governance functions to NGOs, such as monitoring and **reporting** or capacity building. In addition, NGOs (often with other types of actors) are involved in establishing **private regimes** for global environmental governance, such as **labeling and certification** schemes and public–private **partnerships** (Pattberg 2005;

Bernstein and Cashore 2007). This raises questions about how NGOs come to be seen as authoritative actors. In contrast to state actors, whose authority to govern is often taken for granted, NGOs must justify their authority to those who are being governed and often do so by once again appealing to moral arguments as well as their specialized knowledge and expertise.

In theory, NGOs could contribute to "better" decisions and environmental outcomes. They have knowledge and expertise to deal with complex global environmental problems, and by representing diverse stakeholder interests (see **Participation**), they confer legitimacy on decision-making processes, making **compliance and implementation** more likely (Bernstein and Cashore 2007; Betsill and Corell 2008). In practice, this link between NGO participation and outcomes is mediated by political debates about knowledge claims and/or whose voices and interests are being represented (or not).

Arguably, NGOs make global environmental governance more democratic. In creating new forms of governance, NGOs open up alternative space, such as **global deliberative democracy**, for reasoned argument and persuasion. They enhance participatory democracy by giving voice to a wide range of stakeholders whose interests may otherwise be under-represented in decision-making. NGO participation along with monitoring and reporting activities help affected publics hold decision-makers to account (Bäckstrand 2006; Newell 2008). Again, NGOs are susceptible to criticism about their own democratic character. While NGOs often claim to speak on behalf of marginalized populations, do these groups have any say in who represents their interests and how? Is there recourse if NGO programs have negative impacts on a community's livelihoods? This suggests a need to develop strategies for enhancing deliberation, participation, and accountability within NGOs.

Some critical scholars challenge the assumption that NGOs are a positive force in global environmental governance, arguing that they perpetuate environmental degradation by reinforcing the neoliberal economic order (Duffy 2006). NGOs reproduce this dominant ideology, and thereby serve the interests of the global elite, by contributing to the shift towards non-state and market-based forms of environmental governance. In turn, this makes it difficult for weak states in the developing world to exercise **sovereignty** over their natural resources. From this perspective, NGOs must become a counter-hegemonic force for global transformation.

## References

Alcock, Frank. 2008. "Conflicts and Coalitions Within and Across the ENGO Community." *Global Environmental Politics* 8(4): 66–91.

Bäckstrand, Karin. 2006. "Democratizing Global Environmental Governance? Stakeholder Democracy after the World Summit on Sustainable Development." *European Journal of International Relations* 12(4): 467–498.

Bernstein, Steven and Benjamin Cashore. 2007. "Can Non-State Global Governance be Legitimate? An Analytical Framework." *Regulation and Governance* 1(4): 347–371.

Betsill, Michele M. and Elisabeth Corell (Eds.). 2008. *NGO Diplomacy: The Influence of Non-governmental Organizations in International Environmental Negotiations.* Cambridge, MA, MIT Press.

Duffy, Rosaleen. 2006. "Non-governmental Organisations and Governance States: The Impact of Transnational Environmental Management Networks in Madagascar." *Environmental Politics* 15(5): 731–749.

Newell, Peter. 2008. "Civil Society, Corporate Accountability and the Politics of Climate Change." *Global Environmental Politics* 8(3): 122–153.

Pattberg, Philipp. 2005. "The Institutionalization of Private Governance: How Business and Nonprofit Organizations Agree on Transnational Rules." *Governance* 18(4): 589–610.

Raustiala, Kal. 1997. "States, NGOs, and International Environmental Institutions." *International Studies Quarterly* 41(4): 719–740.

Wapner, Paul. 1996. *Environmental Activism and World Civic Politics.* Albany, NY, SUNY Press.

# NONREGIMES

## Radoslav S. Dimitrov

*Western University, Canada*

Nonregimes are most commonly defined as "transnational public policy arena characterized by the absence of multilateral agreements for policy coordination" (Dimitrov et al. 2007: 231). This broad conception accommodates a wide range of intellectual traditions and can be operationalized in a number of ways. In the simplest sense, nonregimes are problems without treaties. Today there are no multilateral policy agreements to combat deforestation or coral reefs degradation (Dimitrov 2006); UN agencies do not regulate biofuels production (Lima and Gupta 2013); and governments have discussed Arctic haze but never attempted to negotiate formal solutions (Wilkening 2011). As most environmental

**treaty negotiations** succeed, the failure of talks on such prominent problems is an interesting but remarkably understudied topic. Identifying a case as a nonregime is not a straightforward matter and requires precise definitions and measures. The number of cases is potentially infinite. For example, states do not cooperate on noise pollution or street litter. Nonregimes are puzzling only when theories create expectations of **regime** creation. A case is relevant only if the potential for mutual gains and conducive conditions are present, such as major power influence, civil society pressure or transaction cost benefits.

From this perspective, it is useful to distinguish public and private nonregimes. Most published studies adopt a state-centric approach and focus on the absence of formal agreements between states (Dimitrov 2006; Wilkening 2011). Alternatively, the absence of transnational corporate or NGO initiatives on a problem would constitute a private nonregime (see **Private regimes**).

It is also possible to distinguish cases of nonregimes with regard to their negotiation records. In some cases, negotiations have commenced and failed, and in other cases negotiations never began. Arctic haze and coral reefs degradation, for instance, have not triggered discussions on policy coordination (Dimitrov 2002; Wilkening 2011). Global forest policy, on the other hand, was under bitter negotiations between 1990 and 2000 that failed to produce a convention (Davenport 2005; Dimitrov, 2006). Cases of this second type are particularly difficult to identify.

At what point do we label a case a nonregime rather than a regime in the making? Negotiations sometimes last decades and remain in deadlock for years. Even at a particular point in time, the outcome may not be clear. The negotiations of the **climate change regime** regarding post-2012 policy have raged since 2007 and failed repeatedly. Eventually, in 2011 states agreed on voluntary emission reductions under an extension of the Kyoto Protocol and launched a new mandate to create a global agreement after 2020—without legal guarantees that it would be binding. Is the current arrangement a regime or nonregime? Scholars may disagree on whether weak policy accords constitute nonregimes. The small community of nonregimes students regards ineffective regimes as regimes nonetheless but the matter is open to debate.

The attempt to investigate cases of non-occurrence immediately raises the question: How can we study something that is not "there"? The task is less challenging than it appears. All nonregimes feature sociopolitical processes involving public discourse, national-level decision-making, multilateral consultations, and occasionally formal negotiations. These processes can be studied more or less in the same manner we study processes that lead to successful regime formation. Although the outcome makes the cases interesting, what we actually investigate is the process. Thus, we can study nonregimes in the same way we explore regimes (Dimitrov et al. 2007).

A fundamental question for nonregimes research pertains to the potential symmetry between theories of regimes and nonregimes. Should regime theory be able to explain also nonregimes? Embracing the notion of symmetry implies that a comprehensive theory must account for failures as well as success in regime creation. Methodologically, this also requires structured comparisons of regime and nonregime cases (Young and Osherenko 1993; Dimitrov 2006). Investigation of "negative" cases can also test regime theories and help build more complete theoretical explanations of collective action.

Alternatively, no single theory may be able to capture both outcomes. Hence, the possibility that nonregime studies may produce novel and original interpretations of regime making. For example, the presence of private regimes may explain the absence of state regimes. Private regimes have arisen to provide solutions to numerous transnational problems as various actors seek to fill the void left by governments' inability or unwillingness to cooperate. The increasing prevalence and apparent **effectiveness** of private governance may offer governments rationale for eschewing interstate regimes.

Thus, beyond theoretical consideration, nonregime research has added value for practical reasons. It can help identify obstacles to negotiations and produce policy recommendations where progress is urgently needed.

## References

Davenport, Deborah. 2005. "An Alternative Explanation of the Failure of the UNCED Forestry Negotiations." *Global Environmental Politics* 5(1): 105–130.

Dimitrov, Radoslav S. 2002. "Confronting Nonregimes: Science and International Coral Reef Policy." *Journal of Environment and Development* 11(1): 53–78.

Dimitrov, Radoslav S. 2006. *Science and International Environmental Policy: Regimes and Nonregimes in Global Governance.* Lanham, MD, Rowman & Littlefield.

Dimitrov, Radoslav S., Detlef Sprinz, Gerald DiGiusto, and Alexander Kelle. 2007. "International Nonregimes: A Research Agenda." *International Studies Review* 9(2): 230–258.

Lima, Mairon G. Bastos and Joyeeta Gupta. 2013. "The Policy Context of Biofuels: A Case of Non-Governance at the Global Level?" *Global Environmental Politics* 13(2): 46–64.

Wilkening, Kenneth. 2011. "Science and International Environmental Nonregimes: The Case of Arctic Haze." *Review of Policy Research* 28(2): 125–148.

Young, Oran R. and Gail Osherenko (Eds.). 1993. *Polar Politics: Creating International Environmental Regimes.* Ithaca, NY, Cornell University Press.

# OZONE REGIME

## David L. Downie
*Fairfield University, United States*

The international **regime** to protect stratospheric ozone is one of the most **effective** cases of global environmental policy. Naturally occurring ozone helps to shield the Earth from harmful ultraviolet radiation emitted by the sun. Destroying this "ozone layer" would be disastrous and a significant depletion would dramatically increase skin cancers and eye cataracts, weaken immune systems, harm many plants and animals, and damage certain food crops and ecosystems.

In the early 1970s, scientists discovered that chlorofluorocarbons (CFCs) release chlorine into the stratosphere, which then destroy ozone (Molina and Rowland 1974). CFCs were employed around the world as coolants in air-conditioning and refrigeration systems and in many other uses and were considered completely benign. Subsequent research revealed that other chemicals were damageable to the ozone layer, including: halons, widely used and effective fire suppressants; methyl bromide, a cheap and toxic pesticide; and HCFCs, which are less ozone damaging CFC-substitutes.

Although preliminary discussions started in the Governing Council of the **United Nations Environment Programme** (UNEP) in the late 1970s, formal global negotiations did not begin until 1982 and only after major EC countries secured agreement that the talks would seek only a framework convention. The resulting agreement, the 1985 Vienna Convention for the Protection of the Ozone Layer, called for international cooperation in monitoring and protection but did not specify regulatory action nor even mention CFCs.

Discovery of severe ozone depletion above Antarctica, often called the ozone hole, allowed lead states to argue successfully that negotiations on a control Protocol were needed, despite the lack of firm evidence linking the hole to CFCs (see **Science**). The new negotiations resulted in the landmark 1987 Montreal Protocol on Substances that Deplete the Ozone Layer, the centerpiece of global ozone policy.

The Montreal Protocol established binding requirements that industrialized countries reduce their production and use of the five most widely used CFCs and freeze production of three halons. Developing countries had to take the same action but were given 10-year extensions to allow them to use CFCs for economic development. The Protocol also includes important and precedent setting **reporting** requirements, prohibitions on trade of control substances with countries that did not ratify the agreement, and procedures for reviewing the treaty's effectiveness and strengthening its controls, including periodic reports by Scientific, Environmental Effects, and Technology Assessment Panels. New chemicals can be added and other changes made to the Protocol by standard amendment procedures, which require formal ratification to take effect. However, the treaty also allows the Meeting of the Parties (MOP) to adjust control measures on chemicals already listed in the Protocol without an amendment. Such adjustments take effect immediately, without the need for time-consuming ratification. Since 1987, parties have used these mechanisms to strengthen the Protocol significantly in response to new scientific information regarding the ozone layer and new commercial developments regarding potential ozone depleting substances substitutes, including important amendments and adjustments agreed to in 1990, 1992, 1995, 1997, 1999 and 2007. Today, the Protocol requires parties to eliminate their production and use of all known ozone depleting substances. Different chemicals have different phase-out schedules. Exemptions allow parties to use small amounts of some substances for limited periods. Broad and controversial exemptions permit the continued use of methyl bromide for many agricultural uses.

Via an historic amendment in 1990, the Protocol also obligates industrialized countries to provide technical and financial assistance to developing countries to help them switch to non-ozone depleting chemicals and fulfill other regime obligations. The Multilateral Fund has disbursed nearly $3 billion to support capacity building, technical assistance, **technology transfer**, training, and industrial conversion projects in nearly 150 countries. The different phase-out schedules for developing countries and creation of the Multilateral Fund were explicit acknowledgements of the principle of **common but differentiated responsibility**. The 1990 London Amendment also created an unprecedented non-compliance procedure that reviews, in a largely facilitative manner, failures by states to meet regime terms and makes recommendations to the MOP for further action (see **Compliance and implementation**).

The Vienna Convention and Montreal Protocol are the only environment treaties to achieve universal ratification. The production and use of new CFCs, halon, carbon tetrachloride, and methyl chloroform has been almost entirely eliminated. Methyl bromide production has declined drastically. HCFCs controls are largely proceeding according to schedule. Ozone depletion has essentially stabilized and if all countries implement their obligations (something that is not guaranteed), the ozone layer could return to normal levels later this century.

Several sets of causal factors played central roles in the creation, content, expansion, and extent success of the ozone regime. Advancing scientific knowledge played an important but not a determinative role (Benedick 1998; Parson 2003; Downie 2012). It gave rise to the issue in the first place, undercut European opposition to starting negotiations, and assisted countries advocating for creating and later strengthening the controls. A relatively influential **epistemic community** that understood the scientific and technological issues also influenced the process (Haas 1992), including framing certain discourses and introducing precautionary and intergenerational perspectives (Litfin 1994).

The economic interests of states and key **business and corporations**, including perceptions of costs and benefits that changed over time, also played central roles. Not surprisingly, since the 1970s, economic interests often impeded efforts to create stronger ODS controls, most recently in the creation and continued use of broad exemptions for methyl bromide (Gareau 2013) and the relatively lengthy phase-out periods for HCFCs. However, during several crucial periods economic interests assisted efforts to strengthen the ozone regime. This included the initial US support for a global treaty to give its industry the same rules as competitors in countries that had not adopted domestic controls, the dramatic policy shifts by major CFCs manufacturers and their governments once they discovered effective alternatives, and the impact of the Multilateral Fund (Downie 2012).

The existence and actions of UNEP greatly assisted efforts to get the issue on the global agenda, to start formal negotiations, and to reach agreement on the Protocol and 1990 Amendment (Downie 1995; Benedick 1998). The evolving structure of the Montreal Protocol itself also proved critical (Downie 2012). The regime could not have been strengthened so quickly if parties had not been able to adjust as well as formally amend the Protocol. The allowance for exemptions prevented isolated interests from keeping a country from joining the regime or blocking its strengthening. Trade restrictions prohibiting parties from exporting ODS and products containing ODS provided powerful incentives for importing countries, especially smaller countries, to join the regime. The Multilateral Fund attracted the participation of large developing countries, assisted developing countries to meet and sometimes exceed the phase-out schedules, and created supporters of ODS control among actors that received funding and transitioned to alternatives. The requirement that parties review the adequacy of control measures was made more impactful by the Assessment Panels and the regime principle that control measures should be guided by scientific understanding of threats to the ozone layer in the way of the precautionary principle.

The ultimate success of the Montreal Protocol is not guaranteed, however. Global ozone policy faces challenges that could delay or even prevent full recovery. These include completing the HCFC and methyl bromide phase-outs, eliminating halon exemptions, preventing future black-market ODS production, ensuring that CFCs trapped in obsolete equipment and insulating foam do not reach the atmosphere, and potential impacts of changing climate conditions (Downie 2012). In addition, HFCs, a key non-ozone-depleting CFC substitute, are strong global warming gases and their use to help solve the ozone depletion problem has exacerbated the climate problem (see **Institutional interactions**).

## References

Benedick, Richard E. 1998. *Ozone Diplomacy*. Cambridge, MA, Harvard University Press.

Downie, David. 1995. "UNEP and the Montreal Protocol." In *International Organizations and Environmental Policy*, Eds. Robert Bartlett, Priya Kurian, Madhu Malik, and David Leonard Downie, 171–185. Westport, CT, Greenwood Press.

Downie, David. 2012. "The Vienna Convention, Montreal Protocol and Global Policy to Protect Stratospheric Ozone." In *Chemicals, Environment, Health: A Global Management Perspective*, Eds. Philip Wexler, Jan van der Kolk, Asish Mohapatra, and Ravi Agarwel, 243–260. Oxford, CRC Press.

Gareau, Brian J. 2013. *From Precaution to Profit: Contemporary Challenges to Environmental Protection in the Montreal Protocol*. New Haven, CT, Yale University Press.

Haas, Peter. 1992. "Banning Chlorofluorocarbons, Epistemic Community Efforts to Protect Stratospheric Ozone." *International Organization* 46(1): 187–224.

Litfin, Karen. 1994. *Ozone Discourses, Science and Politics in Global Environmental Cooperation*. New York, Columbia University Press.

Molina, Mario and F. Sherwood Rowland. 1974. "Stratospheric Sink for Chlorofluoromethanes: Chlorine Atomic Catalyzed Destruction of Ozone." *Nature* 249(5460): 810–812.

Parson, Edward A. 2003. *Protecting the Ozone Layer, Science and Strategy*. Oxford, Oxford University Press.

# PARTICIPATION

## Philippe Le Prestre

*Université Laval, Canada*

International environmental governance rests on the activities of a variety of actors that do not restrict their action to one level of governance or one issue area. The United Nations takes it for granted that **broad public participation in decision-making** is a fundamental prerequisite for the achievement of **sustainable development**. Accordingly, Agenda 21 in 1992, recognized that the "major groups" (local authorities, workers and unions, **indigenous peoples and local communities**, farmers, **business and corporations**, the scientific and technological community, women, children and youth, and **nongovernmental organizations**) have a right to participate in decisions that affect them or touch upon values they promote. Indeed, the United Nations has given civil society a significant role since its creation, a role that has kept expanding although its dimensions vary greatly among agencies and organizations.

The basis for strengthening participation of civil society in environmental policymaking lies in Principle 10 of the Rio Declaration and in Agenda 21 (see **Summit diplomacy**). At the regional level, the 1998 Aarhus Convention aims to encourage states to put into place procedures for effective public participation at the early stages of legislations, policies, and program development. Its theoretical roots are diverse, including pluralist, institutional, and **global deliberative democracy** theories. Its pragmatic roots are also diverse, ranging from the fear of capture of the bureaucracy by organized interests, to the experience of aid agencies and international development banks with controversial projects. Participation is supposed to strengthen democratic values, promote environmental **justice**, and improve **effectiveness**. It is intended to create a sense of ownership of the solution, help reconcile global expectations with local demands, and increase the legitimacy of the decisions and policies adopted. In sum, participation transforms policy subjects into stakeholders.

Though participation is now viewed as a necessity rather than a privilege, the goals it should pursue, how it should be conducted, and its impacts remain contested. A first set of questions touches upon representativeness, process, and its instrumental function.

First, who should participate? In international forums, participation faces logistical, equity, and legitimacy problems. There is always a risk of the process being captured by better organized groups and interests. Indeed, preferences do not automatically translate into group formation. And who should select the participants and the criteria used to assess representativeness? In some developed countries, indigenous peoples and local communities have been granted significant policy roles, which often translates into privileges at the international level, such as membership in national delegations. Their spokespersons in international forums, however, represent group interests above knowledge. Can we also assume that most local problems have local solutions and that local communities always know better? Conversely, how much weight should be given to the majority opinion of representatives of local communities against that of an organized minority financially supported by foreign interests?

Second, what does participation encompass? Is it a process of providing information to affected parties, of convincing people of the soundness of decisions made elsewhere, of identifying emergent needs and demands, or of integrating the perspectives of groups into the definition of the problems and of solutions? Which issues should be given priority and under what conditions? In one extreme example, the United Nations Declaration on the Rights of Indigenous Peoples grants indigenous peoples the rights to exploit natural resources according to their needs, and to participate in the decision-making process of institutions charged with managing these natural resources. These principles are not binding on nation-states, however, and groups vary considerably in terms of the levels of authority they enjoy within bilateral or multilateral institutions. In some cases, representatives of indigenous groups are granted access to closed meetings or, as in the case of the **biodiversity regime**, even co-chair some ad hoc working groups. The Inuit Circumpolar Conference has been an active participant in the scientific committees of the **Arctic Council** and thus able to influence the contents of its reports.

Third, how can one control for the unintended if not perverse effects of participation or prevent it from becoming a tool used for other political ends? Participation can increase inequalities by strengthening the power of local elites acting as go-betweens linking the community with donors or political authorities. For the same reasons, it can exacerbate political conflicts by empowering new individuals at the expense of established hierarchies, as seen in the context of so-called "development brokers." Finally, participation may be used to impose a particular viewpoint (through the selection of participants) and thus steer policy dynamics in a preferred direction.

A second set of questions pertains to the impacts of participation on environmental outcomes. Provisions for public participation may make issues more intractable. There is indeed a debate whether participation encourages gridlock or, rather, helps shift the power balance in favor of more stringent environmental policies (Green 1997; Beierle and Cayford 2002). Even then, there exists a potential trade-off between the environmental soundness of decisions and the **effectiveness** of their implementation (see **Compliance and implementation**) (Fritsch and Newig 2012). The impact of participation thus depends on its context (the political structure, the existence of clear targets and obligations, for example) and on the nature of the issue.

Public participation requirements alone are not sufficient to foster environmental sustainability and environmental justice. Arguably it is not participation that shapes politics but the other way around. The key to international influence may well lie at home, where strong segments of civil society can use domestic channels in order to gain influence at the international level.

### References

Beierle, Thomas C. and Jerry Cayford. 2002. *Democracy in Practice: Public Participation in Environmental Decisions*. Washington, Resources for the Future.

Fritsch, Oliver and Jens Newig 2012. "Participatory Governance and Sustainability: Findings of a Meta-Analysis of Stakeholder Involvement in Environmental Decision-Making." In *Reflexive Governance for Global Public Goods*, Eds. Eric Brousseau, Tom Dedeurwaerdere, and Bernd Siebenhüner, 181–203. Cambridge, MA : MIT Press.

Green, Andrew J. 1997. "Public Participation and Environmental Policy Outcomes." *Canadian Public Policy* 23(4): 435–458.

# PARTNERSHIPS

## Liliana Andonova and Manoela Assayag
*Graduate Institute of International and Development Studies, Switzerland*

The term "partnerships" is a broad umbrella. It covers governance arrangements of various characteristics—more or less decentralized and voluntary; and more or less formal. Partnerships lack traditional top-down steering and regulation and involve actors at a global as well as a local **scale**. Their collaborative dynamics range from initiatives between the private sector and civil society organizations (Austin 2000) such as the Natura Amazonian product line of natural cosmetics developed in partnership with **indigenous and local communities** and **nongovernmental organizations**; between public organizations and non-state actors, for instance, the climate finance instruments facilitated by the **World Bank**, governments, and the private sector (Andonova 2010); and multi-stakeholder arrangements (Glasbergen et al. 2007) such as the Global Alliance for Clean Cookstoves. Partnerships are thus agreements between different actors, public (including national governments, agencies, subnational governments, and intergovernmental organizations) and non-state (including foundations, **business and corporations**, and advocacy nongovernmental organizations), which establish common norms, rules, objectives, decision-making, and **compliance and implementation** procedures for a set of policy problems. Since the 1990s, this mode of environmental governance has proliferated rapidly to thousands of initiatives—from the several hundred partnerships registered as official Type II outcomes of the 2003 Johannesburg Summit to public–private initiatives facilitated by international organizations such as the **United Nations Environment Programme**, the World Bank, United Nations Development Programme (UNDP) and the United Nations Office for Partnerships, and diverse partnerships pursued at the subnational level, such as the initiative of the US Dow Chemical Company and Nature Conservancy on ecosystems or the Cows to Kilowatts partnership in Nigeria for bio-gas plant, which reduces water and greenhouse gas emissions from livestock and produces low-cost cooking gas and natural fertilizers.

The rapid proliferation and diversity of partnerships in environmental governance has prompted a search for cumulative understanding around three core and interrelated questions. Who governs through partnerships, to what effect, and with what degree of accountability? We consider these three layers of partnership politics in turn.

The rise in the power and mobilization of transnational non-state actors has been an important driver of new collaborative governance. The "business case" for partnerships, for instance, includes managing political and business risks associated with environmental failures and scrutiny; improving community relations, developing new **markets** for green products or services, and ultimately increasing corporate reputation and maintaining license to operate in a complex world. The business administration literature distinguishes, however, between more integrative corporate partnerships, which combine environmental or social purpose with the core business of the company, and those that remain largely philanthropic or not necessarily associated with the core environmental impacts of company operations (Austin 2000; Porter and Kramer 2006). For example, the Natura cosmetics line developed in collaboration with

Amazon communities exemplifies an integrative approach, while the Dow partnership with the Nature Conservancy supports research by the environmental organization to inform company strategies to reduce some externalities, but does not pertain directly to the company's core business of chemical production.

For nongovernmental organizations, partnerships are means to engage in direct governance to advance specific normative or implementation agendas. Partnerships also facilitate access to powerful actors such as states, intergovernmental organizations and companies and opportunities to establish a common collaborative purpose. The Amazon Protected Areas Partnership in Brazil for instance entails a substantial reworking of relations between the government, World Wildlife Fund (WWF), the World Bank and other actors toward an implementation-oriented biodiversity and habitat management (Andonova 2014). WWF has also facilitated corporate partnerships such as Climate Savers, whereby companies commit to specific carbon footprint reductions.

The visible non-state agency in environment partnerships has hardly derogated public institutions to insignificance, however. As partnerships evolved in number, purpose, and governance tools over the last twenty years, intergovernmental organizations have been among the most important entrepreneurs of collaborative governance, drawing on agency agendas and autonomy, technical expertise and normative capital. States, and in particular donor countries, provide a significant share of the financial resources that are essential for experimentation with partnership governance. The agency of developing countries has been essential for the implantation and increasing leadership of partnerships initiatives. Rather than retreating, states with some institutional capacity have re-articulated to engage non-state actors in national and sub-national initiatives (Glasbergen et al. 2007; Andonova 2014).

What motivates public and private governors to foster partnerships has important implications for the effects such initiatives produce. Data on partnership effects, although still limited, suggest a potentially dramatic variation. There are governance niches such as clean energy, biodiversity, climate finance, and risks from chemicals and industrial accidents, where partnerships have produced a range of behavioral or environmental outcomes. In clean energy, for instance, the San Cristóbal–Galápagos partnership facilitated the implementation of wind power on the island, reducing by 50 percent its dependence on imported fossil fuels and mitigating environmental externalities. Its broader political effect prompted Ecuador to adopt a government strategy toward zero-fossil-fuel Galapagos. Through its Small Grants Programme the **Global Environment Facility** has similarly contributed to improved access to efficient and cleaner technologies for buildings, cooking, and agriculture of thousands of communities around the developing world.

Such instances of success of many partnerships paradoxically highlight also major hurdles to **effectiveness**. Close to half of the energy partnerships registered by the **Commission on Sustainable Development**, for example, remain non-functional, while the effectiveness of the rest has been variable and highly dependent on the commitment of actors with resources (Pattberg et al. 2012). Successful initiatives remain unevenly clustered, often bypassing **least developed countries** and vulnerable populations that lack capacity or voice to engage partners. Successful partnership experiments have not yet been brought up to scale to make a global dent on pressing issues such as access to clean energy, water, and other **ecosystem services**.

Partnerships as new governance for the environment are thus closely embedded in broader institutional and policy structures. The extent and audiences of partnership accountability (powerful partner constituencies vs. affected populations or national publics) have been an issue for contestation and analysis. The level of **transparency** between partnerships and their policy environment, along with appropriate means for peer, market, and procedural accountability appear to be necessary elements of a complex accountability dynamic (Backstrand 2006; Steets 2010). While collaborative governance does not provide a comprehensive or standard solution to global problems, it often creates significant pockets of implementation capacity, new ideas, and extraordinary reach outcomes across the appropriate scale of action. The frontier of partnerships research has to move beyond the rise and nature of hybrid authority to account for the differential impacts, accountability, and conditions for broader and more equitable up-scaling of successful partnership practices for the environment.

## References

Andonova, Liliana B. 2010. "Public-Private Partnerships for the Earth: Politics and Patterns of Hybrid Authority in the Multilateral System." *Global Environmental Politics* 10(2): 25–53.

Andonova, Liliana B. 2014. "Boomerangs to Partnerships? Explaining State Participation in Transnational Partnerships for Sustainability." *Comparative Political Studies* 47 (3): 481–515.

Austin, James E. 2000. *The Collaboration Challenge: How Nonprofits and Business Succeed through Strategic Alliances*. San Francisco, CA, Jossey-Bass.

Bäckstrand, Karin. 2006. "Multi-stakeholder Partnerships for Sustainable Development: Rethinking Legitimacy, Accountability and Effectiveness." *European Environment* 16(5): 290–306.

Glasbergen, Philipp, Frank Biermann, and Arthur P.J. Mol. 2007. *Partnerships, Governance and Sustainable Development: Reflections on Theory and Practice.* Cheltenham, Edward Elgar.
Pattberg, Philipp, Frank Biermann, Sander Chan, and Aysem Mert. 2012. *Public–Private Partnerships for Sustainable Development: Emergence, Influence, and Legitimacy.* Cheltenham, Edward Elgar.
Porter, Michael E. and Mark R. Kramer. 2006. "Strategy and Society: The Link between Competitive Advantage and Corporate Social Responsibility." *Harvard Business Review* 84(12): 78–92.
Steets, Julia 2010. *Accountability in Public Policy Partnerships.* Basingstoke and New York, Palgrave Macmillan.

# PERSISTENT ORGANIC POLLUTANTS CONVENTION

Jessica Templeton
*London School of Economics and Political Science, United Kingdom*

Adopted in 2001, the Stockholm Convention on Persistent Organic Pollutants (POPs) is a legally binding global agreement designed to protect human health and the environment from exposure to certain hazardous, transboundary chemical pollutants. POPs fall into three categories: pesticides, such as DDT (dichloro-diphenyl-trichloroethane), which is still used for malarial vector control in Sub-Saharan Africa; industrial chemicals, such as the flame retardant hexabromocyclododecane; and unintended by-products of combustion and industrial processes, such as dioxins and furans.

The concept of a POP is socially constructed; the characteristics that define a POP were deliberately selected to include only those chemicals that pose threats to human health and the environment on a global **scale** (Selin 2010). While many chemicals may be hazardous to human health and the environment, the Stockholm Convention addresses only those chemicals that are subject to long-range environmental transport, and are thus capable of traveling thousands of miles from their point of release on air and water currents. This characteristic necessitates global collective action to protect people from exposure to these substances, which tend to concentrate in the Arctic (Downie and Fenge 2003). POPs are also toxic, bioaccumulative (increasing in concentration as they are passed upward through the food chain), and persistent (breaking down very slowly, if at all, in the environment).

Policy decisions to ban or limit production and use of POPs are based on **science**. Substances nominated for listing in the Stockholm Convention are evaluated by the POPs Review Committee, a subsidiary science advisory body composed of thirty-one technical experts affiliated with parties to the Convention. The design of this committee is intended to reflect regional diversity, gender balance, and a variety of areas of expertise. Kohler (2006) argues that such diversity is essential to the perceived legitimacy of **boundary organizations** such as the POPs Review Committee. These bodies works at the interface of science and policy, and their credibility is crucial for the credibility of the treaties they support.

The Stockholm Convention is one of three global treaties that address different aspects of global chemical pollution; the other two are the Basel Convention on **hazardous wastes** and the Rotterdam Convention on **hazardous chemicals**. While these conventions were established independently and are legally autonomous, a recent "synergies" initiative by the **United Nations Environment Programme** has formalized administrative and programmatic linkages among them. This is intended to enhance the cooperation of these instruments in areas of overlapping responsibility (see **Institutional interactions**). Most visibly, this has resulted in the combination of the three **secretariats** into one body to increase administrative efficiency. However, this process also has significant implications for the implementation of the conventions, such as through integration of technical assistance for developing countries seeking to implement their obligations under both the Stockholm and Basel conventions. Such changes will further strengthen the vertical and horizontal linkages among the chemicals and wastes conventions, and may facilitate policymaking by enhancing cooperation and efficiency (Selin 2010). However, strengthening linkages can also create obstacles to agreement; e.g. when controversy in one policy forum spills over to another. In such cases, linking issues across policy forums "raises the political stakes," making agreement harder to achieve (Selin 2010: 194).

### References

Downie, David Leonard and Terry Fenge (Eds.). 2003. *Northern Lights against POPs: Combatting Toxic Threats in the Arctic*. Montreal, McGill-Queen's University Press.

Kohler, Pia. 2006. "Science, PIC and POPs: Negotiating the Membership of the Chemical Review Committees under the Stockholm and Rotterdam Conventions." *Review of European Community and International Environmental Law* 15(3): 293–303.

Selin, Henrik. 2010. *Global Governance of Hazardous Chemicals: Challenges of Multilevel Management*. Cambridge, MA, MIT Press.

# POLICY DIFFUSION

## Katja Biedenkopf

*University of Amsterdam, Netherlands*

Policy diffusion describes the process through which policies spread among a group of jurisdictions or even globally. It can be observed at and across different **scales** of governance, from the local to the global. Authors distinguish several causal mechanisms and a number of scope conditions. Mechanisms describe a sequence of events that explains how one policy triggers or influences a policy change in another jurisdiction. Whereas the number and types of mechanisms differ between studies, a growing consensus on coercion, competition, learning, and emulation has emerged (Gilardi 2012: 460–461).

*Coercion* is the imposition of a policy change by one jurisdiction on another, mainly by means of sanctions and conditionality. This includes trade sanctions, conditions attached to market access such as the 1983 European Economic Community (EEC) law prohibiting the import of seal pup products, which led to Canada ceasing commercial whitecoat seal pup hunting. Coercive measures also include incentives in the form of payments or admission to, for example, an international organization as a reward for a demanded policy change. Countries wanting to join the European Union (EU) (see **Regional governance**) must fulfill the condition of adopting the Union's entire set of environmental laws. In the case of the Central and Eastern European countries that acceded in the 2000s, this obligation was accompanied by incentivizing financial and administrative capacity-building measures (Andonova 2003: 6–9).

*Competition* is based on jurisdictions' struggle to retain or attract resources and investment. If one jurisdiction lowers its environmental regulation so that doing business becomes cheaper, it might attract more investment (see **Dumping**). In response, another jurisdiction could equally lower its environmental regulation to compete for the same investment, which is commonly labeled a "race to the bottom." Yet, the globalization of production chains and sales markets can also lead to the opposite effect: a "race to the top." If a jurisdiction with a large and attractive market adopts ambitious environmental regulation, all companies that are active in this market must comply. Out of efficiency considerations, some companies can decide to apply the more stringent requirements to all of their products. Having made the initial compliance investments, companies can decide to actively advocate policy change in other jurisdictions where they operate to level the playing field with domestic competitors that otherwise would not make the investments (Vogel 1997: 561–563). In 1960, California enacted a standard for limiting car emissions, which led to the adoption of an identical federal standard five years later. In the 1970s, the EEC and Japan adopted identical standards to the US. The global nature of car manufacturing is often cited as the main reason for this race to the top (Carlson 2008). *Learning* means drawing lessons from another jurisdiction's experiences. Policymakers use other jurisdictions' experiences and material for inspiration and to gauge the consequences of possible policy options. Environmental ministries and agencies have diffused rapidly since the 1970s. Busch and Jörgens (2005: 875) argue that international communication and exchange of experiences contributed to this diffusion process, through for instance **transgovernmental networks** and **epistemic communities.**

*Emulation* is the adoption of policy similar to another jurisdiction's policy based on normative grounds. Viewing a certain policy as appropriate and legitimate is the motivation for this process. Jurisdictions follow others' policy examples because of their adherence to the same norms, their high esteem for the jurisdiction that adopted the policy first, and as a result of socialization efforts by the early adopters of the respective policy. The diffusion of the practice of eco-labels, labeling products based on their environmental performance (see **Labeling and certification**) was first introduced in the 1970s by a few countries. In the late 1980s/ early 1990s, their diffusion rate surged rapidly. One explanation for this can be found in the international cooperation and socialization among the adopting countries (Tews et al. 2003: 583–585). Empirically, emulation and learning can be difficult to distinguish.

Diffusion can occur through a combination of mechanisms, which can reinforce or weaken each other. One example of mutual reinforcement is an EU law that requires electronic products to be (re)designed so that they do not contain certain hazardous substances (apart from designated exemptions, see **Hazardous wastes regime**). Through the competition mechanism, the EU has leverage over countries such as China, which produces many electronics components for global supply chains. Leading by example, the EU additionally influenced China's own regulation on the restriction of hazardous substances through learning and, to a lesser degree, emulation (Biedenkopf 2012).

Diffusion only occurs under certain conditions. These can pertain to the first-adopting jurisdiction, the follower jurisdiction(s), and the diffused policy's properties. In the above-mentioned example of substance restrictions, the structure of the Chinese economy, China's administrative capacity and its legal system explain why the Chinese regulation that resulted from the diffusion process has not only similarities but also differences from the EU law (Biedenkopf 2012). Many policy diffusion studies take little account of agency. The role of individuals and organizations in fostering or impeding diffusion processes is often overshadowed by structural variables. For this reason, the politics of diffusion remain rather understudied. This relates to the broader question of how insights from policy diffusion research could be used for increased purposeful use of diffusion as a governance tool by jurisdictions (Biedenkopf and Dupont 2013: 190–192).

## References

Andonova, Liliana B. 2003. *Transnational Politics of the Environment: The European Union and Environmental Policy in Central and Eastern Europe*. Cambridge, MA, MIT Press.

Biedenkopf, Katja. 2012. "Hazardous Substances in Electronics: The Effects of European Union Risk Regulation on China." *European Journal of Risk Regulation* 3(4): 477–488.

Biedenkopf, Katja and Claire Dupont. 2013. "A Toolbox Approach to the EU's External Climate Governance." In *Global Power Europe*, Eds. Astrid Boening, Jan-Frederik Kremer, and Aukje van Loon, 181–199. Heidelberg, Springer.

Busch, Per-Olof and Helge Jörgens. 2005. "The International Sources of Policy Convergence: Explaining the Spread of Environmental Policy Innovations." *Journal of European Public Policy* 12(5): 860–884.

Carlson, Anne E. 2008. *California Motor Vehicle Standards and Federalism: Lessons for the European Union*, Working Paper 2008(4). Berkeley, Institute of Governmental Studies.

Gilardi, Fabrizio. 2012. "Transnational Diffusion: Norms, Ideas, and Policies." In *Handbook of International Relations*, Eds. Walter Carlsnaes, Thomas Risse, and Beth A. Simmons, 453–477. London, Sage.

Tews, Kerstin, Per-Olof Busch, and Helge Jörgens. 2003. "The Diffusion of New Environmental Policy Instruments." *European Journal of Political Research* 42(4): 569–600.

Vogel, David. 1997. "Trading Up and Governing Across: Transnational Governance and Environmental Protection." *Journal of European Public Policy* 4(4): 556 571.

# POLLUTER PAYS PRINCIPLE

## Nicolas de Sadeleer

*Université Saint-Louis - Bruxelles, Belgium*

The use of environmental goods typically gives rise to what economists call externalities where social costs linked to environmental degradation are passed on to the community. In accordance with the theory of externalities developed by English economist Pigou, such external costs should be internalized: that is, integrated into the price of the goods or services in question, by charging those responsible for them. As long as these costs remain hidden, markets will react to distorted price signals and make inefficient economic choices. Against this background, the polluter pays principle mirrors an economic rule of cost allocation whose source lies precisely in the theory of externalities. Accordingly, it requires polluters to take responsibility for the external costs arising from their pollution (de Sabran-Pontevès 2007).

Besides having been endorsed since the 1970s by the Organisation of Economic Co-operation and Development (OECD) and the European Union (EU), the polluter pays principle has been expressly enshrined either in the preamble or in the operative provisions of a number of environmental agreements, the majority of which aim at protecting regional seas (Sands and Peel 2012). At the 1992 Rio Conference, the principle was proclaimed in the Declaration on Environment and Development, albeit in aspirational rather than obligatory terms:

> National authorities should endeavor to promote the internalization of environmental costs and the use of economic instruments, taking into account the approach that the polluter should, in principle, bear the cost of pollution, with due regard to the public interest and without distorting international trade and investment. (principle 16)

In contrast to other parts of the world where the principle has never been endorsed, it has been gathering momentum within EU countries, most of which are imposing environmental charges on polluters (de Sadeleer 2002; de Sadeleer 2012). In addition, several national lawmakers (France, Belgium) have expressly recognized it as a guiding norm or a fundamental principle of their environment policy.

The history of the polluter pays reflects a gradual shift in meaning. At first, the principle was carved out by both the OECD and the EU in the course of the 1970s as a means of preventing the distortion of competition (instrument of harmonization intended to ensure the smooth functioning of the internal market); later, in the course of the 1980s it formed the basis both for internalizing chronic pollution (instrument of redistribution through the use of environmental funds) and preventing it (instrument of prevention through the use of **taxation**); finally, it served more recently to guarantee the integrated reparation of damage (curative instrument thanks to liability schemes).

Last, the polluter pays principle juxtaposes two terms whose meanings appear self-evident at first glance but become more elusive as one attempts to define them. The act of definition is thus best approached from two different angles. First: who is the polluter? And second: how much must the polluter pay? The polluter should be the person who causes pollution. However, in the case of diffuse pollution, where multiple causes produce single effects and single causes produce multiple effects, the identification of the polluter would be somewhat difficult. Once identified, the polluter will have to pay, but it still remains to agree on a price. Furthermore, the question arises as to whether the polluter pays principle entails a full or a partial internalization of externalities. However, pricing environmental costs remains embroiled with controversies.

## References

de Sadeleer, Nicolas. 2002. *Environmental Principles*. Oxford, Oxford University Press.

de Sadeleer, Nicolas. 2012. "The Polluter-Pays Principle in EU Law—Bold Case Law and Poor Harmonisation." In *Festskrift til H.-C. Bugge*, Eds. Lorange Backer, Ole Kristian Fauchald, and Christina Voigt, 405–419. Oslo, Universitetsforlaget.

De Sabran-Pontevès, Elzeéar. 2007. *Les transcriptions juridiques du principe pollueur-payeur*. Aix-en-Provence, Presses universitaires d'Aix-Marseille.

Sands, Philippe and Jacqueline Peel. 2012. *Principles of International Environmental Law*. Cambridge, Cambridge University Press.

# POPULATION SUSTAINABILITY

## Diana Coole
*Birkbeck University of London, United Kingdom*

Population sustainability may be construed in three ways. First, it concerns the demographic viability of a particular population: does it have sufficient critical mass, resilience, and fecundity to maintain itself over time? Second, it refers to the material capacity of the external environment to support existing or projected numbers. This is sometimes related to a third, more prescriptive sense in which a sustainable population is equated with an optimum population. During the 1920s there were attempts at fixing an optimal range and this is still sometimes related to the **carrying capacities paradigm**, although critics regard definite numbers as overly rigid.

The second meaning is most pertinent to environmental sustainability. In pre-modern cultures there is evidence of populations disappearing as they outgrew natural resources. The issue emerged more forcefully during Europe's fertility transition when Malthus (1798) cited famine, disease, and war as consequences of exponential demographic growth. During the 1960s and 1970s these warnings were reignited by a post-war baby boom that amplified the West's rising per capita consumption to trigger concerns over resource shortages and environmental degradation. Paul Ehrlich's *The Population Bomb* (1972) and the Club of Rome's *Limits to Growth* (Meadows et al. 1972) recommended population stabilization and a steady state economy. The UN Conference on the Human Environment (Stockholm 1972) refers in its fifth proclamation to continuous population growth as a source of problems for environmental preservation and its sixteenth principle recommends appropriate demographic policies where population growth rates or concentrations adversely affect the environment, provided these respect **human rights**.

The topic of unsustainable population growth subsequently fell into abeyance as population control policies became politically contentious, the growth rate slowed, and neoliberals seized upon anti-Malthusian demographic revisionism. This argues that more people are a spur to economic growth and technological innovation, thereby rendering resources elastic while increasing the revenue for managing ecological **services** more effectively. At the Rio Earth Summit (1992) an eighth principle merely tacked "appropriate demographic policies" onto eliminating unsustainable patterns of production and consumption. By Rio+20 (2012) demographic policies had disappeared entirely from the **sustainable development** toolbox. Ironically, although environmental declarations on sustainability routinely eschew "the numbers game," population policies are widely used to influence growth and fertility rates for economic purposes. The UN's *World Population Policies 2011* (United Nations 2013) shows 119 governments making policy interventions to raise (39) or lower (70) growth rates, while 118 similarly strive to increase (67) or reduce (51) the fertility rate. In the case of raising these variables, Australia's population policy (Australian Government 2011) is exemplary of a focus on the number of productive working-age people, with sustained economic growth providing the principal framework. Most **least developed countries** treat population growth as a threat to resource security and development but here, too, environmental concerns have lower priority.

In light of continued high population growth in some **emerging countries**, increasing numbers of middle class consumers worldwide, the UN's upwardly revised projection of almost eleven billion by 2100, and evidence that environmental destruction persists, some studies—such as The Royal Society's *People and the Planet* (2012)—are again claiming population numbers as crucial to the sustainability puzzle. Satisfying unmet needs for contraception and incentivizing small family norms are recognized as cost-effective ways to mitigate **tragedy of the commons** outcomes such as climate change and biodiversity loss.

### References

Australian Government. 2011. *Sustainable Australia—Sustainable Communities: A Sustainable Population Policy for Australia.* Canberra, Commonwealth of Australia.

Ehrlich, Paul. 1972. *The Population Bomb,* 2nd Edition (first published 1968). London, Pan/Ballantine.

Meadows, Donella H., Dennis L. Meadows, Jorgen Randers, and William W. Behrens III. 1972. *The Limits to Growth.* New York, Universe Books.

The Royal Society. 2012. *People and the Planet.* London, The Royal Society.

United Nations. 2013. *World Population Policies Report 2011.* New York, United Nations.

# POST-ENVIRONMENTALISM

## Chiara Certomà

*Sant'Anna School of Advanced Studies, Italy, and*
*Ghent University, Belgium*

Post-environmentalism theory emerged in the 1990s as part of a larger corpus of theoretical critiques pointing out the weakness of the **sustainable development** paradigm and the inefficacy of mainstream environmental politics (see also **Critical political economy**). It affirms that from the 1980s onward **summit diplomacy, business and corporations** and large **nongovernmental organizations** put forward a process of de-politicization of environmental issues in the pursuit of establishing consensus-seeking global environmental governance. This process went together with the search for technical solutions to environmental problems that have weakened the socio-political strengths of environmental claims, disempowered social agency, and produced largely ineffective policy measures, such as tradable permits and other **market**-based solutions.

The term post-environmentalism was introduced into the political philosophy debate by John Young (1992) and a few years later it was picked up by the critical philosopher Klaus Eder (1996), who envisages post-environmentalism as a master frame for a further development of the cognitive and moral modern rationality in the public space.

In 2004 consultants Michael Shellenberger and Ted Nordhaus published a pamphlet titled "The Death of Environmentalism" that gave rise to a large debate in the US public policy sector and in the environmental sociology field (Latour 2008). They criticized environmental movements for not making any effort to link with other social movements and thus for determining their marginalization in the political debate. The naïve presentation of environmental issues as merely pertaining to nature **conservation and preservation** undermined their high political relevance and the possibility for environmental campaigns to be successfully addressed, such as in the case of the failure to reform and deepen the **climate change regime**.

By critically building upon the mentioned contributions, political scientist Ingolfur Blühdorn (2000) proposed a theoretical advancement from post-environmentalism to post-ecologism, in order to overcome the conventionally accepted definition, knowledge-production processes, and political practices of environmentalism itself. He claims that the full acceptance of strictly environmental values is incompatible with the practices of modern capitalist consumer democracies and this determines a no-way-out situation for mainstream environmental politics (Blühdorn 2011). In order to disclose the paradox determined by the coexistence of the hyper-ecologism of declaratory commitments toward sustainability goals and the immutable faith of infinite growth, he adopts a constructivist approach. The critical analysis of the social construction of environmental issues in the theory of **ecological modernization** reveals it to be a mere peacekeeping strategy and calls for a new sociology for the post-ecologist era.

## References

Blühdorn, Ingolfur. 2000. *Post-Ecologist Politics: Social Theory and the Abdication of the Ecologist Paradigm*. London, Routledge.
Blühdorn, Ingolfur. 2011. "The Politics of Unsustainability: COP15, Post-Ecologism and the Ecological Paradox." *Organization and Environment* 24(1): 34–53.

Eder, Klaus. 1996. *The Social Construction of Nature*. London, Sage.
Latour, Bruno. 2008. "'It's the Development, Stupid!' or How to Modernize Modernization?.'" Available at www.bruno-latour.fr.
Young, John. 1992. *Post-Environmentalism*. London, Belhaven Press.

# PRECAUTIONARY PRINCIPLE

**Aarti Gupta**

*Wageningen University, Netherlands*

The precautionary principle is often touted as one of the most important principles of global environmental governance. Its central premise is that scientific uncertainty about the nature and extent of environmental or human health risks and harm should not be a reason for policy inaction (Foster et al. 2000, see **Science**). One of the most well-known articulations of the precautionary principle is that contained in the Rio Declaration adopted during the 1992 Earth Summit (see **Summit diplomacy**). Principle 15 of this declaration states that "Where there are threats of serious or irreversible damage, lack of full scientific certainty shall not be used as a reason for postponing cost-effective measures to prevent environmental degradation."

The policy domain of global environmental and risk governance has seen the most intense debates over precaution, given persisting scientific uncertainties about cause, impact, and distribution of harm and risk (Pellizzoni and Ylönen 2008). The historical antecedents of the precautionary principle go back to the German notion of *vorzorgeprinzip*, first articulated in a domestic context in the 1970s, and implying the need for preventive and forward-looking (rather than reactive) action on environmental problems (O'Riordan and Jordan 1995). Much scholarly attention has focused since then on the challenges of defining and operationalizing the precautionary principle, particularly in an international context (Löfstedt et al. 2001).

The principle has continued to generate controversy in both scholarly and policy debates over the last decades, with strong advocates (Sachs 2011) and equally strong and influential detractors (Sunstein 2005). One reason for such contrary reactions relates to the proliferating definitions of the concept, with resultant uneven and contested policy implications. Many scholars have noted that at least fourteen definitions are identifiable in various international declarations and treaties (Foster et al. 2000). This definitional diversity implies that there is little shared understanding of key elements of the precautionary principle, including appropriate triggers for precautionary action or where the burden of proof should lie in claiming harm or lack thereof. This lack of shared understanding extends to whether precaution should even be considered a "principle" or merely an "approach" to environmental policymaking. While the United States (US) prefers this latter characterization, the European Union (EU) has long been a strong advocate for the precautionary principle as a cornerstone of its regional environmental policy (Pellizzoni and Ylönen 2008).

A longstanding scholarly debate turns on whether the precautionary principle's "vagueness" and openness to multiple interpretations is its key strength or a fatal flaw. While some claim that the precautionary principle "will remain politically potent as long as it continues to be tantalizingly ill-defined" (O'Riordan and Jordan 1995: 193), others view the lack of definitional clarity as leaving the principle open to abuse. These definitional debates are also linked to identifying and critiquing "weak" versus "strong" versions of the precautionary principle. Strong versions include those that seem to call for zero risk or "full" scientific certainty. In a cogent critique, Sunstein (2005) argues that strong versions of the precautionary principle that preclude taking (uncertain) risks are paralyzing since, taken to their logical conclusion, they permit neither action nor inaction, given that both carry with them corresponding risks and foregone opportunities. From such a perspective, the precautionary principle as a guide to policy is useless.

Others allege that its vagueness allows the precautionary principle to serve as a front to further protectionist trade agendas. For example, the principle has been implicated in the transatlantic conflict between the US and EU over trade in genetically modified organisms (GMOs), given that the EU evokes the precautionary principle to justify its restrictions on GMO imports from the US (Tait 2001). This conflict is linked to similar longstanding disputes and **institutional interactions** over how precaution is being conceptualized in international environmental versus trade **regimes**. One of the most closely analyzed relationships is that between the international environmental treaty governing GMO transfers, the Cartagena Protocol on Biosafety negotiated under the **biodiversity regime**, and the science-based regulation of environmental risks and safety under the **World Trade Organization**'s Agreement on Application of Sanitary and Phytosanitary Measures (SPS Agreement).

The SPS Agreement requires that national sanitary and phytosanitary standards relating to plant, animal, and human health and safety have a scientific justification, to prevent their becoming non-tariff barriers to trade. Article 5.7 of the SPS Agreement allows, however, that:

> in cases where relevant scientific evidence is insufficient, a Member may provisionally adopt . . . [restrictive] measures [while seeking] to obtain the additional information necessary for a more objective **assessment** of risk, and review the sanitary or phytosanitary measure accordingly within a reasonable period of time.

Thus, the SPS Agreement permits recourse to trade restrictive precautionary measures, including for GMOs, as long as these are time-bound and efforts are underway to generate concrete scientific evidence of harm. In contrast, the 2000 Cartagena Protocol appears to provide greater leeway to countries to take precautionary action, insofar as it does not require a review of precautionary measures within a specified period of time. Nonetheless, scholarly debates persist about how to interpret the articulation of the precautionary principle in each global regime (Gupta 2001).

The United Nations Framework Convention on Climate Change (UNFCCC) in its Article 3 also evokes a version of the precautionary principle in mandating that "lack of full scientific uncertainty should not be used as a reason for postponing . . . [climate mitigation] measures" (see **Climate change regime**). This issue area highlights, as do many others, a need to go beyond definitional conflicts to embed operationalization of precaution into the growing institutionalization of science and (different types of) uncertainty in global environmental governance (Pellizzoni and Ylönen 2008).

### References

Foster, Kenneth R., Paolo Vecchia, and Michael H. Repacholi. 2000. "Science and the Precautionary Principle." *Science* 288(5468): 979–981.

Gupta, Aarti. 2001. "Advance Informed Agreement: A Shared Basis for Governing Trade in Genetically Modified Organisms?" *Indiana Journal of Global Legal Studies* 9(1): 265–281.

Löfstedt, Ragnar E., Baruch Fischhoff, and Ilya R. Fischhoff. 2001. "Precautionary Principles: General Definitions and Specific Applications to Genetically Modified Organisms." *Journal of Policy Analysis and Management* 21(3): 381–407.

O'Riordan, Timothy and Andrew Jordan. 1995. "The Precautionary Principle in Contemporary Environmental Politics." *Environmental Values* 4(3): 191–212.

Pellizzoni, Luigi and Marja Ylönen. 2008. "Responsibility in Uncertain Times: An Institutional Perspective on Precaution." *Global Environmental Politics* 8(3): 51–73.

Sachs, Noah M. 2011. "Rescuing the Strong Precautionary Principle from its Critics." *University of Illinois Law Review* 4: 1285–1338.
Sunstein, Cass. 2005. *Laws of Fear: Beyond the Precautionary Principle.* New York, Cambridge University Press.
Tait, Joyce. 2001. "More Faust than Frankenstein: The European Debate about the Precautionary Principle and Risk Regulation for Genetically Modified Crops." *Journal of Risk Research* 4(2): 175–189.

# PREVENTIVE ACTION PRINCIPLE

## Hélène Trudeau

*Université de Montréal, Canada*

The principle of preventive action is associated with the concept of **sustainable development.** This principle means that states should take necessary measures to protect the environment and to prevent harm caused by activities on their territory, not only from a transboundary perspective but also from a global one. These measures can include, for example, the regulation of products and activities that can be toxic or harmful and the **assessment** and authorization of projects that could generate risks for the environment.

It is important to distinguish the **precautionary principle** from the principle of preventive action. Although connected because preventive measures and action can be warranted in face of all risks (Trouwborst 2009), the principle of preventive action applies more specifically to known risks to the environment (see **Risk society**). The precautionary principle is an advanced articulation of prevention that applies to risks framed with scientific uncertainty (De Sadeleer 2002) (see **Science**).

The principle of preventive action finds its origin in the rules governing state **liability.** In 1941, in the Trail Smelter dispute, Canada was held responsible for the damage caused to American farmers by emissions emanating from a plant on the Canadian side of the border. The arbitral tribunal said that a state is not allowed to use its territory in a way that can harm the territory of another state. In international law, states have a responsibility to prevent damages they can cause outside their territory, in spite of their **sovereignty** over their natural wealth and resources. With respect to the protection of the environment, a correlating duty has emerged imposing on states the responsibility to control and correctly manage activities based on their territory if they can impact on the territory of another state (Sands 1995; Paradell-Trius 2000; Trouwborst

2009). This obligation is limited to a conduct of "due care" or "due diligence": a state will not be held liable for damages if it took reasonable measures to prevent them from happening (Crawford et al. 2010). That duty has been articulated during **summit diplomacy** in both Principle 21 of the Stockholm Declaration and Principle 2 of the Rio Declaration. It has found application in situations of transboundary harm and pollution and has been clearly stated as a customary rule of international law in several international litigations and **dispute settlement mechanisms** (Trail Smelter, Lac Lanoux, Gabcikovo-Nagymaros) (Sands 1995). Its precise normative content is provided for in bilateral and multilateral treaties such as the Convention on Environmental Impact Assessment and the **transboundary air pollution regime**, which formulate concrete measures of prevention applicable between states (**assessments**, consultation, cooperation, monitoring sources of potential transboundary harm). Moreover, in 2001, the International Law Commission codified the specific elements resulting from that due care obligation in the Draft Articles on Prevention of Transboundary Harm from Hazardous Activities (Barboza 2011).

## References

Barboza, Julio. 2011. *The Environment, Risk and Liability in International Law*. Leiden, Boston, Martinus Nijhoff Publishers.

Crawford, James, Alain Pellet, and Simon Olleson. 2010. *The Law of International Responsibility*. Oxford, Oxford University Press.

de Sadeleer, Nicolas. 2002. *Environmental Principles*. Oxford, Oxford University Press.

Paradell-Trius, Lluis. 2000. "Principle of International Environmental Law: An Overview." *Review of European, Comparative and International Environmental Law* 9(2): 93–99.

Sands, Philippe. 1995. *Principles of International Environmental Law*. Manchester, Manchester University Press.

Trouwborst, Arie. 2009. "Prevention, Precaution, Logic and Law: The Relationship between the Precautionary Principle and the Preventative Principle in International Law and Associated Questions." *Erasmus Law Review* 2(2): 105–127.

# PRIVATE REGIMES

## Jessica F. Green

*Case Western Reserve University, United States*

States are no longer the sole actors responsible for governing global environmental problems. Increasingly, private regimes, which are transnational rules created by non-state actors (including **nongovernmental organizations**, **business and corporations**, and **partnerships**), are managing environmental issues (Pattberg 2007; Green 2014; see also **regimes**).

The trend toward private regimes can be traced, in part, back to the 1992 Conference on Environment and Human Development, where states called on non-state actors to promote environmental protection through **partnerships** and other activities. The most prominent type of private regime takes the form of environmental **labeling and certification**. These are rules created by non-state actors that set standards for the environmental attributes of various products. For example, these private regimes decide what constitutes "sustainable" fish or "organic" food. These are driven by **market** logic: consumers from developed nations demand products that have a reduced environmental impact, for which they are willing to pay a premium (Vogel 2008).

Codes of conduct for **corporate social responsibility** are examples of self-regulation, which can also be considered a type of private regime. The chemical industry created the Responsible Care program to improve the environmental safety and public accountability of chemical manufacturers. The majority of global chemical producers are now members, and have adopted principles of behavior to improve their conduct.

Information-based standards are a third form of private regime. They require organizations—usually firms—to collect and report their activities with respect to some environmental practice (see **Audits**). Thus, the Global Reporting Initiative (see **Reporting**) provides a framework for organizations to report on the economic, social, and environmental impacts of their activities. The Carbon Disclosure Project does the same, but is focused largely on carbon emissions. Environmental management systems, such as ISO14001, can also be considered a private regime: these standards are created by private actors to improve their internal operations (Prakash and Potoski 2006). They are process-based rules, and as such do not have any requirements about outcomes.

There are a few different views about why private regimes emerge; ultimately, the answer depends in part on who creates the rules and who adopts them. Private regimes constituted by and for business often confer some benefit to members. This may include an improved corporate reputation, or the ability to forestall more stringent public regulation. Others see private regimes, and especially, labeling and certification, as the result of globalization. Supply chains now span the length of the globe, and cannot be regulated by any single nation; private regimes have emerged to fill this gap. Since fish sold in the United States may have been caught in one nation and processed in another, no single nation can regulate this product. Thus, the demand for these private regimes may come from consumers or from firms. In other cases, the demand comes from NGOs who seek to reduce the environmental impacts of firms (Bartley 2007).

Since private regimes are voluntary, and not required by law, they have been critiqued as being weak and ineffective. Weak regimes are viewed as a form of "green washing"—making claims about improving environmental quality without really doing so. Even with strong rules, private regimes may also be ineffective, since they cannot compel organizations to join. For example, although the Marine Stewardship Council now certifies almost one-tenth of the world's fish catch, most of the world's fisheries are still dangerously overexploited despite the parallel existence of the **fisheries governance**. Recently, studies have begun to examine whether and how private regimes can be strengthened through governmental action. For example, many EU nations now accept timber certified by forest labeling schemes such as the Forest Stewardship Council. This public policy creates more demand and in theory, enhances the **effectiveness** of labeling schemes. Of course, if governments are needed for the proper functioning of private regimes, this raises the question of whether they are really necessary forms of governance.

Private regimes are also vulnerable to legitimacy critiques. Since they are not endowed with authority by the state, there is a question of whether non-state actors are viewed as rightful rule-makers (Bernstein and Cashore 2007). Perceptions of legitimacy are closely tied to the ability to govern, since legitimacy provides private actors with authority. Some works discuss the specific measures that private regimes have adopted to cultivate legitimacy, including **transparency** and **participation** procedures to ensure that they are held accountable to those that they regulate, and to the public at large.

Despite these potential problems, private regimes are growing rapidly. Their growth raises questions about competition: what happens when multiple regimes compete to regulate the same issue (see **Institutional interactions**)? Since private regimes are voluntary, actors can choose not to join or to join those regimes with weak rules. Thus, a big question in research on private regimes is whether competition among standards can produce a "ratcheting up" effect, so that weak regimes are either driven out of business or are forced to strengthen their rules, or a "race to the bottom," where private regimes weaken their rules to compete for adherents. Thus far, the findings on the question of the **policy diffusion** of private regimes are mixed.

## References

Bartley, Tim. 2007. "Institutional Emergence in an Era of Globalization: The Rise of Transnational Private Regulation of Labor and Environmental Conditions." *American Journal of Sociology* 113(2): 297–351.

Bernstein, Steven and Benjamin Cashore. 2007. "Can Non-State Global Governance be Legitimate? An Analytical Framework." *Regulation and Governance* 1(4): 347–371.

Green, Jessica F. 2014. *Rethinking Private Authority: Agents and Entrepreneurs in Global Environmental Governance*. Princeton, NJ, Princeton University Press.

Pattberg, Phillip. 2007. *Private Institutions and Global Governance: The New Politics of Environmental Sustainability*. Cheltenham, Edward Elgar.

Prakash, Aseem and Matthew Potoski. 2006. *The Voluntary Environmentalists: Green Clubs, ISO 14001, and Voluntary Environmental Regulations*. Cambridge, Cambridge University Press.

Vogel, David. 2008. "Private Global Business Regulation." *Annual Review of Political Science* 11: 261–282.

# REDD

## Heike Schroeder
*University of East Anglia, United Kingdom*

With a dwindling forest cover, the problem of massive deforestation in tropical forest countries has come center stage in addressing climate change, accounting for 13–17 percent of annual global greenhouse gas emissions (van der Werf et al. 2009). After the newly formed Coalition for Rainforest Nations lobbied for addressing deforestation in the post-Kyoto negotiations under the **climate change regime** and Stern (2007) famously framed deforestation as a cheap mitigation option compared to ongoing international and domestic mitigation efforts, avoiding deforestation was adopted as international climate change policy in the Bali Action Plan in 2007.

The Bali Action Plan took up the idea of creating incentives to keep forests intact by making trees standing more valuable than felled. It launched the designing of a mechanism to compensate tropical forest countries keeping forests standing and thereby to reduce emissions from deforestation and forest degradation (REDD) as part of the ongoing post-2012 climate change negotiations. The 2009 Copenhagen Accord committed to funding activities toward REDD as well as conservation, sustainable management of forests, and enhancement of forest carbon stocks (REDD+). The 2010 Cancun Agreements include provisional language on social and environmental safeguards and provide guidance on REDD+ readiness activities. During 2011 and 2012, much attention was focused on finance and developing guidelines for measuring, **reporting**, and verifying reductions in deforestation (Lyster et al. 2013).

Meanwhile, **market**-based schemes have been set up and funds have been flowing to tropical forest countries to develop capacity on the ground, experiment with various schemes, and gain a head start in finding ways to reduce emissions while providing benefits to forest dependent people. In 2008, two programs were set up: UN-REDD to supporting countries in developing and implementing national REDD+ strategies and the **World Bank** Forest Carbon Partnership Facility (FCPF) to fund partner countries to get ready for REDD+. In addition, several bilateral, transnational and nongovernmental schemes and pilot projects are being carried out (Angelsen et al. 2012).

It has been widely acknowledged that governance issues are the central challenge for REDD+ (Corbera and Schroeder 2011). REDD+ will not be effective in avoiding deforestation without causing social and environmental harm unless a number of crucial governance challenges at both the international design level and the country implementation level are sufficiently addressed (see **Scale**). These include the problem of leakage, i.e. forest saved in one location may lead to deforestation elsewhere if the global and/or domestic drivers of deforestation are not addressed at the same time; permanence, i.e. how to engage with recipient country stakeholders on donor countries' demands for long-term contracts over avoiding deforestation; and additionality, i.e. how to calculate sufficiently precisely the degree of difference to the business as usual trajectory of deforestation that the international payment has enabled.

## References

Angelsen, Arild, Maria Brockhaus, William D. Sunderlin, and Louis V. Verchot (Eds.). 2012. *Analysing REDD+: Challenges and Choices.* Bogor, CIFOR.

Corbera, Esteve and Heike Schroeder. 2011. "Governing and Implementing REDD+." *Environmental Science and Policy* 14(2): 89–99.

Lyster, Rosemary, Catherine MacKenzie, and Constance McDermott. 2013. *Law, Tropical Forests and Carbon: The Case of REDD.* Cambridge, Cambridge University Press.

Stern, Nicholas. 2007. *The Economics of Climate Change.* Cambridge, Cambridge University Press.

Van der Werf, Guido, Douglas C. Morton, Ruth S. DeFries, Jos G.J. Olivier, Prasad S. Kasibhatla, Robert B. Jackson, Jim Collatz, and James T. Ranaderson. 2009. "$CO_2$ Emissions from Forest Loss." *Nature Geoscience* 2: 737–738.

# REFLEXIVE GOVERNANCE

## Tom Dedeurwaerdere

*Université catholique de Louvain, Belgium*

Reflexive governance denotes a mode of governance where feedback on multiple regulatory frameworks generates social learning processes that influence actors' core beliefs and norms (Dedeurwaerdere 2005; Voß et al. 2006; Brousseau et al. 2012). These processes complement political-administrative hierarchy and economic incentives as mechanisms for governance.

Two main models of reflexive governance have been developed to complement conventional state-based and market-based modes of governance, which rely respectively on the seminal works of Jürgen Habermas and Ulrich Beck. The model of Habermas (1998) was one of the first attempts to justify the **participation** of civil society actors in the governance of post-conventional societies, where democratic legitimacy is no longer built on the basis of common conventions shared by a group with a common history at the level of a nation or the belonging to a social class. Instead, democratic legitimacy is built through social learning processes among state and civil society actors based on open participation in the debates on new collective values and norms. This theory influenced experimentation with several deliberative processes, such as citizen juries, consultations with **nongovernmental organizations** (such as stakeholder consultations in the EU prior to the adoption of new regulations) and **global deliberative democracy** (such as stakeholder consultations and international United Nations conferences). A weakness of this first model is that social learning not always leads to the adoption of new policies at the level of the political-administrative hierarchy.

The second model was proposed by Ulrich Beck in the context of his work on the regulation of **risk society**. According to Beck (1992), the building of efficient and legitimate rules for dealing with risks that might have important unanticipated side effects should involve so-called sub-politics, where nongovernmental actors (including social movements) are directly involved in social learning processes for solving collective action problems without relying on the administrative state.

Illustrations of sub-politics are direct negotiations between environmental associations and **business and corporations** (see **Private regimes**), to make corporate activities or products more sustainable, and the participation of representatives of **indigenous peoples and local communities** in meetings of international research federations (such as the meeting in Belem on ethnobotanical research in 1988 that led to a first formulation of the principles of "prior informed consent" in the **biodiversity regime**). An important strength of sub-politics is their direct impact on the strategic decisions of collective actors. An important weakness is the possible isolation of sub-politics from more encompassing issues and broader social groups.

The key lesson that can be drawn from this literature is that reflexive governance cannot be reduced to the cognitive aspect only (for example values and social identity play an important role in social learning, in addition to purely cognitive aspects such as providing the best argument and transparency of the debate). Instead, reflexive governance has to be analyzed as a social and political process of reframing our core collective values and norms when facing unprecedented unsustainability problems.

## References

Beck, Ulrich. 1992[1986]. *Risk Society*. London, Sage Publications.

Brousseau, Eric, Tom Dedeurwaerdere, and Bernd Siebenhüner (Eds.). 2012. *Reflexive Governance and Global Public Goods*. Cambridge, MA, MIT Press.

Dedeurwaerdere, Tom. 2005. "From Bioprospecting to Reflexive Governance." *Ecological Economics* 53(4): 473–491.

Habermas, Jürgen. 1998 [1992]. *Between Facts and Norms*. Cambridge, MA, MIT Press.

Voß, Jan-Peter, Dierk Bauknecht, and René Kemp. 2006. *Reflexive Governance for Sustainable Development*. Cheltenham, Edward Elgar.

# REGIMES

Amandine Orsini

*Université Saint-Louis - Bruxelles, Belgium*

## Jean-Frédéric Morin

*Université libre de Bruxelles, Belgium*

The concept of international regimes is not specific to, but frequently used in, the study of global environmental governance. Building on the definition by Stephen Krasner, specialists have defined environmental regimes as intergovernmental institutions that give rise to social practices, assign roles, and govern interactions to address situations of ecosystem degradation through overuse (for instance the **fisheries governance**) or through pollution (for instance the **climate change regime**) (Young et al. 2008). Regimes occupy an intermediary position. They are shaped by structures in place, including power distribution or prevailing ideas, but they also guide and constrain the behavior of actors.

International regimes are not necessarily centered on a formal treaty or an intergovernmental organization. For example, no universal intergovernmental organization and no multilateral treaty is dedicated to fresh water, but there is arguably a **transboundary water regime** made of a set of implicit rules that lay out actors' expectations. However, most regimes are formalized by international treaties. These **treaty negotiations** tend to evolve in a path dependency manner: from political declarations to framework conventions, to protocols, follow-up annexes and decisions.

Research on environmental regimes kicked off at the end of the 1980s. Initially, scholars focused on the reasons and the conditions leading to the establishment of such regimes. They found that **science** and the agency of **epistemic communities** were instrumental in explaining the adoption of environmental regimes such as the acid rain regime, the **ozone regime**, or the Mediterranean sea regime.

In the 1990s, while scholars in other fields abandoned the concept of international regimes to its detractors, researchers in environmental governance worked to adapt it in several manners (Vogler 2003). First, to answer the critics that viewed regime analysis as functionalist, environmental scholars demonstrated that "issue areas," as defining criteria of regimes, depended on social and cognitive constructions. Second, in reaction to the accusation of state centrism, global environmental governance specialists studied in detail the **participation** of non-state actors and the development of **private regimes**. Third, against the claim that regime theory was biased in favor of positive cases, environmental scholars developed extensive regime databases to identify recurring patterns (Breitmeier et al. 2006) and looked at **nonregimes** to refine scope conditions.

In the 2000s, environmental scholars developed conceptual and methodological tools to assess regime **effectiveness**. They show that regimes have various impacts, including on neighboring regimes. Indeed, regimes can collide, compete against each other, develop synergies, or even merge. Therefore, since the beginning of the 2010s, regime analysts have been investigating **institutional interactions** between different regimes known as "regime complexes." This concept announces a rebirth of regime analyses in global environmental governance.

### References

Breitmeier, Helmut, Arild Underdal, Oran R. Young, and Michael Zürn. 2006. *Analyzing International International Environmental Regimes: From Case Study to Database.* Cambridge, MA, MIT Press.

Vogler, John. 2003. "Taking Institutions Seriously: How Regime Analysis can be Relevant to Multilevel Environmental Governance." *Global Environmental Politics* 3(2): 25–39.

Young, Oran, Leslie L. King, and Heike Schroeder. 2008. *Institutions and Environmental Change: Principal Findings, Applications, and Research Frontiers.* Cambridge, MA, MIT Press.

# REGIONAL GOVERNANCE

## Tom Delreux

*Université catholique de Louvain, Belgium*

In the environmental sphere, "governance" refers to "structures of authority that manage collective environmental problems and resolve conflicts between stakeholders" (Elliott and Breslin 2011: 3). Such structures are not only developed at the global, state, or sub-state **scales**, but also at the regional level, where it is called "regional governance." Although there is no commonly accepted definition of "region", political scientists agree that a region implies a limited number of states within geographical proximity and exposed to a certain degree of mutual interdependence.

It is generally acknowledged that regional governance constitutes an important component of the international environmental politics architecture. When the national or the global level do not provide the appropriate scale for tackling a particular environmental problem, the regional level may emerge as an in-between solution to effectively deal with these challenges. Indeed, regional governance initiatives can contribute to solving common action problems where national or intra-state action is not sufficient, mostly due to the transboundary nature of the environmental problem at stake. Furthermore, they often emerge when the global level fails or when global environmental governance is deadlocked. The **compliance and implementation** problems faced by several multilateral environmental agreements, the lowest common denominator outcomes of global negotiations, the fuzziness of the distribution of work between various **regimes**, or the fatigue in environmental **summit diplomacy** all raise questions about the continued feasibility of negotiating agreements at the global level and open the door for an increased belief in regional initiatives (Conca 2012). However, scholars do not agree whether regional environmental governance is rather a (contributing) building block or a (hindering) stumbling block for global initiatives (Balsiger and Debarbieux, 2011).

Besides regional governance initiatives that establish **transgovernmental networks** and structures of authority between public and private actors such as **partnerships**, most regional environmental governance arrangements are concluded between states. The two main instruments of regional environmental governance are regional agreements and regional organizations.

On the one hand, regional environmental agreements are treaties between states on environmental issues, mostly touching upon ecologically defined geographical areas such as river basins, mountain ranges, or regional seas. An example of the latter is the Barcelona Convention for the Protection of the Mediterranean Sea against Pollution. A reliable count of regional environmental agreements is lacking, but it is clear that their number is still growing substantially (Balsiger and VanDeveer 2012). Although single-issue environmental agreements are still the norm, many regional economic integration organizations have adopted environmental agreements. In North America, for instance, environmental concerns are not only addressed in the North American Free Trade Agreement (NAFTA) itself, but also in a separate side-treaty to NAFTA, the North American Agreement on Environmental Cooperation (NAAEC).

On the other hand, regional environmental organizations are international governmental organizations, which include states from a single region among their membership and which are created through an international agreement. Regional environmental organizations can be found around the globe and they take many different forms. Some regional environmental organizations were especially created to deal with environmental issues, such as the International Commission for the Protection of the Danube River (operative since 1998), whereas others initially were focused on economic or security integration but gradually began to develop activities in the environmental domain, such as the European Union (EU) or the Association of Southeast Asian Nations (ASEAN) (Elliott and Breslin 2011).

Regional organizations can be a forum for environmental policy and an actor in global environmental politics. First, organizations such as the EU or to a lesser extent also ASEAN have harmonized environmental policies or practices of their member states. Whereas environmental cooperation in a regional organization such as ASEAN is characterized by non-binding agreements, non-interference in domestic politics of its member states, and project-based cooperation (Elliott 2012), the EU has adopted a broad range of legally binding environmental policies with a deep impact on the policy autonomy of its member states. Having adopted hundreds of pieces of environmental legislation, it has the strongest and most comprehensive regional environmental regulatory framework in the world, covering almost all environmental issues, including chemicals, biodiversity, waste, noise, and climate change (Jordan and Adelle 2013). Whereas EU environmental policy has for a long time been characterized by a top-down regulatory approach, yet also with implementation problems in the member states, an evolution towards more freedom for the member states and towards softer instruments of environmental governance can be gradually observed.

Second, regional organizations can be important actors in global environmental negotiations. The EU is again the most illustrative example here. Since the 1990s, the EU has been a major force in promoting strong environmental protection at the international level and has ratified more than sixty multilateral environmental agreements. The EU has attempted to play a leadership role in many **regimes** and **treaty negotiations**. Although the EU's leadership ambitions are certainly not limited to this area, it has been most visible and most widely discussed in the literature with regard to negotiations under the **climate change regime** (Jordan et al. 2010). EU leadership was badly damaged at the 2009 Copenhagen climate change conference, although the EU seems to have found a new bridge-building and coalition-making role in the following conferences. Scholars currently debate to what extent the EU is still able to lead in international environmental politics and what the scope conditions are under which a regional organization such as the EU is able to exert actorness and to be influential in global negotiations.

## References

Balsiger, Jörg and Bernard Debarbieux. 2011. "Major Challenges in Regional Environmental Governance Research and Practice." *Procedia Social and Behavioral Sciences* 14: 1–8.

Balsiger, Jörg and Stacy D. VanDeveer. 2012. "Navigating Regional Environmental Governance." *Global Environmental Politics* 12(3): 1–17.

Conca, Ken. 2012. "The Rise of the Region in Global Environmental Politics." *Global Environmental Politics* 12(3): 127–133.

Elliott, Lorraine. 2012. "ASEAN and Environmental Governance: Strategies of Regionalism in Southeast Asia." *Global Environmental Politics* 12(3): 38–57.

Elliott, Lorraine and Shaun Breslin (Eds.). 2011. *Comparative Environmental Regionalism*. London, Routledge.

Jordan, Andrew and Camilla Adelle (Eds.). 2013. *Environmental Policy in the EU: Actors, Institutions and Processes*, 3rd Edition. London, Routledge.

Jordan, Andrew, Dave Huitema, Harro van Asselt, Tim Rayner, and Frans Berkhout (Eds.). 2010. *Climate Change Policy in the European Union: Confronting the Dilemmas of Mitigation and Adaptation?* Cambridge, Cambridge University Press.

# REPORTING

## Klaus Dingwerth
*University of St. Gallen, Switzerland*

As environmental policymaking has matured, information-based policy instruments and **transparency** issues have been gaining a prominent role. As one such instrument, reporting standards do not demand a particular environmental performance from their targets, but instead ask for the provision of information about environmental performance. The central idea behind reporting is that such information is valuable for the targets themselves—for instance because it allows them to identify strengths and weaknesses in their environmental performance—as well as for a variety of stakeholders who can sanction poor and reward good environmental performance.

Environmental reporting has its role in both intergovernmental and transnational environmental governance. At the intergovernmental level, reporting is closely tied to monitoring and verification of environmental performance standards. It thus primarily includes treaty provisions that require member states to report on their **compliance and implementation** review with goals set in environmental agreements. Most treaty systems require contracting parties to report to their treaty **secretariat** on an annual basis in accordance with relatively precise and often fine-grained reporting templates. Yet data quality varies greatly, both across states and across treaty systems, as does the degree to which national reports are independently verified. Moreover, national reports are rarely used beyond treaty bodies and their function therefore remains limited to compliance and implementation review (Wettestad 2007).

In contrast to the intergovernmental level, transnational reporting schemes such as the Global Reporting Initiative (GRI) and the Carbon Disclosure Project (CDP) are not connected to explicit environmental performance standards. The GRI is a multi-stakeholder organization that seeks to harmonize corporate sustainability reporting through its Sustainability Reporting Guidelines. Founded in 2002, the GRI has gone through a rapid and thorough institutionalization process. With strong network ties to the UN Global Compact, the **United Nations Environment Programme** and the **Commission on Sustainable Development** as well as occasional support from governments that have made GRI reporting mandatory for some types of corporate actors, the GRI has become a key player in global environmental governance (Brown et al. 2009). By mid 2013, a significant number of large multinational **business and corporations** based their non-financial reports on the GRI Guidelines, with variation across sectors as well as societies. Yet as independent verification is optional for reporters, academic studies take note of the limited quality of data (Hedberg and Malmborg 2003). Moreover, the commercialization of information infrastructures means that environmental information contained in such reports is primarily translated in ways that are useful to market actors, in particular investors (Brown 2011; Dingwerth and Eichinger 2014).

The latter group is even more central in the CDP where more than 300 institutional investors demand greenhouse gas emissions reporting from the corporations they invest in (Kolk et al. 2008; Kim and Lyon 2011). Conventional accounts see the reason behind investors' initiative to establish the CDP in the financial risks that excessive greenhouse gas emissions may pose for investments. Such risks are framed either in terms of **liability** for damage incurred by excessive emissions or in terms of corporate costs to adapt to stricter emission targets that may become mandatory in the future (see **Audit**). As with the GRI, however, most studies are critical when it comes to the actual value of current carbon reporting for investors and other stakeholder groups. As a result, the CDP is often seen as either an innovative starting point for a stronger scheme or as merely symbolic action meant to signal to stakeholders a level of control that is currently unavailable in practice. Analytically, the move toward information-based policy instruments such as reporting puts states in a managerial position. The main function of states remains to set the core parameters for "regulation by revelation" (Hamilton 2005), either through mandatory rules, through providing information infrastructures, or through economic incentives for voluntary reporting. At the same time, environmental reporting itself has become an industry of its own in which many actors and interests intersect.

## References

Brown, Halina Szejnwald. 2011. "The Global Reporting Initiative." In *Handbook of Transnational Governance*, Eds. Thomas N. Hale and David Held, 281–289. Oxford: Polity Press.

Brown, Halina Szejnwald, Martin de Jong, and Teodorina Lessidrenska. 2009. "The Rise of the Global Reporting Initiative: A Case of Institutional Entrepreneurship." *Environmental Politics* 18(2): 182–200.

Dingwerth, Klaus and Margot Eichinger. 2014. "Tamed Transparency and the Global Reporting Initiative: The Role of Information Infrastructures." In *Transparency in Global Environmental Governance*, Eds. Aarti Gupta and Michael Mason, 225–247. Cambridge, MA, MIT Press.

Hamilton, James. 2005. *Regulation through Revelation: The Origins, Politics, and Impacts of the Toxic Release Inventory Program*. Cambridge, Cambridge University Press.

Hedberg, Carl-Johan and Fredrik von Malmborg. 2003. "The Global Reporting Initiative and Corporate Sustainability Reporting in Swedish Companies." *Corporate Social Responsibility and Environmental Management* 10(3): 153–164.

Kim, Eun-Hee and Thomas P. Lyon. 2011. "The Carbon Disclosure Project." In *Handbook of Transnational Governance*, Eds. Thomas N. Hale and David Held, 213–218. Oxford, Polity Press.

Kolk, Ans, David Levy, and Jonatan Pinkse. 2008. "Corporate Responses in an Emerging Climate Regime: The Institutionalization and Commensuration of Carbon Disclosure." *European Accounting Review* 17(4): 719–745.

Wettestad, Jørgen. 2007. "Monitoring and Verification." In *Oxford Handbook of International Environmental Law*, Eds. Daniel Bodansky, Jutta Brunnée, and Ellen Hey, 974–994. Oxford: Oxford University Press.

# RISK SOCIETY

## Ulrich Beck

*Ludwig Maximilian University Munich, Germany*

Environmental **disasters** such as Chernobyl, 9/11, global financial crises, and climate change are manufactured uncertainties and incalculable global risks resulting from the triumphs of modernity and mark the human condition at the beginning of the twenty-first century. Speaking very generally, the theorem of "(world) risk society" (Beck 1986, 2009) is conceived of as a radicalized form of the dynamic of modernization that is dissolving the familiar formulae of "first" modernity. The first—the "classical", or "high"—modernity associated specifically with industrial society was characterized by a logic of organization and action that involved the establishment of extremely fine divisions between categories of people and of activities and the distinctions between spheres of action and forms of life such as to facilitate an unambiguous institutional ascription of competence, responsibility, and jurisdiction. Today, the limitations of this logic of fine division and unambiguousness are becoming ever more evident. The *logic of unambiguousness*—one might speak here, metaphorically, of a "Newtonian" social and political theory of the first modernity—is now being replaced by a *logic of ambiguity*— which one might envisage, to extend the metaphor, in terms of a new "Heisenbergian fuzziness" of the social and the political.

For the institutions of advanced societies, the transition to a "second" modernity entails the challenge of developing a new logic of action and decision-making, which finds its orientation no longer in the principle "either this or that" but rather in the principle "this and that both." In various spheres—from **science** and technology through the state and the economy, individualized life-worlds and social structures right up to the level of the present debates and confrontations regarding the new ordering of global politics—one thing is becoming ever clearer: that great body of distinctions, standardizations, norms, and role-systems essential to the very institutions of the first modernity can no longer be treated as valid; they describe ever less adequately the current normal condition of societies, of nation-states, and of inter-state relations. The reality we face today is rather that of a (more or less) acknowledged plurality in respect of forms of work, of family life, of lifestyle, of political **sovereignty**, and of politics in general. We live—to recur to a metaphor already current in the social sciences—in the "era of flows": of capital flow, of cultural flow, of flows of human beings, information, and risks.

The collapse of boundaries and the new mobility of risks (Arnoldi 2009; Rosa et al. 2014) have fundamental implications for the social sciences inasmuch as it helps us to the insight that sociology (as well as historiography, political science, economics, jurisprudence etc.) remain bogged down in a "methodological nationalism." Methodological nationalism rests on the assumption that "modern society" and "modern politics" are synonymous with a society and a politics organized in terms of nation-states. The state is understood as creator, supervisor, and guarantor of society. Societies (the number of which is equal to the number of nation-states) are understood as mere containers, arising and subsisting in a space defined by the power of the state.

### References

Arnoldi, Jakob. 2009. *Risk: An Introduction.* Cambridge, Polity Press.
Beck, Ulrich. 1992 [1986]. *Risk Society: Towards a New Modernity.* London, Sage.
Beck, Ulrich. 2009. *World at Risk.* Cambridge, Polity Press.
Rosa, Eugene A., Ortwin Renn, and Aaron M. McCright. 2014. *The Risk Society Revisited: Social Theory and Governance.* Philadelphia, PA, Temple University Press.

# SCALE

## Kate O'Neill

*University of California at Berkeley, United States*

Scale in global environmental governance (GEG) is defined in different ways. The concept applies to different levels at and across which governance can occur. These are often jurisdictional: local, national, regional, and global. It is also used in the sense of scaling out, capturing how phenomena and events broaden out to or manifest at scales from micro (individuals, communities) to macro levels (regional or global). Researchers who study scale often examine vertical linkages between and across scales, and movement of ideas, policies, and actors between scales (as opposed to horizontal linkages such as **institutional interactions**). Some also examine the social construction of scales (Marston 2000). It has become an important concept in GEG because of the emergence of institutions that operate at different scales and because of the growing interest in the role of local and regional knowledge, politics, and communities in the instigation, **compliance, and implementation** of GEG (Andonova and Mitchell 2010).

Several important examples demonstrate how scale and vertical linkages matter in contemporary GEG. For example, the role of city governments in climate governance is one area where local actors are, through **transgovernmental networks**, reaching the global scale (Betsill and Bulkeley 2006). Conversely, regional centers who implement terms of the chemicals agreements at local levels are another way in which vertical linkages are made across jurisdictional levels (Selin 2010). The emergence of **REDD** as a multilevel governance institution that directly engages **indigenous peoples and local communities, business and corporations**, states, and the **World Bank** needs to be understood through the lens of scale, as REDD initiatives may also have divergent impacts across levels (Doherty and Schroeder 2011). Cases of the incorporation of indigenous peoples' knowledge into **regimes** such as the **biodiversity regime** highlight how ideas and knowledge flow upwards to the global level as well as down (Jasanoff and Martello 2004).

Although it is often a hard concept to pin down and operationalize, the development and use of scale has pushed researchers to engage more effectively with a new generation of GEG initiatives. Scale and vertical linkages are important in understanding various dimensions of some of the more complex environmental issues we face, including climate change, biodiversity, and deforestation, their governance, and their socioeconomic impacts. They shed light on dynamics of transnational activism and policymaking, and on practical questions of how global governance institutions can connect to local communities and actors.

## References

Andonova, Liliana B. and Ronald B. Mitchell. 2010. "The Rescaling of Global Environmental Politics." *Annual Review of Environment and Resources* 35: 255–282.

Betsill, Michele M. and Harriet Bulkeley. 2006. "Cities and the Multilevel Governance of Global Climate Change." *Global Governance* 12(2): 141–159.

Doherty, Emma and Heike Schroeder. 2011. "Forest Tenure and Multi-Level Governance in Avoiding Deforestation under REDD+." *Global Environmental Politics* 11(4): 66–88.

Jasanoff, Sheila and Marybeth Long Martello (Eds). 2004. *Earthly Politics: Local and Global in Environmental Governance*. Cambridge, MA, MIT Press.

Marston, Sallie A. 2000. "The Social Construction of Scale." *Progress in Human Geography* 24(2): 219–242.

Selin, Henrik. 2010. *Global Governance of Hazardous Chemicals: Challenges of Multilevel Management*. Cambridge, MA, MIT Press.

# SCARCITY AND CONFLICTS

**Alexis Carles**

*Université libre de Bruxelles, Belgium*

The assumption that environmental scarcity leads to interstate conflicts has become prevalent, notwithstanding numerous contributions putting into question this causal inference. Despite specific case studies' analyses and concrete theoretical inputs, the debate on whether or not environmental scarcity is a triggering factor of conflicts still divides the academic world.

Historical contributions suggest this causal relation dates back to the works of Malthus under the **carrying capacities paradigm**, who predicted that at some point in time the world's population would exceed the food supply, leading to conflicts upon resource allocation. Garrett Hardin's theorization of the **tragedy of the commons** in the late 1960s also predicted environmental conflicts in the case of overexploitation of common environmental resources. The modern debate started during the last years of the Cold War, along with the redefinition of the traditional concept of security to include environmental **security**.

A well-known author linking environmental scarcity with conflict is the political scientist Homer-Dixon (1994, 1999), who defines environmental scarcity as "scarcity of renewable resources such as cropland, forests, river water and fish stocks" (1999: 4). Informed by realist approaches shaped by neo-Malthusian geopolitical arguments, he argues that the consequent social changes due to environmental scarcity trigger or exacerbate tensions between parties sharing the same resource. According to Homer-Dixon, environmental scarcity is composed of three dimensions: resource degradation and depletion (supply scarcity); higher socioeconomic and demographic needs (demand scarcity); and unequal distribution of the resource (structural scarcity). These lead to both a decline in economic productivity and an increase in the number of **migrants**, which eventually generate ethnic, socioeconomic, or political conflicts. Among numerous case studies, Homer-Dixon showed that land scarcity combined with flooding gave rise to massive migrations of Bengalis to India in the 1980s, which critically altered inter-ethnic relations, land distribution arrangements, and power relations in the border regions.

The main criticism of neo-Malthusian assumptions is their overly deterministic character. Indeed, advocates of this perspective postulate that scarcity will occur. By doing so, they tend to overlook other crucial social and economic variables driving environmental resources' management, such as **market** mechanisms and technological innovation or substitution for resources (Haas 2002). First, the neglect of market mechanisms implies that neo-Malthusians do not take into account the variations of prices and thus the potential for social **adaptation** to resource scarcity. The recent boom of solar, wind, or biofuel energies is as much the consequence of price signals from markets of traditional energy sources such as coal and oil, as of the growing awareness of environmental issues worldwide. Second, humans have historically proven to be innovative in the face of scarcity, either by developing new technologies, or by using other resources to substitute them for traditional ones. For instance, as an example of innovation, the development of drip irrigation—watering agricultural products through a drop-by-drop system—saves tremendous amounts of water in water-scarce areas. Also, the progressive replacement of copper wires (land lines) by fiber optics and more recently satellite technologies shows that a resource given as disappearing at some point in time (such as copper in the mid 1970s) can subsist thanks to substitution through innovation.

"Cornucopians," or "resource optimists," see in scarcity an opportunity for states to cooperate rather than fight. Their theoretical assumptions are close to liberal and neoliberal institutionalist authors. If they acknowledge that there is a risk inherent in resource scarcity, they argue that humans will rather cooperate, notably through creation of institutions for resource allocation (Simon 1998). Recent theoretical and empirical findings on the role of regional and international institutions as catalysts of cooperation offer a window of opportunity to minimize the influence of environmental scarcity as a component of international conflicts. Scarcity should be grasped as an issue of common interest, a motivation for creating **regimes** on transboundary environmental resources in order to coordinate actors' arrangements toward rational win–win solutions. The Southern African Development Community (SADC), certainly the most advanced regional integration process after the European Union, was founded on cooperation over **transboundary water regimes**. Water is very diversely distributed in the region, and the first SADC protocol was on shared watercourse systems. The SADC is now driven by twenty-six protocols on various issues (trade, mining, health . . .). Following that stance, some argue that cooperation on resource scarcity is a catalyzing factor for profounder cooperation on other issues.

Most empirical contributions on the subject are qualitative analyses of precise case studies. At the international level, they often refer to transboundary water issues, which are grasped as the most risky resources, despite a clear empirical trend in favor of cooperation. A few qualitative analyses of case studies revealed that water scarcity, under specific circumstances, could contribute to enhancing the probability of violent conflict occurring, thereby confirming Homer-Dixon's findings (Hauge and Ellingsen 1998). Other studies demonstrated the prevalence of other political and socioeconomic factors as more significant explanatory independent variables for conflicts to occur. Theisen et al. (2012), for instance, showed that drought has minimal impact on civil conflicts in Africa, compared to other factors such as the political and economic marginalization of ethnic groups, among others. In reality, this hypothesized causal inference faces more counter-examples than empirical confirmations. Haas goes even further and argues: "no one has been killed in direct international conflict over any resource" (2002: 7).

Despite these different viewpoints, most academics agree that resource scarcity can sometimes contribute to catalyzing existing sociopolitical tensions. Referring to Israel–Palestine relations on water, Lowi, who strongly doubts that there could be war on resources, admits that it could happen in extreme cases where the resource is in short supply, where parties are both adversarial and highly dependent on it, with constraining geographical positions and power configurations (Lowi 1999: 385). Finally, for some scholars, environmental scarcity may actually be the consequence rather than the cause of conflicts (see **Military conflicts**).

## References

Haas, Peter M. 2002. "Constructing Environmental Conflicts from Resource Scarcity." *Global Environmental Politics* 2(1): 1–11.

Hauge, Wenche and Tanja Ellingsen. 1998. "Beyond Environmental Scarcity: Causal Pathways to Conflict." *Journal of Peace Research* 35(3): 299–317.

Homer-Dixon, Thomas F. 1994. "Environmental Scarcities and Violent Conflict: Evidence from Cases." *International Security* 19(1): 5–40.

Homer-Dixon, Thomas F. 1999. *Environment, Scarcity, and Violence*. Princeton, NJ, Princeton University Press.

Lowi, Miriam R. 1999. "Water and Conflict in the Middle East and South Asia: Are Environmental Issues and Security Issue Linked?" *The Journal of Environment Development* 8(4): 376–396.

Simon, Julian L. 1998. *The Ultimate Resource II: Peoples, Materials and Environment*. Princeton, NJ, Princeton University Press.

Theisen, Ole M., Holtermann Helge, and Halvard Buhaug. 2012. "Climate Wars? Assessing the Claim that Drought Breeds Conflict." *International Security* 36(3): 79–106.

# SCENARIOS

**Stacy D. VanDeveer**
*University of New Hampshire, United States*

**Simone Pulver**
*University of California, Santa Barbara, United States*

Most social **science** methods are designed to build knowledge about the world as it is now, or as it was before. In contrast, scenarios are a unique set of techniques intended to think about how the world might be in the future, and are often commissioned with the stated goal of aiding decision-makers (in the public, private, and civil society sectors) in envisioning, understanding, and planning for the future. Commonly defined as "plausible, challenging and relevant stories about how the future might unfold" (Raskin 2005: 36), scenarios generally combine quantitative biophysical models and qualitative storylines of social and political trends. The quantitative modeling elements ensure internal consistency and impose structural limitations, e.g. maximum possible rates of technology replacement, while the narrative storylines accommodate the possibility of rapid social transformation, e.g. a significant change in ecosystem function.

Scenario techniques were first developed in the security and business arenas (Raskin 2005), but over the past two decades they have become a ubiquitous part of environmental politics, policymaking, and social learning, at multiple governance **scales**. Prominent examples in the global environmental arena include the Intergovernmental Panel on Climate Change (IPCC) (see **Boundary organizations**) and the Millennium Ecosystem Assessment scenarios (Pulver and VanDeveer 2009) (see **Assessments**). Decision-makers use scenarios to envision likely alternative futures (forecasting scenarios), identify pathways to an ideal future (backcasting scenarios), and assess the robustness of decisions across the range of possible futures (van Notten et al. 2003). In all three uses, scenario exercises achieve dual outcomes—a final product that summarizes the results of the scenario exercise and a process of social and organizational learning based on dialogue across diverse perspectives. Scenario exercises tend to emphasize one or the other goal. For example, the primary goal of the IPCC scenarios is to create a set of emissions trajectories that can be "plugged in" to a host of other climate change and energy related modeling, scenarios, and assessment exercises. In the Millennium Ecosystem Assessment, scenarios were used to bring together people from diverse disciplinary, sectorial, educational, and/or social backgrounds to "think through" identified issues and explore opportunities to learn via processes of scenarios construction and output production (O'Neill et al. 2008).

Despite the remarkable spread of scenarios in global environmental governance, they remain a relatively unexamined methodology. Unlike purely quantitative modeling exercises, whose limitations have been explored (Craig et al. 2002), systematic analysis of the application of scenarios and their impact on policy outcomes remains in its early stages. Scholars and practitioners disagree on the usefulness of information generated through scenarios, on how to characterize and interpret uncertainty in scenario outcomes, and on how to best structure scenario processes. Current research focuses on formalizing expert input to developing storylines, on techniques to estimate likelihoods associated with scenario outcomes, on the political and social dynamics of scenarios as knowledge processes and objects, and on the actual use of scenarios in decision-making (Wright et al. 2013).

## References

Craig, Paul, Ashok Gadgil, and Jonathan Koomey. 2002. "What Can History Teach Us? A Retrospective Examination of Long-Term Energy Forecasts for the United States." *Annual Review of Energy and the Environment* 27: 83–118.

O'Neill, Brian, Simone Pulver, Stacy VanDeveer, and Yaakov Garb. 2008. "Where Next with Global Environmental Scenario." *Environmental Research Letters* 3(4): 5–8.

Pulver, Simone and Stacy VanDeveer 2009. "'Thinking About Tomorrows': Scenarios, Global Environmental Politics, and Social Science Scholarship." *Global Environmental Politics* 9(2): 1–13.

Raskin, Paul 2005. "Global Scenarios in Historical Perspective." In *Ecosystems and Human Well-Being: Scenarios—Findings of the Scenarios Working Group Millennium Ecosystem Assessment Series*, Eds. Stephen Carpenter, Prabhu Pingali, Elena Bennett, and Monika Zurek, 35–44. Washington, Island Press.

van Notten, Phillip, Jan Rotmans, Marjolein Van Asselt, and Dale Rothman. 2003. "An Updated Scenario Typology." *Futures* 35(5): 423–443.

Wright, George, George Cairns, and Ron Bradfield. 2013. "Scenario Methodology: New Developments in Theory and Practice." *Technological Forecasting and Social Change* 80(4): 561–565.

# SCIENCE

**Tim Forsyth**

*London School of Economics and Political Science, United Kingdom*

Science in global environmental governance refers to the underlying knowledge about environmental problems. The main political controversies for science, however, arise from the legitimacy and authority it has within political debates. For many environmental scholars, scientific debates have to be clearly demarcated from political debates in order to gain a politically neutral understanding of environmental change, and to provide a compelling basis for environmental policy (Pielke 2007). But many other analysts—including both supporters of environmental policy and those resistant to it—argue that science has either been misused by political interests, or cannot escape from political and social influences. Consequently, various analysts argue there is a need to make science more transparent and open to governance. This requirement also applies to the expert groups that produce or summarize research such as **epistemic communities** or certain **boundary organizations**.

One key theme of debate is scientific certainty. Many environmental analysts argue environmental policy needs to be based on scientific certainty about the existence of environmental problems and human influences on them. Sometimes, the standards for certainty are relaxed under the **precautionary principle** when causal links are not yet certain, but when there is consensus that potential risks are sufficiently worrying. On certain occasions, scientific statements of certainty have been challenged as motivated by political interests, and skeptics have invoked contrasting science. For example, the skeptic Global Warming Policy Foundation uses a chart of twenty-first-century global average temperatures to suggest that no overall temperature rise has taken place. On a parallel theme, the US has also challenged the European Union in the **World Trade Organization** to demonstrate that its restrictions on importing genetically modified crops should be based on "sound science" rather than the precautionary principle.

But these debates about scientific certainty rarely take place without some reference to the credibility and legitimacy of the science and scientific organizations speaking. During the "Climate-gate" scandal of 2009, climate change skeptics used emails hacked from the University of East Anglia Climate Research Centre to imply that scientists had deliberately manipulated data in order to maintain evidence for the proposed Hockey Stick chart of rising global temperatures (these claims were refuted). The aim of this strategy was to cast doubt on the ethics and politics of climate change scientists and the Intergovernmental Panel on Climate Change (IPCC). Yet, simultaneously, environmental political scientists have also argued that most information challenging climate science has been shaped by conservative think tanks, and have questioned the accuracy of their claims (Jacques et al. 2008).

Consequently, other scholars have argued that the debate about science in global environmental governance should look more holistically at how facts and normative values are connected. Scholars in science and technology studies (STS) for example, argue that scientific certainty should not just refer to statistical trends, but to the social and political forces that stabilize public debate about which statistics to gather, or the meaning given to observed trends. Accordingly, STS scholars analyze the social conditions that give rise to the generation of science, and to the perceived status of experts and organizations that legitimize science. This approach does not question the possibility of worrying environmental changes, or the need to regulate human activities, but it suggests that diverse societies will always disagree about the objectives and legitimacy of scientific measurement (Hulme 2009). STS therefore asks two important questions: what visions of social order are reproduced when scientific information is presented as universally accurate and applicable for all society? And, which normative perspectives or options for physical environmental management are excluded when science is presented as politically neutral and not open to public debate?

An important example is the use of national statistics of climate change emissions to indicate the political responsibility for undertaking climate change policy (see **Scenarios**). For example, the Indian think tank, the Centre for Science and Environment, famously argued that simply comparing national statistics of emissions overlooked per capita usage; the number of years that countries have been industrialized; and whether developed countries had already cut down forests in order to expand agricultural land (Agarwal and Narain 1991; Beck 2011).

Moreover, climate models that focus on atmospheric greenhouse gas concentrations overlook the role of social vulnerability and resilience on the ground that is related to levels of development or international assistance (Forsyth 2012). The implications here are that "global" representations of risk or crisis sometimes understate the diversity by which different societies or individuals respond to environmental change. Hence, using climate change models or frameworks such as the Hockey Stick to indicate risk universally might impose assumptions about social identity and behavior upon different societies in ways that do not address their experience of risk or undermine trust in **treaty negotiations** (Jasanoff and Martello 2004).

Analysts therefore debate how to govern hybrid scientific and policy-advocacy bodies and scientific assessments that engage across the boundaries between science and politics. STS scholars see "boundary work" as the means by which science is rendered non-political, and consequently no longer open to public debate. Earth-system scientists, however, see boundary work as the ways scientists can interact with policymakers without appearing biased. The IPCC, for example, has been urged to make data more transparent, and to establish clearer procedures for considering information from non-peer reviewed sources (InterAcademy Council 2010).

Another theme is the social **participation** within **assessments**, where the objective is to diversify social perspectives on complex environmental problems in order to increase the relevance of policies for different stakeholders (for example, the Ecosystem Approach under the **biodiversity regime**).

## *References*

Agarwal, Anil and Narain S. 1991. *Global Warming in an Unequal World*. Delhi, Center for Science and Environment.

Beck, Silke. 2011. "Moving beyond the Linear Model of Expertise? IPCC and the Test of Adaptation." *Regional Environmental Change* 11(2): 297–306.

Committee to Review the Intergovernmental Panel on Climate Change. 2010. *Climate Change Assessments: Review of the Processes and Procedures of the IPCC*. Amsterdam, InterAcademy Council.

Forsyth, Tim. 2012. "Politicizing Environmental Science does not Mean Denying Climate Science nor Endorsing it Without Question." *Global Environmental Politics* 12(2): 18–23.

Hulme, Michael. 2009. *Why we Disagree about Climate Change: Understanding Controversy, Inaction and Opportunity*. Cambridge, Cambridge University Press.

Jacques, Peter, Riley E. Dunlap, and Mark Freeman. 2008. "The Organization of Denial: Conservative Think Tanks and Environmental Scepticism." *Environmental Politics* 17: 349–385.

Jasanoff, Sheila and Marybeth Martello. 2004. *Earthly Politics: Local and Global in Environmental Governance*. Cambridge, MA, MIT Press.

Pielke, Roger A. 2007. *The Honest Broker: Making Sense of Science in Policy and Politics*. Cambridge, Cambridge University Press.

# SECRETARIATS

## Bernd Siebenhüner

*Carl von Ossietzky University of Oldenburg, Germany*

Almost all international environmental treaties foresee a secretariat to fulfill fundamental administrative and some executive functions in implementing the agreement (see **Compliance and implementation**). They organize meetings and conferences, prepare documentation and monitoring, and implement practical projects and campaigns. In the field of global environmental governance, secretariats play a particularly prevalent role given the absence of a strong **World Environment Organization**. However, there is variation with regard to the scope of their actual activities and related influence in international environmental governance. While some have only a few staff members, others employ hundreds of international civil servants, such as the secretariat of the **climate change regime**.

Following Biermann and Siebenhüner (2009: 6) convention secretariats take the form of international bureaucracies that can be defined as:

> agencies that have been set up by governments or other public actors with some degree of permanence and coherence and beyond formal direct control of single national governments (notwithstanding control by multilateral mechanisms through the collective of governments) and that act in the international arena to pursue a policy.

In most cases, treaty secretariats as international bureaucracies are characterized through a hierarchically organized group of international civil servants with a given mandate, given resources, identifiable boundaries, and a set of formal rules and procedures within the context of a policy area.

Different approaches argue about the actual influence of treaty secretariats. For instance, political realism in the field of international relations theory views international bureaucracies as derivatives of different national governmental interests with almost no independent influence. More recent studies from the field of sociological institutionalism find significant autonomy with international bureaucracies of major UN agencies (Barnett and Finnemore 2004). A particular source of influence is found in expertise and knowledge that is provided by the secretariats to negotiators and other stakeholders (e.g. Haas 1990). Other institutional approaches identified fields of influence in the area of fostering international agreements and norm-setting since international secretariats prepare, organize, and often arrange **treaty negotiations** (Biermann and Siebenhüner 2009). Explanatory schemes for this influence refer to the characteristics of the underlying environmental problem such as political salience and visibility, to economic incentive structures as conceptualized in principal–agent approaches, or to personalities involved. The actor quality in international bureaucracies is often focused in their top executives, such as the Executive Secretaries who lend their face to this bureaucratic personality (Andresen and Agrawala 2002, see **Influential individuals**). Considering perspectives from organizational theory, it is also the organizational culture, the institutional setting in which it acts, and the processes it performs that make the difference for the effects an international bureaucracy such as an environmental treaty secretariat has (Bauer et al. 2009).

Key examples can be drawn from the issue areas of climate change and biodiversity governance. Both global UN processes were launched in 1992 with the **climate change regime** and the **bio-diversity regime** mandating secretariats with key administrative tasks. While the climate regime was seen as an independent process with a secretariat only accountable to the respective Conference of the Parties and the UN General Assembly, the CBD process remained formally under the responsibility of the **United Nations Environment Programme**. However, the mandates for both affiliated secretariats are almost equal whereas the actual performance and influence differ significantly (Bauer et al. 2009).

Since its formal establishment in 1996, the climate secretariat, located in Bonn, has remained limited in its influence on the negotiation processes in the climate field. Its main function has been to translate parties' political agreements into functioning technical systems and procedures. During the negotiation processes, parties relied on the secretariat to provide consensus documents and texts that find the common ground of all parties. The secretariat has been reluctant to promote an own political agenda, like other secretariats, nor was it successful in putting through particular issues in the negotiations. The climate secretariat focuses less on shaping discourses related to the regime and limits itself to disseminating largely factual and descriptive information to stakeholders. In this sense, it is more a technical administrator of the treaty.

By contrast, the biodiversity secretariat, located in Montreal, enjoys a reputation among parties and is trusted as a credible and balanced facilitator of international cooperation. Governments as well as **non-governmental organizations** changed their behavior because of their experiences with the work of the secretariat. In general, the biodiversity secretariat helps to organize the negotiations rather inclusively and thereby facilitates the implementation of the convention. Since it does not interfere autonomously with any discourses related to the regime, it can be described as an environmentalist facilitator.

By way of explanation, this variation can be attributed in part to the problem structure that involves significantly higher stakes in the climate regime than any other international environmental agreement. These high stakes have motivated parties to be extremely wary of any of the secretariat's activities and, by imposing considerable constraints on the secretariat, to rule out initiatives by the secretariat. In the case of the biodiversity secretariat, its organizational and conceptual expertise constitutes an important source of influence that has earned it the reputation of a trusted provider of information and knowledge at large.

## References

Andresen, Steinar and Shardul Agrawala. 2002. "Leaders, Pushers and Laggards in the Making of the Climate Regime." Global Environmental Change 12(1): 41–51.

Barnett, Michael N. and Martha Finnemore. 2004. *Rules for the World: International Organizations in Global Politics.* Ithaca, NY, Cornell University Press.

Bauer, Steffen, Per-Olof Busch, and Bernd Siebenhüner. 2009. "Treaty Secretariats in Global Environmental Governance." In *International Organizations in Global Environmental Governance*, Eds. Frank Biermann, Bernd Siebenhüner, and Anna Schreyögg, 174–191. London, Routledge.

Biermann, Frank and Bernd Siebenhüner (Eds.). 2009. *Managers of Global Change: The Influence of International Environmental Bureaucracies.* Cambridge, MA, MIT Press.

Haas, Ernst B. 1990. *Where Knowledge is Power: Three Models of Change in International Organizations.* Berkeley, CA, University of California Press.

# SECURITY

## Hiroshi Ohta

*Waseda University, Japan*

The concept of environmental security is still a contested one. The concept of security as such is elusive and open to many different interpretations. Yet, Arnold Wolfers summed up succinctly: "security, in an objective sense, measures the absence of threats to acquired values, [and] in a subjective sense, the absence of fear that such values will be attacked" (Wolfers 1962: 150). With the two oil crises of the 1970s, the end of the Cold War, and the 1992 Rio Earth Summit, it became clear that the acquired values to be protected go beyond strict military concerns and cover economic, energy, food, and environmental values as well.

Reflecting both sides of Wolfers' definition, Rita Floyd (2013) epistemologically divides environmental security studies into empirical studies on how environmental security matters in practice and critical or/and normative studies on the conditions of environmental security. While the former positivist and analytical environmental security studies focus on research about causal relations between resource scarcity (or abundance) and acute conflicts (see **Scarcity and conflicts**), the latter reflectivist and critical environmental security studies interact with various security concerns such as ecological security, human security, and climate security.

A prominent example of the second perspective is the Copenhagen School (Buzan et al. 1998). One of the key concepts developed by this School is "securitization," an attempt to go beyond the traditional conceptualization of security by addressing the issue of who invokes security response to an emergency situation and who or what is endangered in such a situation. When we attach the term "security" to certain issues, such as climate security and human security, and if they are accepted by a concerned community whether national or inter-national, those issues take politics beyond the established rules and they are framed as a special kind of politics that can generate emergency response. However, both climate security and human security have not necessarily shown securitization effects. One of the greatest beneficiaries of securitization of environmental change would be the military in developed nations, particularly when "environmental refugees" in developing countries are perceived as threats to national security (see **Migrants**) (Dalby 2009). Under this perspective, more appropriate responses to environmental security may be preventive approaches and risk management based on the logic of a **risk society**.

However, we have to dig deeper to arrive at security concerns regarding the relationship between humans and the Earth ecosystem. Skeptics of the concept of environmental security stress the difference between military violence and environmental **disasters**. Violence perpetrated by humans is highly intentional and could arguably be prevented by centralized and hierarchical military organizations, while environmental degradation is partly unintentional and requires the participation of everyone involved in preserving fragile ecosystems at national, regional, and global **scales**. All in all, environmental security is a muddled concept and can connote inappropriate responses to environmental problems (Deudney 1999). However contestable this concept is, it poses the ultimate question of who we are.

## References

Buzan, Barry, Ole Wæver, and Jaap de Wilde. 1998. *Security: A New Framework for Analysis*. Boulder, CO, Rienner.
Dalby, Simon. 2009. *Security and Environmental Change*. Cambridge, Polity.
Deudney, Daniel. 1999. "Environmental Security: A Critique." In *Contested Grounds: Security and Conflict in the New Environmental Politics*, Eds. Daniel H. Deudney and Richard A. Matthew, 187–222. Albany, NY, SUNY Press.
Floyd, Rita. 2013. "Analyst, Theory and Security: A New Framework for Understanding Environmental Security Studies." In *Environmental Security: Approaches and Issues*, Eds. Rita Floyd and Richard A. Matthew, 21–34. London, Routledge.
Wolfers, Arnold. 1962. *Discord and Collaboration: Essays on International Politics*. Baltimore, MD, Johns Hopkins University Press.

# SHAMING

## Charlotte Epstein

*The University of Sydney, Australia*

"Shaming" refers to a set of strategies mobilized by international actors in order to obtain that states honor their international obligations, notably with regards to environmental protections (see **Compliance and implementation**). This behavior speaks to the anarchical structure of the international system, which lacks a centralized political authority. Indeed in the absence of an overarching enforcement mechanism, in a peaceful international system, actors cannot be forced into a course of action. They can, however, be shamed into complying with their obligations; for example, to avert the extinction of a species (see **CITES**). Human rights and the environment constitute the main issue areas where shaming has been deployed and studied.

The targets of shaming strategies have included states and multinational **business and corporations**. For example, pharmaceutical companies have been brought into the limelight through their being awarded the Captain Hook Award for their profiteering of **indigenous peoples and local communities**' genetic resources by a coalition of

**nongovernmental organizations** (NGOs) in their campaign against biopiracy. The actors deploying the strategies range from NGOs, international organizations, or states, who can use international fora to shame other states into complying with international norms. An example constitutes the annual meetings of the **International Whaling Commission**, where a coalition of anti-whaling states, together with anti-whaling NGOs, have sought over the last three decades to shame Japan into halting its commercial and scientific whaling activities.

Conceptually, "shaming" has been analyzed through both rationalist and constructivist accounts of international politics. Rationalist explanations focus on the material effects of shaming strategies, whether on their costs to actors who are shamed (Lebovic and Voeten 2009) or on their benefits to international cooperation (Franklin 2008). Shaming enters into the neoliberal institutionalist analysis of cooperation as a corollary to the interest-based analysis of reputation and the effect of the shadow of the future upon inter-state interactions (Hafner Burton 2008).

However, insofar as it involves complying with normative behavior, shaming beckons constructivist accounts that emphasize the intrinsic power of norms. Here, two lines of enquiry have been pursued successively; how shaming strategies operate, and why they are successful. With regards to the first, shaming constitutes the linchpin to "leverage politics" applied upon states (Keck and Sikkink 1988) or a key mechanism of their socialization into international norms. In seeking to understand why states actually respond to this form of leverage the second foregrounds the role of identities. States are sensitive to shaming because of the moral damage to their self-images and identities (Epstein and Barclay 2013).

## References

Epstein, Charlotte and Kate Barclay. 2013. "Shaming to 'Green': Australia–Japan Relations and Whales and Tuna Compared." *International Relations of the Asia-Pacific* 13(1): 195–123.

Franklin, James C. 2008. "Shame on You: The Impact of Human Rights Criticism on Political Repression in Latin America." *International Studies Quarterly* 52(1): 187–211.

Hafner Burton, Emilie M. 2008. "Sticks and Stones: Naming and Shaming the Human Rights Enforcement Problem." *International Organization* 62(4): 689–716.

Keck, Margaret E. and Kathryn Sikkink. 1998. *Activists beyond Borders: Advocacy Networks in International Politics.* Ithaca, NY, Cornell University Press.

Lebovic, James H. and Erik Voeten. 2009. "The Cost of Shame: International Organizations and Foreign Aid in the Punishing of Human Rights Violators." *Journal of Peace Research* 46(1): 79–97.

# SOVEREIGNTY

**Jean-Frédéric Morin**

*Université libre de Bruxelles, Belgium*

**Amandine Orsini**

*Université Saint-Louis - Bruxelles, Belgium*

"The Earth is one but the world is not" begins the Brundtland Report of the World Commission on Environment and Development (1987: 27). Indeed, states are divided whereas the biosphere exists as a unit. This fact makes environmental politics an interesting case of reflection for the principle of sovereignty.

In the 1960s, during the decolonization process, developing countries insisted upon controlling their natural resources. Many were suspicious of the Western environmental intentions, fearing a form of neo-colonialism (see **Critical political economy**). In 1962, they strongly advocated for the adoption of the United Nations Resolution 1803 on the *Permanent Sovereignty Over Natural Resources*, recognizing "the inalienable right of all states freely to dispose of their natural wealth and resources in accordance with their national interests." Still today, developing countries frequently refer to this principle and make sure that negotiated texts explicitly recall it (Conca 1994; Hochstetler et al. 2000).

The idea of a full, exclusive, and supreme sovereignty might seem incompatible with the "common preoccupation of mankind," equally stated in numerous international agreements. Several environmentalists, especially in the 1970s and 1980s, feared that such behavior would impede environmental protection.

Under this line of reasoning, two options are frequently mentioned as means to limit sovereignty and favor environmental protection. The first consists in extending the **common heritage of mankind**. This would allow, for example, for the establishment of a global system of inspection and **taxation** for resources traditionally under state sovereignty. The second route for a post-Westphalian order is to increase the rights of non-state actors: **nongovernmental organizations**, **business and corporations**, **epistemic communities**, or **indigenous peoples and local communities** (Shadian 2010).

However, the supremacy of state sovereignty is not universally accepted as an impediment to environmental protection. International law already includes principles that limit sovereignty. Following the **preventive action principle**, for example, a state cannot use its territory in a way that damages the environment of another state. It was politically endorsed by **summit diplomacy** in the Stockholm (1972) and the Rio (1992) Declarations, and legally recognized by the International Court of Justice (Sands 1995).

State sovereignty is additionally limited by international conventions, which often qualify sovereignty rights by assigning specific obligations to states (Schrijver 1997. The **Law of the Sea Convention**, for example, extends sovereignty rights to 200 nautical miles from the coasts but provides for environmental duties. This led some legal experts to affirm that sovereign rights "over certain environmental resources are not proprietary, but fiduciary" (Sand 2004: 48). Here, sovereignty is seen as a form of public trusteeship granted to states with specific obligations and limitations.

Other requirements also create conditions that push states towards cooperation and joint action. For instance, several environmental treaties prohibit trade with non-parties. The Montreal Protocol (see **Ozone regime**) bans imports, even from non-parties, of products containing substances that are harmful to the ozone layer. The **hazardous wastes regime** bans imports and exports of toxic wastes with non-parties. Consequently, a country whose firms produce sprays or process toxic wastes has a high incentive to respect these treaties (DeSombre 2005). Global interdependence prevents regulatory autarcy.

With time, it appeared that sovereign rights could even consolidate environmental cooperation. As the **tragedy of the commons** suggests, a clear definition of rights can provide incentives for the **conservation and preservation** of natural resources. For example, the 1992 **biodiversity regime** and its 2010 Nagoya protocol placed genetic resources under national sovereignty, rejecting the common heritage principle that was formerly found in the 1983 FAO International Undertaking on Plant Genetic Resources. Through their sovereign rights, states can now control the access to their biodiversity and ask bio-technology **business and corporations** to compensate for the use of their national genetic resources.

Arguably, concerning **effectiveness**, states are often the best actors to enforce and control environmental measures. Not only are they able to impose regulations, levy taxes, offer subsidies, and define education programs, they also have the political and legal capacity to challenge actors that damage their natural resources. Fish stocks are unsustainably fished and extra-atmospheric space hazardously over-polluted partly because of the lack of national sovereignty over these resources.

The debates between sovereignty as an obstacle or as a means for environmental protection could be somewhat resolved by breaking down the concept. Karen Litfin (1997) divides sovereignty into authority, control, and legitimacy. She argues that states engage in "sovereignty bargains" along these dimensions. For instance, tying emission targets to domestic ownership of green technology could increase autonomy but reduce legitimacy, while delegating emission targets to an internationally recognized scientific body (see **Boundary organizations**) could increase legitimacy but decrease autonomy. Here, sovereignty is not understood as an absolute attribute but as a multidimensional concept in constant flux, and in constant social redefinition (Conca 1994; Chayes and Chayes 1998; Hochstetler et al. 2000).

To further understand the complex interaction between the principle of sovereignty and environmental protection, it might be useful to differentiate environmental problems. The quality of scientific knowledge (see **Science**), the level of ecological interdependence, the availability of international institutions, and the type of national resources might affect the desirability for a strong sovereignty norm and the bargains settled between sovereignty dimensions. One hypothesis is that the protection of local resources benefits from the direct involvement of transnational and supranational actors, whereas transboundary resources are better protected when states guard their sovereign rights.

## References

Chayes, Abram and Antonia H. Chayes. 1998. *The New Sovereignty: Compliance with Treaties in International Regulatory Regimes.* Cambridge, MA, Harvard University Press.

Conca, Ken. 1994. "Rethinking the Ecology-Sovereignty Debate." *Millennium* 23(3): 701–711.

DeSombre, Elizabeth R. 2005. "Fishing under Flags of Convenience: Using Market Power to Increase Participation in International Regulation." *Global Environmental Politics* 5(4): 73–94.

Hochstetler, Kathryn, Ann Marie Clark, and Elisabeth J. Friedman. 2000. "Sovereignty in the Balance: Claims and Bargains at the UN Conference on the Environment, Human Rights, and Women." *International Studies Quarterly* 44(4): 591–614.

Litfin, Karen T. 1997. "Sovereignty in World Ecopolitics." *Mershon International Studies Review* 41(2): 167–204.

Sand, Peter H. 2004. "Sovereignty Bounded: Public Trusteeship for Common Pool Resources." *Global Environmental Politics* 4(1): 47–71.

Sands, Philippe. 1995. *Principles of International Environmental Law.* Manchester, Manchester University Press.

Schrijver, Nico. 1997. *Sovereignty over Natural Resources: Balancing Rights and Duties.* Cambridge, Cambridge University Press.

Shadian, Jessica, 2010. "From States to Polities: Reconceptualizing Sovereignty through Inuit Governance." *European Journal of International Relations* 16(3): 485–510.

United Nations World Commission on Environment and Development. 1987. *Our Common Future.* Oxford, Oxford University Press.

# SUMMIT DIPLOMACY

## Arild Underdal

*University of Oslo and Center for International Climate and Environmental Research, Norway*

In the study of international relations, a "summit" is usually defined as a meeting involving heads of state or government (typically presidents or prime ministers) in direct face-to-face communication in the same room (Dunn 1996: 16f.). Meetings of this format have a long history, but Winston Churchill seems to have been the first, in 1950, to label them "summits."

Churchill used this label restrictively for (rare) meetings where the leaders of the Great Powers negotiated important high politics issues such as World War II strategies and peace settlements. Over the past three to four decades, summit diplomacy has expanded and become more institutionalized. Leaders of the most important states still meet in exclusive club-like settings, notably G8 and G20, but now they meet regularly, the "clubs" are larger, and their agendas are more diverse. Moreover, meetings of heads of state or government have become an integral component of the political system of several regional organizations including the European Union and the African Union, and of forums such as the Asia-Pacific Economic Cooperation (see **Regional governance**). Most of these meetings cover multiple issues, but overall attention to environmental concerns seems to have been growing.

Today, two main types of summits play important but different roles in environmental governance. First, regional organizations such as the EU and club-like forums such as the G20 play more or less important roles in governing human activities that cause environmental damage. Environmentalists may dismiss the summits that take place in these settings as focusing on policies for economic growth and stability rather than on environmental protection. Yet, if we measure importance in terms of environmental consequences, summits that take place in these settings and that focus primarily on economic issues will often—for better or worse—be the most important. The EU's importance is further boosted by its direct involvement in environmental policymaking and by its unique institutional capacity.

The other important type of summit is that called specifically to strengthen environmental governance. Most such summits take place in the context of UN global conferences and **regimes**. Prominent examples include the 1972 Stockholm Conference on the Human Environment, the 1992 Rio Conference on Environment and Development (also known as the Earth Summit), the 2002 Johannesburg World Summit on **sustainable development**, and the 2012 Rio Conference on Sustainable Development. Here, the ideal is universal participation. The setting is traditionally dominated by environmental ministries, agencies, experts (often forming **epistemic communities**), and **nongovernmental organizations**. What these actors presumably have in common is a genuine commitment to environmental values—and a weak mandate to intervene in the human activities that threaten these values. The active involvement of heads of government or state may be thought of as particularly important to ensure that environmental values and policies in fact penetrate other policy domains. Available evidence confirms that meetings of leaders indeed can provide unique opportunities for enhancing environmental policies (see **Influential individuals**). The current institutional reform of the **Commission on Sustainable Development** is an attempt to take advantage of such opportunities. However, particularly in its present format of mega-gatherings with sprawling agendas and a rich flora of side events, global conference diplomacy can hardly provide a conducive setting for some of the most important leadership functions that summits are supposed to serve (Victor 2011).

Let us nevertheless begin on the bright side. First, global conferences often serve as an effective tool for raising awareness, setting political agendas, and simultaneously focusing the attention of governments and stakeholders worldwide on the same problem (Seyfang and Jordan 2002). All these effects are amplified, sometimes substantially, if the conference includes a summit attended by presidents or prime ministers of the most important states. In fact, preparations for such summits often lead to unilateral upgrading of a state's policies and/or its institutional capacity (Meyer et al. 1997). Second, summit diplomacy generates, particularly for the leaders involved, positive stakes in its own success. Summits thus provide windows of opportunity for environmental ministries, agencies, and NGOs to influence policy (Seyfang and Jordan 2002), and they usually end with some kind of joint declaration. Third, the active participation of heads of government and state enhances aggregation capacity. These leaders can modify positions, link issues, and make trade-offs that their ministers, let alone ordinary ambassadors, have no mandate to make. In short, at its best, summit diplomacy can cut deadlocks and strike deals that qualify as important breakthroughs for global environmental governance.

Summit diplomacy also involves significant risks. First, plenary sessions with political leaders in the spotlight provide fertile ground for ideological posturing. Particularly in areas characterized by stark asymmetries between large groups of countries ("North" and "South"), leaders can use summits to mobilize domestic support. Under these circumstances, the risk of deadlock over basic principles and beliefs may increase when leaders meet. Second, high public expectations sometimes create strong incentives for leaders to (over)emphasize achievements. Announcements of lofty goals with no implementation plans attached are a common symptom of this "disease" (see **Compliance and implementation**). Third, to deliver what is expected, leaders depend heavily on the preparations made at lower levels. When these preparations fail to come up with coherent texts or clear policy alternatives, leaders may respond by some combination of withdrawal and improvisation (Jepsen 2013). Fourth, as seen from the perspective of seasoned diplomats, summitry inevitably involves risks of magnifying mistakes. These risks are inherent in the institutional order itself. Ambassadors may be corrected by their superiors; presidents and prime ministers may be overruled only through parliamentary refusal to ratify (legally binding) agreements.

For these and other reasons, enthusiasm for global conference summitry is muted in many of the assessments of environmental governance published by scholars (e.g. Susskind 1994; Victor 2011) as well as practitioners (e.g. Tolba and Rummel-Bulska 1998).

### References

Dunn, David H. 1996. *Diplomacy at the Highest Level*. Basingstoke, Macmillan.

Jepsen, Henrik. 2013. *"Nothing is Agreed until Everything is Agreed": Issue Linkage in the International Climate Change Negotiations*. Århus, Politica.

Meyer, John W., David J. Frank, Ann Hironaka, Evan Schofer, and Nancy Brandon Tuma. 1997. "The Structuring of a World Environmental Regime, 1870–1990." *International Organization* 51(4): 623–651.

Seyfang, Gill and Andrew Jordan. 2002. "The Johannesburg Summit and Sustainable Development: How Effective are Mega-Conferences?" In *Yearbook of International Co-operation on Environment and Development 2002–2003*, Eds. Stokke, Olav S., and Øystein B. Thommessen, 19–26. London, Earthscan.

Susskind, Lawrence E. 1994. *Environmental Diplomacy: Negotiating More Effective Global Agreements*. Oxford, Oxford University Press.
Tolba, Mostafa K. and Iwona Rummel-Bulska. 1998. *Global Environmental Diplomacy*. Cambridge, MA, MIT Press.
Victor, David G. 2011. *Global Warming Gridlock—Creating More Effective Strategies for Protecting the Planet*. Cambridge, Cambridge University Press.

# SUSTAINABLE DEVELOPMENT

## Edwin Zaccai

*Université libre de Bruxelles, Belgium*

Sustainable development was defined in the Brundtland Report in 1987 as a "development that meets the needs of the present without compromising the ability of future generations to meet their own needs" (World Commission on Environment and Development, 1987: 43). This remains by far its most known definition, even though the World Conservation Strategy was one of the first to use the term (IUCN et al. 1980). The Brundtland report is a product of the World Commission on Environment and Development, an international expert panel that was commissioned by the UN General Assembly in 1983 to define a new type of global development that reconciles environment and development in both the North and the South.

In this definition *intergenerational equity* stands out as the clearest specificity of sustainable development, compared with former formulas of development (see **Justice**). The expression *future generations* encompasses not only the next generation, but several generations, obliging one to consider a time frame well beyond that of current policy decisions. The capacities to be sustained in order to meet people's needs (with a priority for essential needs) in the distant future are not limited to the environment, but include economic, social, and institutional aspects as well. Brundtland's approach to sustainable development recognizes also that there are limits to be set in the exploitation of the environment, but these have to be dealt with in combination with technical developments and social equity.

As regards global governance, the major historic step in the sustainable development discourse was the United Nations Conference on Environment and Development (UNCED, Rio, 1992), also referred to as *Earth Summit* (see **Summit diplomacy**). It was held shortly after the end of the East–West divide, and attracted high expectations. The Rio

Declaration includes prominent environmental governance principles, such as the **polluter pays principle**, the **preventive action principle**, or the **precautionary principle**. In addition, it contains a major principle, namely one arguing for **common but differentiated responsibility**.

The academic literature provides a multiplicity of definitions of sustainable development and often describes the concept as being fuzzy (Lélé 1991). Broadly a general objective, it is specified by different actors depending on their context, be it **ecological modernization**, more suitable in industrial countries (Mol et al. 2009), greener forms of development in agrarian developing countries (Adams 2008), or local projects in towns or regions under the banner of Local Agenda 21. In any case the symbolic and political value of the concept should be highlighted. It is consensual, federating a number of interests, previously seen as in conflict, at least potentially. Arguably, it enabled a broad participation in the conferences and institutions that were dedicated to sustainable development, rallying **business and corporations**, developing countries, institutions for economic development, or associations of workers or of environmentalists.

The ecologist or environmental view tends to stress ecological constraints, or the **carrying capacities paradigm** of a territory, prior to allowing for the expansion of development. For instance, the *Strategy for Sustainable Living*, which was endorsed by the International Union for Conservation of Nature (IUCN) in 1991, the **United Nations Environment Program** (UNEP), and the World Wild Fund (WWF). The latter, that ties in with this vein, describes sustainable development as "improving the quality of human life while living within the carrying capacity of supporting ecosystems." In addition, **nongovernmental organizations** have frequently stressed the importance of **participation** of citizens for implementing sustainable development, especially at a local level (see **Compliance and implementation**).

Since the mid 1990s the concept of sustainable development has been increasingly understood as a balance between environmental, social, and economic pillars, dimensions, or objectives. In practice, the balance between these objectives remains contingent on the indicators used, the time scale chosen, or the actors that are included or excluded. A variety of indexes aiming at measuring sustainable development have been elaborated, such as the Index of Sustainable Economic Welfare (ISEW), or the Genuine Progress Indicator (GPI).

From the start, the sustainable development formula set the stage, among other "win–win" objectives, for reconciling environmentalism and business and corporations' interests. One of the chapters of the

Brundtland report is entitled *Producing More with Less*, which illustrates this environment–business tandem. The Business Council for Sustainable Development, which later became World Business Council for Sustainable Development (WBCSD), is a group of major global transnational corporations that was founded before the Rio Conference in order to participate actively in the discussions, and has influenced these orientations. Since the mid 1990s, a multitude of links have developed between corporate sustainable development and **corporate social responsibility.**

Economists interested in sustainable development introduced a distinction between strong and weak sustainability (Pearce 1993). Weak sustainability assumes substitutability between various forms of capital (economic capital, but also natural capital, several forms of social or even cultural capitals). The most common substitution would be if a decrease in natural capital (i.e. deforestation) were compensated by an increase in economic capital. Under the weak sustainability paradigm, development is considered successful when the total capital stock grows, no matter its composition. In contrast, strong sustainability considers some natural capital to be "critical," which implies limited substitutability and the need for certain nature conservation at any cost.

In a synthesis paper Hopwood et al. (2005) present a classification and "mapping" of different trends of thought on sustainable development through two broad axes. One is the ability of using technological solutions in order to solve environmental problems versus the conservation of a more intact environment. The other axis relates to the degree of presence of inequality or social concerns (see **Justice**) within the work of the authors that are considered. The Organisation for Economic Co-operation and Development (OECD), the EU, or the Ecological Modernizers stand not too far from each other on one side of the figure, in modes of sustainable development that may fit with **liberal environmentalism**. At the opposite side we find environmental justice or anti-capitalist movements, that might also refer to sustainable development emphasizing transformational change. In the middle of the figure stand the Brundtland Report and mainstream environmental groups, among others.

A controversial issue in the sustainability discourse that has been debated at length is the compatibility between economic growth and sustainable development (Jackson 2009). Some ecological economists consider sustainable development, and especially sustainable growth, to be an oxymoron, based on the argument that a development path based on ever-increasing production cannot be sustainable in a finite world. On the other hand, the Brundtland Report and many scholarly works draw a strong distinction between economic growth and development.

Economic growth would be desirable only insofar as it improves people's quality of life, respecting equity and environmental protection. But these conditions have not proven to be attained yet, raising critiques against the power of sustainable development policies to really make a structural difference, even though improvements have been obtained for some impacts (Zaccai 2012).

## References

Adams, Bill. 2008. *Green Development: Environment and Sustainability in a Developing World.* London, Routledge.

Hopwood, Bill, Mary Mellor, and Geoff O'Brian. 2005. "Sustainable Development: Mapping Different Approaches." *Sustainable Development* 13(1): 38–52.

IUCN, UNEP, WWF. 1980. *World Conservation Strategy: Living Resource Conservation for Sustainable Development.* Gland, IUCN.

IUCN, UNEP, WWF. 1991. *Caring for the Earth: A Strategy for Sustainable Living.* Gland, IUCN.

Jackson, Tim. 2009. *Prosperity without Growth.* London, Routledge.

Lélé, Sharachchandra. 1991. "Sustainable Development: A Critical Review." *World Development* 19(6): 607–621.

Mol, Arthur P.J., David A. Sonnefeld, and Gert Spaargaren (Eds.). 2009. *The Ecological Modernisation Reader: Environmental Reform in Theory and Practice.* London and New York, Routledge.

Pearce, David W. 1993. *Blueprint 3, Measuring Sustainable Development.* London, Earthscan.

United Nations World Commission on Environment and Development. 1987. *Our Common Future.* Oxford, Oxford University Press.

Zaccai, Edwin. 2012. "Over Two Decades in Pursuit of Sustainable Development: Influence, Transformation, Limits." *Environmental Development* 1(1): 79–90.

# TAXATION

## Bernard P. Herber

*University of Arizona, United States*

Taxation not only provides government revenues, it also may promote economic efficiency by internalizing unpriced externalities back into the price system (see **Polluter pays principle**). These taxation functions normally occur within a sovereign nation, but technological progress and globalization have made them increasingly important between nations due to the emergence of major inter-nation externalities. In environmental governance, such externalities include pollution of the global oceans and excess carbon emissions into the global atmosphere, the latter resulting in global warming with its destructive climate change effects. Externalities distort economic efficiency since they escape market pricing.

Two policy instruments proposed by economists to reduce carbon emissions are the carbon tax and carbon market (cap and trade) devices (Nordhaus 2007; Metcalf and Weisbach 2009; Aldy and Stavins 2012; also, see **Markets**). The carbon tax, an excise form of sales tax, is normally levied upon the mining or distribution of fossil fuels, which emit carbon in providing energy for economic production and consumption. It is a pigovian tax that enters into the prices of fossil fuels, thus "internalizing" previously unpriced carbon pollution costs into the prices of the economic goods that the fuels produce.

An ideal carbon tax design would levy a tax rate that is highest on coal, which has the highest carbon content per unit of energy produced, a lower rate on oil, which has less carbon content than coal, and lowest on the least carbon-emitting fuel, natural gas. A carbon tax attacks the core of the climate change problem by reducing carbon emissions. Meanwhile, its revenues may be used for such purposes as **adaptation** to already existing climate change effects and for the creation of a global trust fund to address normative inter-nation distributional issues associated with a global carbon tax.

Implementation of such a tax is a formidable undertaking (see **Compliance and implementation**). Taxation is inherently unpopular due to its "compulsory" nature, as compared to the "free choice" nature of market transactions. Moreover, it faces even greater resistance at the supranational level where sovereign political authority is absent. Efforts to compensate for this void often utilize international treaties, whereby nations "delegate" **sovereignty** to a supranational entity via binding agreements. However, treaty decision-making is hindered by the unwieldy consensus-voting rule (see **Treaty negotiations**).

Optimally, a sovereign "global political authority" that corresponds to the "global geographical space" of climate change externalities would levy the tax (Herber 1992). Otherwise, significant free rider incentives would arise if only one, or a few, nations, or even a regional affiliation of nations, levy the tax. Yet, the world has no sovereign global political body nor is it likely to create one in the foreseeable future.

Nonetheless, a "second-best" approach, albeit one using the flawed treaty mechanism, could establish a functional "de facto" global carbon tax (Cooper 2008; Silverstein 2010; Nordhaus 2011). The treaty would delegate sovereignty from national governments to a nonsovereign supranational government for the purpose of harmonizing a network of national carbon taxes across national political boundaries. This supranational entity could be either an existing body, such as the United Nations, or a newly created nonsovereign supranational government. The resulting tax domain would correspond to the geographical scope of global climate change externalities.

Although such a treaty would face considerable opposition, the gravity of the climate change threat—as voiced by a large majority of global climate scientists—lends support for strong action. Moreover, the tax could be made more acceptable if nations were allowed to retain some of the revenues generated by the tax. Meanwhile, a policy framework for definitive global climate policy already exists in the **climate change regime**. Furthermore, a conceptual foundation for such policy, the **common heritage of mankind** principle, is part of international law in the **Law of the Sea Convention**. Also, a recent study by the United Nations (2012) provides enhanced support for global taxation initiatives.

## References

Aldy, Joseph and Robert Stavins. 2012. "The Promise and Problems of Pricing Carbon: Theory and Experience." *Journal of Environment and Development* 21(2): 152–180.

Cooper, Richard. 2008. *The Case for Charges on Greenhouse Gas Emissions*. Discussion Paper 08–10, Harvard Project on International Climate Agreements. Cambridge, MA, Harvard Kennedy School.

Herber, Bernard. 1992. *International Environmental Taxation in the Absence of Sovereignty*. WP/92/104, Washington, International Monetary Fund.

Metcalf, Gilbert and David Weisbach. 2009. "The Design of a Carbon Tax." *Harvard International Law Review* 33: 499–556.

Nordhaus, William. 2007. "To Tax or Not to Tax: Alternative Approaches to Slowing Global Warming." *Review of Environmental Economics and Policy* 1(1): 26–44.

Nordhaus, William. 2011. "The Architecture of Climate Economics: Designing a Global Agreement on Global Warming." *Bulletin of the Atomic Scientists* 67(1): 9–18.

Silverstein, David. 2010. *A Method to Finance a Global Climate Fund with a Harmonized Carbon Tax*. Munich Personal RePEc Archive, Paper No. 27121.

United Nations. 2012. *World Economic and Social Survey 2012: In Search of New Development Finance*. New York, United Nations.

# TECHNOLOGY TRANSFER

## Joanna I. Lewis

*Georgetown University, United States*

Achieving environmental goals frequently requires the utilization of specific technology; for instance pollution control technology, low emission technology, or energy efficient technology. As many of these environmental technologies originate in the industrialized world but must be implemented in the developing world in order to achieve global environmental goals, such technology must be transferred from the North to the South. It is this phenomenon that dominates the discussions of technology transfer in the global environmental governance literature, although the concept of "South–South" technology transfer is also gaining interest as such opportunities increase.

Technology transfer is closely tied to the concept of "technology leapfrogging," or the skipping of some generations of technology or stages of development, including through technology transfers (Goldemberg 1998). This concept has particular resonance in the area of climate change mitigation, suggesting that developing countries might be able to follow more sustainable, low carbon development pathways and avoid the more emissions-intensive stages of development that were previously experienced by industrialized nations (Watson and Sauter 2011).

Technology transfers may be facilitated by the efforts of government, international organizations, research institutes, or **business and corporations**, and can occur through many different models, including technology licensing, mergers and acquisitions, joint development, and foreign direct investment. Barriers to the transfer of environmental technologies have been documented across multiple industries and technologies, from cleaner automobiles to $SO_2$ scrubbers for acid rain control (Taylor et al. 2003; Gallagher 2006). Cases have demonstrated that the transfer of technology without supplemental "know-how" or tacit knowledge may detract from the lasting effectiveness of the technology transfer, and that "absorptive capacity," or the ability to adopt, manage and develop new technologies, is an important indicator of the technology recipient's ability to fully implement an effective technology transfer (Davidson et al. 2000; Watson and Sauter 2011).

The role of intellectual property protections in facilitating or inhibiting technology transfers has been examined extensively. There is some evidence that stronger protection in developing countries facilitates technology transfer from industrialized countries through exports, foreign

207

direct investment, and licensing by limiting the risk for foreign firms of intellectual property theft or imitation (Hall and Helmers 2010). The high costs of accessing intellectual property have been demonstrated to obstruct technology transfer in some cases, including when technology is still in pre-commercial stages and the initial investor has not yet recovered the initial research and development investments. In other cases, however, intellectual property rights have not served as a barrier to technology transfer, and licensing or other fees to acquire intellectual property rights have been minimal (Lewis 2013).

Almost all multilateral environmental agreements contain some provision to facilitate technology transfer to developing countries in order to assist them in meeting their obligations. For example, technology transfer is encouraged by the **climate change regime**, the **hazardous wastes regime**, the **ozone regime**, and the **biodiversity regime**, and is a key aim of the **Global Environment Facility.** Due to differences in treaty objectives and the types of technologies involved, there is no universal framework for the transfer of environmental technologies under multilateral environmental agreements. While most agreements provide for developed countries to make some effort to promote the transfer of technology to developing countries, in most cases the specific obligations are rather vague, making **compliance and implementation** challenging (Shepherd 2007).

Perhaps the most successful technology transfer mechanism to date was the one created by the parties to the Montreal Protocol to assist developing countries in phasing out their use of ozone depleting substances (see **Ozone regime**). A Multilateral Fund, managed by both developed and developing countries and funded by contributions from developed countries, was created to finance the implementation of developing countries' obligations to phase-out their use of ozone depleting substances on an agreed schedule. Over US $3 billion has been spent from the Multilateral Fund since 1991. While much of the successful technology transfer under the Montreal Protocol is attributed to payments from the Fund directed at industrial conversion projects, it has also supported a variety of technical assistance, training, and capacity building activities that have also played an important role.

The **climate change regime** has taken a different approach to technology transfer from the Montreal Protocol, primarily due to the complexity of the climate challenge, the wide range of technologies needed for mitigation, and the enormous costs involved. Years of technology transfer negotiations under the **climate change regime** have produced a Technology Mechanism consisting of two components: a Technology

Executive Committee and a Climate Technology Center and Network. The mandate of these entities involves a wide variety of activities that may facilitate technology transfer, primarily by linking actors across countries and regions from the public and private sectors, and facilitating training, capacity building, and international **partnerships**. While still in its early stages, it is unlikely the Technology Mechanism will be sufficient to facilitate the scale of technology transfers needed to address the climate change mitigation and adaptation challenge. Yet given the politically charged nature of the technology transfer debate involving complex choices about equity, intellectual property rights, and wealth transfers, it is perhaps a notable first step.

## References

Davidson, Ogunlade, Bert Metz, and Sascha van Rooijen. 2000. *Methodological and Technological Issues in Technology Transfer, International Panel on Climate Change (IPCC)*. New York: Cambridge University Press.

Gallagher, Kelly. 2006. *China Shifts Gears: Automakers, Oil, Pollution, and Development*. Cambridge, MA, MIT Press.

Goldemberg, Jose. 1998. "Leapfrog Energy Technologies." *Energy Policy* 26(10): 729–741.

Hall, Bronwyn H. and Christian Helmers. 2010. *The Role of Patent Protection in (clean/green) Technology Transfer*. Working Paper 16323. Washington, National Bureau of Economic Research.

Lewis, Joanna I. 2013. *Green Innovation in China: China's Wind Power Industry and the Global Transition to a Low-Carbon Economy*. New York: Columbia University Press.

Shepherd, James. 2007. "The Future of Technology Transfer Under Multilateral Environmental Agreements." *Environmental Law Reporter* 37(7): 10547–10561.

Taylor, Margaret R., Edward S. Rubin, and David A. Hounshell. 2003. "Effect of Government Actions on Technological Innovation for $SO_2$ Control." *Environmental Science and Technology* 37(20): 4527–4534.

Watson, Jim, and Raphael Sauter. 2011. "Sustainable Innovation through Leapfrogging: A Review of the Evidence," *International Journal of Technology and Globalisation* 5(3/4): 170–189.

# THERMOECONOMICS

**Kozo Mayumi**

*University of Tokushima, Japan*

Thermoeconomics usually refers to applying thermodynamics to engineering or socioeconomic systems with the aim of improving energy efficiency and of reducing economic cost. The concept has been used in global environmental governance because thermoeconomics at the global scale covers not only the thermodynamic application to these systems, but also the material circulation aspects of **ecosystem services** including mineral resources that maintain **sustainable development**. Frederick Soddy was one of the first to use thermodynamic analysis for global governance to distinguish biophysical wealth (available energy) from monetary wealth (Soddy 1926). Nicholas Georgescu-Roegen (1971) extended Soddy's work by placing the entropy law at the center stage of the economic process. Entropy is a general index of unavailable energy. Available energy is irrevocably transformed into unavailable energy: after burning oil, it is impossible to recover the dissipated energy. Georgescu-Roegen claimed that energy shortage and scarcity of mineral resources ultimately limit human survival (see also **Carrying capacities paradigm**). Factors such as the oil shocks of the 1970s, concern about peak oil, and climate change have triggered scientific investigations and theories about how to tackle entropy and material circulation for sustainability. To make quantitative **assessments** of energy quality on a global **scale**, Charlie Hall (Hall et al. 1986) proposed the EROI (Energy return on investment) concept that was originally designed as surplus energy by Fred Cottrell (Cottrell 1955). EROI is the ratio of energy produced from an energy-gathering activity compared to the energy used in that process. It indicates whether a fuel is a net energy gainer or loser.

On the other hand, industrial ecology, a branch of thermodynamics for global scale, initiated by Ayres and Kneese (1969) emphasizes the importance of the first law of thermodynamics (conservation of energy and matter) in the economic process. On a global level, industrial ecology is the study of material and energy flows through a network of industrial systems. One important question of how the Earth as a whole has been functioning was investigated by Atsushi Tsuchida (Tsuchida and Murota 1987, see also **Gaia theory**). The Earth is an open system with respect to energy but is closed materially, so it would be useful to describe a mechanism by which the Earth could discard dissipated energy due to various activities including economic ones into outer space. According to Tsuchida, the Earth can be regarded as a big thermal engine powered by the temperature difference between the sun and outer space. Water in a vapor form is much lighter than air, therefore our planet could effectively discard dissipated thermal energy into outer space through water and air circulating systems. Yet global climate change is a threat to this important mechanism.

At least five practical problems appear when applying thermoeconomics in practice. First, a thermodynamic consideration *per se* does not necessarily produce useful scientific information. For example, *exergy* (maximum obtainable mechanical work) cannot be used as a benchmark value for practical purposes because environmental conditions are continuously changing and the system in question moves among those various environmental conditions. Second, EROI by itself is not enough to judge the virtues or vices of particular fuels or energy sources because, as Georgescu-Roegen emphasized, the roles of mineral resources and energy must be simultaneously incorporated into thermoeconomics. Third, industrial systems need different forms of energy carriers such as fuels, process heat, and electricity (or biomass for rural society), depending on where these industrial systems are situated. Fourth, energy efficiency is an important consideration for thermodynamic systems, but improving energy efficiency does not necessarily lead to a reduction in the total amount of energy carriers used for socioeconomic systems (Jevons Paradox). Fifth, the material circulation aspect of ecology (closing circle concept) proposed by Barry Commoner (1971) is not fully reached for industrial ecology.

### References

Ayres, Robert U. and Allen V. Kneese. 1969. "Production, Consumption, and Externalities." *American Economic Review* 59(3): 282–297.

Commoner, Barry. 1971. *The Closing Circle*. New York, Alfred A. Knopf.

Cottrell, Fred. 1955. *Energy and Society*. Westport, CT, Greenwood Press.

Georgescu-Roegen, Nicholas. 1971. *The Entropy Law and the Economic Process*. Cambridge, MA, Harvard University Press.

Hall, Charles A., Cleveland, Cutler, J., and Robert Kaufmann. 1986. *Energy and Resource Quality: The Ecology of the Economic Process*. New York, John Wiley.

Soddy, Frederick. 1926. *Wealth, Virtual Wealth and Debt*. London, George Allen & Unwin.

Tsuchida, Atsushi and Murota, Takeshi. 1987. "Fundamentals in the Entropy Theory of Ecocycle and Human Economy." In *Environmental Economics: The Analysis of a Major Interface*, Eds. G. Pillet and T. Murota, 11–35. Geneva, Leimgruber.

# TRAGEDY OF THE COMMONS

**Thomas Falk**
*University of Marburg, Germany*

**Björn Vollan**
*University of Innsbruck, Austria*

**Michael Kirk**
*University of Marburg, Germany*

The "tragedy of the commons" is a social dilemma arising from a situation in which members of a group make independent rational decisions that lead to the depletion of a natural resource, even though this will eventually result in a welfare loss for every group member. Garrett Hardin in his 1968 *Science* article stimulated this discussion and emphasized the increasing pressure on natural resources as a consequence, in particular, of population growth induced by a supportive welfare state (see **Population sustainability**). According to Hardin, these developments require a change in human values, ideas of morality, or rules instead of technological solutions. To shape his arguments he introduced the much debated parable of a pasture jointly used by a group of herders and implicitly assumed the absence of any coordination between the users. Each individual herder of the group of herders managing such an unregulated pasture will receive all of the profits from his own animals. Simultaneously, the negative consequences of pasture degradation caused by his animals will be shared by all group members. Imagine a local grazing area of limited size. The value of one additional cow grazing on it depends on the total number of grazing cows. With too many cows on the pasture competing for fodder, the animals will give less milk, lose weight, and the regeneration of the ecosystem will be disturbed. Thus, each additional cow generates a negative externality for the other cows as there is rivalry in consumption. Adding together the component of partial utilities, the rational herdsman concludes that the only sensible course for him to pursue is add another animal to his herd—and another, and another. This is the conclusion reached by each and every rational herdsman sharing a commons. Therein is the tragedy of the commons (Hardin 1968; see also Townsend and Wilson 1987). Hardin's example of a social dilemma can be applied to overexploitation of various common pool resources such as **fisheries** or forests, as well as to the problem of maintaining and contributing to **global public goods** such as clean air.

Both social dilemmas represent situations of conflicting private and social interest.

Ostrom (2005) defines such common pool resources as resource systems marked by a) high costs of excluding somebody from resource use and b) the subtractability of resource use. Difficulties to enforce exclusion emerge for instance in the case of large resource systems with undefined borders and mobile resource units, such as watersheds or marine systems. The degree of subtractability describes how strongly one person's resource use affects other people's ability to use the resource. The difference of a common-pool resource to a public good is that public goods can be enjoyed by everyone without decreasing the utility of other users (low subtractability of resource use). The nature of a good therefore has an immediate impact on the requirements of the governance system. Many global natural resources such as atmosphere, biodiversity, or oceans are according to Ostrom's definition common pool resources or public goods.

The main criticism of Hardin's argumentation refers to equating the commons (or common property) with the situation of open access common pool resources. Open access describes a management system where no property rights are assigned and no institutions regulate relations between individual users (Gordon 1954). Open access is, however, a rare case in reality even though particular global natural resources such as the oceans are to a large extent open accessible. Many common pool resources are managed as common property regimes that give ownership over resources to a user group. It is important to note that common-pool resources can in effect be owned by individuals, a group of people, or the government. Nevertheless, common property regimes are more likely to be established in cases where costs of exclusion are high.

Applying Hardin's misinterpretation the conclusion was drawn that all commons under scarcity will inevitably be overused unless the state controls resource use or private property rights are assigned to them. Therefore, non-diluted and bundled property rights are supposed to be assigned to a powerful state that regulates resource use or to autonomous individuals who reach social optimal use levels by internalizing the damage one cow incurs on the other cows (Hardin 1968; Ophuls 1973). With individual property rights on land there are no incentives for farmers to stock their pasture below or above its **carrying capacity**. The farmer will produce until his marginal costs of production equals the market price (this is also the ideal situation for society).

In response to these rather orthodox lines of thinking, Nobel laureate Elinor Ostrom and her scholars argued that also in many cases people using the commons can avoid its overexploitation (Ostrom 1990). Building on numerous case and experimental studies it was found that people can avoid becoming trapped in social dilemmas when certain minimum "design principles" are met. Under common property regimes as the third governance alternative a group of people hold rights of use in a resource system and effectively exclude non-group members, thereby preventing the tragedy of the commons and allowing the capture of future benefit streams to the collective. Formal and informal institutions such as bylaws or customary community norms regulate each member's resource use even though no individual rights to particular resource units are usually given to group members.

It is possible to find examples of both success or failure of state, private, and common property regimes (Ostrom 1990). Ostrom (2007) highlighted that no governance regime is per se superior to the other and that there are no panaceas to prevent the tragedy of the commons. Chhatre and Agrawal (2008) analyzed a data set spanning fifteen years and 152 forests in nine different countries and found that forest management success is independent of ownership to the forest—most important is local monitoring and enforcement. Assessing the likelihood of institutions to succeed, it is important to be aware of transaction costs, such as costs of identifying possible consequences of an action, costs of negotiation as well as costs of monitoring and enforcing rules. Transaction costs thus differ depending on the features of the natural and social systems.

Common property regimes have mainly been studied on the local **scale** and there is skepticism of the degree to which successful experience can be scaled up to **global public goods** (Berkes 2006). One approach is to treat nations as unitary actors. Similar to local level self-organization agreements such as the Montreal Protocol or **CITES** are reached on the basis of informal strategies such as subtle social sanctions for achieving **compliance and implementation** (Dietz et al. 2003). Still, many other examples exist where such coordination failed.

A classical state regime is difficult to imagine on a global scale as it would require a global authority holding a power monopoly. The difficulties to sanction are a major problem of international agreements (Dietz et al. 2003). Yet, through national **sovereign** powers state mechanisms strongly contribute to the governance of global commons. Also market-based systems are increasingly applied. **Markets** theoretically allow reaching a pre-defined emission target in the most efficient way (Dietz et al. 2003). At the same time, policymakers need to be aware of risks of market failures such as in the case of the trade with body parts of endangered species.

## References

Berkes, Fikret. 2006. "From Community-Based Resource Management to Complex Systems: The Scale Issue and Marine Commons." *Ecology and Society* 11(1): 45.

Chhatre, Ashwini and Arun Agrawal. 2008. "Forest Commons and Local Enforcement." *Proceedings of the National Academy of Sciences* 105(36): 13286–13291.

Dietz, Thomas, Elinor Ostrom, and Paul C. Stern. 2003. "The Struggle to Govern the Commons." *Science* 302(5652): 1907–1912.

Gordon, Scott H. 1954. "The Economic Theory of a Common-Property Resource: The Fishery." *The Journal of Political Economy* 62(2): 124–142.

Hardin, Garrett. 1968. "The Tragedy of the Commons." *Science* 162: 1243–1248.

Ophuls, William. 1973. "Leviathan or Oblivion?" In *Toward a Steady-State Economy*, Ed. Herman E. Daly, 215–230. San Francisco, CA, Freeman & Company.

Ostrom, Elinor. 1990. *Governing the Commons—The Evolution of Institutions for Collective Action.* Cambridge, Cambridge University Press.

Ostrom, Elinor. 2005. *Understanding Institutional Diversity.* Princeton, NJ, Princeton University Press.

Ostrom, Elinor. 2007. "A Diagnostic Approach for Going beyond Panaceas." *Proceedings of the National Academy of Science* 104(39): 15181–15187.

Townsend, Ralph and James A. Wilson. 1987. "An Economic View of the Tragedy of the Commons." In *The Question of the Commons: The Culture and Ecology of Communal Resources*, Eds. B.J. MacCay and J.M. Acheson, 311–326. Tucson, AZ, University of Arizona Press.

# TRANSBOUNDARY AIR POLLUTION REGIME

**Delphine Misonne**

*Université Saint-Louis - Bruxelles, Belgium*

The Long-Range Transboundary Air Pollution Convention, the so-called Geneva Convention, originates from the need to combat acid rain. It is typically a framework convention, instituting dynamics that allow for the adoption of further protocols (see **Treaty negotiations**).

At the time of its adoption in 1979, at the invitation of the United Nations Economic Commission for Europe, the convention made history. It was the first multilateral treaty addressing transboundary air pollution and the first agreement between East and West on environmental issues (Fraenkel 1989). By contrast, the weakness of its obligations raised concerns (Birnie et al. 2009) and questions were asked as to its possible impact, beyond symbolism (Wetstone and Rosencranz 1984).

The convention led to the adoption of eight protocols and gathered together fifty-one parties, all located in the United Nations Economic Commission for Europe region, from North America to Central Asia, including Europe. It had a considerable impact on other regional **regimes**, such as on European Union Law.

Its strength lies in the cooperation mechanisms it installed, which pushed forward scientific and political dialogue on international air pollution issues (see **Science**), instituting a decisive forum for sharing knowledge on air pollution issues (Wettestad 2002) but also for proposing new policy instruments. The encounter of science and policy crystallized in progressively imposing differential national obligations based on the **carrying capacity** of local ecosystems (Lidskog and Sundqvist 2011), making central the concept of "critical load," the quantitative estimate of an exposure to one or more pollutants below which significant harmful effects on specified sensitive elements of the environment do not occur according to current knowledge. The strong reliance on science was also soon demonstrated by the crucial role given to modeling for assessing the presence and impact of air pollution (see **Assessment**), among which the Regional Acidification Information System (RAINS) model (Tuinstra et al. 2006).

From its first focus on acid deposition (Helsinki Protocol) and on one pollutant (sulfur dioxide), the convention rapidly moved on to other pollutants and to other environmental effects. The Gothenburg Protocol of 1999 to abate acidification, eutrophication, and ground-level ozone broke new ground as it endorsed the challenge of a multi-pollutant and a multi-sector approach and introduced the concept of "national emissions ceilings," fixing the maximum amount of a substance expressed in kilotons that may be emitted from a party in a calendar year, but leaving the party with a large margin of appreciation regarding the measures that are the most suitable and the most cost-efficient on its own territory to reach these obligatory results.

The proposed regime was once described as ambitious and sophisticated but it also made air pollution work more complicated, so smart that only a few experts could understand its mechanisms (Lidskog and Sundqvist 2011). The important leeway left to national public authorities in order to meet the national ceilings did not ease **compliance and implementation**. Not all ceilings were fully met by the fixed target of 2010. The protocol was amended in 2012 and now includes "national emission reduction commitments," to be achieved in 2020 and beyond.

## References

Birnie, Patricia, Alan Boyle, and Catherine Redgwell. 2009. *International Law and the Environment.* Oxford, Oxford University Press.

Fraenkel, Amy. 1989. "The Convention on Long-Range Transboundary Air Pollution: Meeting the Challenge of International Cooperation." *Harvard International Law Journal* 30(2): 447–476.

Lidskog, Rolf, and Göran Sundqvist. 2011. *Governing the Air.* Cambridge, MA, MIT Press.

Tuinstra, Willemijn, Hordijk, Leen, and Carolien Kroeze. 2006. "Moving Boundaries in Transboundary Air Pollution Co-Production of Science and Policy under the Convention on Long Range Transboundary Air Pollution." *Global Environmental Change* 16(4): 349–363.

Wetstone, Gregory and Armin Rosencranz. 1984. "Transboundary Air Pollution: The Search for an International Response." *Harvard Environmental Law Review* 89, 100–106.

Wettestad, Jørgen, 2002. *Clearing the Air: European Advances in Tackling Acid Rain and Atmospheric Pollution.* Aldershot, Ashgate.

# TRANSBOUNDARY WATER REGIME

## Shlomi Dinar

*Florida International University, United States*

Pundits, policymakers, and prominent international figures have long prophesied that the next war will likely be over water. Water is not only necessary for all of humanity's needs, but is becoming increasingly scarce, is unequally distributed and is often transboundary in nature. Transboundary freshwater refers to water bodies such as lakes and rivers that are shared between two or more states thus making conflict over the allocation or management of the resource possible (see **Scarcity and conflicts**). While there have been a number of militarized disputes over shared water resources, the last war over water took place 4,500 years ago between the city-states of Lagash and Umma in modern day Iraq over the Tigris River (Wolf and Hamner 2000).

The more impressive history regarding international hydro-politics is that of cooperation in the form of international water agreements (see **Regional governance**). This is not to suggest that the past is devoid of instances of non-violent conflict over water. Examples abound of political disputes from Europe (e.g. Rhine Basin) to Asia (e.g. Indus Basin) over pollution and unilateral dam projects, respectively. Nor does the impressive record of agreements suggest that cooperation has been without incident or perhaps even taken other forms, less formalized or conventional. Scholars have pointed to inequity and strategic maneuvering enabled by power differentials (Zeitoun and Warner 2006) while other researchers have highlighted alternative forms of coordination and water governance such as networks of professionals, social movements, and international legal principles (Conca 2005). Still, the sheer number of inter-state agreements (more than 400 since 1820) is impressive and the cooperation these treaties engender (governing issues such as flood control and hydroelectric production) is noteworthy, suggesting that the characteristics that explain conflict over water may also explain inter-state cooperation. In this context, studies (e.g. Dinar 2008) have considered incentives to cooperation, oftentimes stipulated in the agreement, including issue-linkage and side-payments (see **Services** and **Polluter pays principle**).

The hydro-politics literature is rich with case studies. Too numerous to mention here, they have covered almost every region and major river basin in the world (e.g. Elhance 1999). More recently, large-n (or quantitative) studies have proliferated. Many of these published works have utilized the theories developed in the aforementioned case-study literature to examine hypotheses allowing for more generalizable inferences. Water scarcity, for example, has been identified as an important variable. Scholars studying conflict have uncovered some inconclusive results regarding scarcity and militarized conflicts between states yet have found some evidence to suggest that countries with low average rainfall are at more risk of interstate conflict (Gleditsch et al. 2006; Hensel et al. 2006). Those studying cooperation have found more conclusive results suggesting that increased water scarcity motivates formalized international cooperation (Tir and Ackerman 2009). Still, very high scarcity levels (and very low scarcity levels) lead to decreased instances of cooperation (Dinar et al. 2011). Other sociopolitical, economic, and geographic variables have also been examined in these quantitative studies (see Dinar et al. 2013 for a survey of many of these works).

Given the effects of climate change on international rivers, researchers have turned to investigating the impact of water variability, floods, and droughts (see **Disasters**). Some have argued that such environmental effects will have adverse social consequences (Chellaney 2011). Yet others have focused on the ability of river basin states to adapt to the effects of climate change by considering the treaties governing the basin and their make-up—a measure of institutional capacity (Drieschova et al. 2008).

These latter studies, combined with the research on climate change and instability, suggest that despite the impressive history of cooperation over water, global warming could potentially destabilize inter-state hydro-relations, particularly if the institutional capacity needed to deal with these abrupt changes is lacking (De Stefano et al. 2012). Disputes and conflicts over shared resources, such as water, may, in turn, lead to instability across other political spheres.

## References

Chellaney, Brahma. 2011. *Water: Asia's New Battleground.* Washington, DC, Georgetown University Press.

Conca, Ken. 2005. *Governing Water: Contentious Transnational Politics and Global Institution Building.* Cambridge, MA, MIT Press.

De Stefano, Lucia, James Duncan, Shlomi Dinar, Kerstin Stahl, Kenneth Strezepek, and Aaron T. Wolf. 2012. "Climate Change and the Institutional Resilience of International Rivers Basins." *Journal of Peace Research* 49(1): 193–209.

Dinar, Ariel, Shlomi Dinar, Stephen McCaffrey, and Daene McKinney. 2013. *Bridges over Water: Understanding Transboundary Water Conflict, Negotiation, and Cooperation.* Singapore, World Scientific.

Dinar, Shlomi. 2008. *International Water Treaties: Negotiation and Cooperation along Transboundary Rivers.* London, Routledge.

Dinar, Shlomi, Ariel Dinar, and Pradeep Kurukulasuriya. 2011. "Scarcity and Cooperation along International Rivers." *International Studies Quarterly* 55(3): 809–833.

Drieschova, Alena, Mark Giordano, and Itay Fischhendler. 2008. "Governance Mechanisms to Address Flow Variability in Water Treaties." *Global Environmental Change* 18(2): 285–295.

Elhance, Arun. 1999. *Hydropolitics in the 3rd World: Conflict and Cooperation in International River Basins.* Washington, United States Institute of Peace Press.

Gleditsch, Nils Petter, Kathryn Furlong, Håvard Hegre, Bethany Lacina, and Taylor Owen. 2006. "Conflict over Shared Rivers: Resource Scarcity or Fuzzy Boundaries." *Political Geography* 25(4): 361–382.

Hensel, Paul, Sara McLaughlin Mitchell, and Thomas Sowers. 2006. "Conflict Management of Riparian Disputes." *Political Geography* 25(4): 383–411.

Tir, Jaroslav and John Ackerman. 2009. "Politics of Formalized River Cooperation." *Journal of Peace Research* 46(5): 623–640.

Wolf, Aaron and Jesse Hamner. 2000. "Trends in Transboundary Water Disputes and Dispute Resolution." In *Water for Peace in the Middle East and Southern Africa,* Ed. Green Cross International, 55–66. Geneva, Green Cross International.

Zeitoun, Mark and Jerown Warner. 2006. "Hydro-hegemony: A Framework of Analysis of Transboundary Water Conflicts." *Water Policy* 8(5): 435–460.

# TRANSGOVERNMENTAL NETWORKS

**Harriet Bulkeley**

*Durham University, United Kingdom*

As the study of global environmental governance has moved beyond a focus on **regimes** scholars have sought to understand the alternative ways in which governance is undertaken and coordinated transnationally. Transnational governance is undertaken not only through **private regimes** and **partnerships** of **business and corporations** and **nongovernmental organizations**, but also through networks of state-based actors that operate transnationally—transgovernmental networks. Interest in transgovernmentalism was revived in the 1990s as central to an emerging "new world order" (Slaughter 1997). For Slaughter (1997) the disaggregation of the state combined with an increasing number of global challenges had served to create dense webs of transgovernmental networks that in turn proved more flexible and more effective for those engaged in seeking to govern. As a result, some have argued that "much contemporary international cooperation is not inter-national at all; rather, it is occurring among discrete, specialized agencies of [national] governments" (Raustiala 2002: 3).

Perhaps curiously, there has been relatively little examination of the roles that transgovernmental networks have played in global environmental governance. Bäckstrand (2008: 91) finds that transgovernmental networks gathering the specialized agencies of national governments in the climate change domain were "represented by voluntary agreements between governments involving cooperation for clean technology, renewable energy, clean coal and carbon sequestration" (see **Climate change regime**). Analysis by Bulkeley et al. (2012) also finds such networks to be relatively rare in the transnational climate governance arena. This suggests that, at least in the climate change domain, such networks of nation-state-based actors are either to be found only in **regimes** or that transgovernmental networks of this type are relatively rare, with collaboration usually involving other non-state actors. In contrast, at the regional level, including within the EU (Martens 2008) and Association of Southeast Asian Nations (ASEAN) (Elliot 2012) researchers have found that transgovernmental networks are active across a range of environmental policy areas.

While originally developed to analyze national level governmental agencies and their transboundary activities, the term "transgovernmental" can also be applied to those networks that have been formed between sub-national state-based agencies (Bäckstrand 2008) (see **Scale**). Since the early 1990s, researchers have documented a growing number of transnational networks organized by and orchestrated through sub-national tiers of government—regions and municipalities—that have mobilized in response to climate change (Betsill and Bulkeley 2006; Kern and Bulkeley 2009). Such transgovernmental networks are regarded as important in mobilizing sub-national responses because they have provided a sense of collective purpose, political support, access to knowledge, and the sharing of best practice. In some cases, transgovernmental networks have also offered a means through which specific policies and tools are developed and deployed, and access to financial resources. During the past two decades, the number of such networks has grown and their membership has diversified. At the same time, networks have sought to distinguish themselves from one another while also coordinating their actions. The result is a complex "ecology" of transgovernmental networks at work within and between cities and regions. While these networks have predominantly emerged in the climate change domain, the broad way in which climate change is approached has meant that a number of urban development challenges—from poverty and development, air pollution, transportation, and energy security—are now being governed not only locally and nationally, but transnationally through the work of transgovernmental networks.

## References

Bäckstrand, Karin. 2008. "Accountability of Networked Climate Governance: The Rise of Transnational Climate Partnerships." *Global Environmental Politics* 8(3): 74–102.

Betsill, Michele M. and Harriet Bulkeley. 2006. "Cities and the Multilevel Governance of Global Climate Change." *Global Governance* 12(2): 141–159.

Bulkeley, Harriet, Liliana Andonova, Karin Bäckstrand, Michele Betsill, Harriet Bulkeley, Daniel Compagnon, Rosaleen Duffy, Matthew Hoffmann, Ans Kolk, David Levy, Tory Milledge, Peter Newell, Matthew Paterson, Philipp Pattberg, and Stacy VanDeveer. 2012. "Governing Climate Change Transnationally: Assessing the Evidence from a Database of Sixty Initiatives." *Environment and Planning C: Government and Policy* 30(4): 591–612.

Elliot, Lorraine. 2012. "ASEAN and Environmental Governance: Strategies of Regionalism in Southeast Asia." *Global Environmental Politics* 12(3): 38–57.

Kern, Kristin and Harriet Bulkeley. 2009. "Cities, Europeanization and Multilevel Governance: Governing Climate Change through Transnational Municipal Networks." *Journal of Common Market Studies* 47(2): 309–332.

Martens, Maria. 2008. "Administrative Integration through the Back Door? The Role and Influence of the European Commission in Transgovernmental Networks within the Environmental Policy Field." *Journal of European Integration* 30(5): 635–651.

Raustiala, Kal. 2002. "The Architecture of International Cooperation: Trans-governmental Networks and the Future of International Law." *Virginia Journal of International Law* 43(1): 2–92.

Slaughter, Anne-Marie. 1997. "The Real New World Order." *Foreign Affairs* 76(5): 183–197.

# TRANSNATIONAL CRIME

**Lorraine Elliott**

*Australian National University, Australia*

Transnational environmental crime (TEC)—one of the fastest growing areas of cross-border criminal enterprise—is the knowing violation (usually by individuals and private entities) for illegal gain, of prohibition or regulation **regimes** established by multilateral environmental agreements or by the criminal provisions of legislation adopted by individual states. This includes the trafficking of illegally logged timber, the smuggling of endangered species, the black market in ozone-depleting substances, the transboundary dumping of toxic and hazardous waste, and the illegal exploitation of marine living resources (see Banks et al. 2008; UNODC 2010: 149–69; Interpol 2012). These crimes are serious because of their environmental consequences, because of their links with violence, corruption, and a range of cross-over crimes such as money-laundering, and because they undermine the rule of law and good governance at local, national, and global levels (Elliott 2012).

As with many other forms of transnational crime, TEC challenges conventional assumptions that criminal activity is managed through hierarchical cartels and mafia-type organizations. Rather, those engaged in this clandestine sphere rely on the operational advantages offered by network structures: that they are flexible, decentralized, and "highly resistant to decapitation and more difficult to contain" (Williams 2001: 73). Much of that involves commodity-specific smuggling networks but it also includes criminal groups involved in other forms of illegal activity and, in some cases, politically motivated organizations such as militia groups for whom TEC generates income to support other activities. For example, timber that is illegally logged in the Congo Basin, often with militia involvement, is transported to Burundi, Rwanda, and Uganda, then exported to the EU, the Middle East, China, and other Asian countries with support from financiers in the US (Nellerman 2012: 6).

The global governance complex (see **Institutional interaction and Scale**) for TEC constitutes a form of multilevel governance, characterized by effort across multiple agencies and sites of authority. There is no international treaty designed specifically to prevent, suppress, and punish the kinds of trafficking and smuggling that constitute transnational environmental crime. Existing transnational crime agreements such as the 2000 UN Convention against Transnational Organized Crime and the 2003 UN Convention against Corruption pay little attention to environmental crime. Key multilateral environmental agreements (such as **CITES**, the **ozone regime**, and the **hazardous wastes regime**) were adopted to strengthen environmental protection, not to address transnational crime.

Since the adoption of these respective multilateral environmental agreements, parties have moved to take illegal trade and associated criminal activity more seriously. Agencies whose mandate is more oriented to cross-border illegality—such as the World Customs Organization, Interpol, and the UN Office of Drugs and Crime—have made TEC more prominent in their individual agendas. One of the key themes in contemporary global governance is that "networked threats [and this would include TEC] require a networked response" (Slaughter 2004: 160) or, as United Nations Environment Programme (UNEP) (2002) puts it, networking counts . The proposition is yet to be tested fully with respect to TEC. However, in pursuit of effective policy and operational responses, the multilateral core has been actively supplemented with regional inter-agency arrangements (such as wildlife enforcement networks) (see **Regional governance**) and formal and informal **partnerships** between Multilateral Environmental Agreements (MEA) secretariats and international organizations (such as the International Consortium for Combating Wildlife Crime, established in 2010 as a collaborative arrangement between CITES, Interpol, the World Customs Organization, the **World Bank**, and the UN Office of Drugs and Crime to provide support for national and regional wildlife enforcement efforts). TEC also offers a lens on contemporary forms of agency beyond the state and the role of **nongovernmental organizations**. The involvement of NGOs in coordination and knowledge network arrangements with governments and intergovernmental organizations extends the boundaries of relevant **epistemic communities**. NGOs also conduct undercover operations and intelligence gathering of the kind usually taken to be the responsibility of governments (see Environmental Investigation Agency 2013, for example). This not only challenges expectations that environmental governance remains fundamentally the preserve of states but it also brings into question statist models of global governance.

## References

Banks, Debbie, Charlotte Davies, Justin Gosling, Julian Newman, Mary Rice, and Fionnuala Walravens. 2008. *Environmental Crime: A Threat to our Future.* London, Environmental Investigation Agency.

Elliott, Lorraine. 2012. "Fighting Transnational Environmental Crime." *Journal of International Affairs* 66(1): 87–104.

Environmental Investigation Agency. 2013. *Hidden in Plain Sight: China's Clandestine Tiger Trade.* London, Environmental Investigation Agency.

Interpol. 2012. *Environmental Crime, It's Global Theft.* Lyon, Interpol Environmental Crime Programme.

Nellerman, Christian (Ed.). 2012. *Green Carbon, Black Trade: Illegal Logging, Tax Fraud and Laundering in the World's Tropical Forests, a Rapid Response Assessment.* Norway, UNEP, GRID-Arendal.

Slaughter, Anne-Marie. 2004. "Disaggregated Sovereignty: Towards the Public Accountability of Global Government Networks." *Government and Opposition* 39(2): 159–190.

Williams, Phil. 2001. "Organizing Transnational Crime: Networks, Markets and Hierarchies." In *Combating Transnational Crime: Concepts, Activities and Responses,* Eds. Phil Williams and Dimitri Vlassis, 57–87. London, Frank Cass.

United Nations Environment Programme. 2002. *Networking Counts: Montreal Protocol Experiences in Making Multilateral Environmental Agreements Work.* Paris, UNEP.

United Nations Office of Drugs and Crime. 2010. *The Globalization of Crime: A Transnational Organized Crime Threat Assessment.* Vienna, UNODC.

# TRANSPARENCY

## Michael Mason

*London School of Economics and Political Science, United Kingdom*

Right-to-know is a legal principle affording individuals an entitlement to information from governmental authorities and private entities. Mandatory disclosure of information is now a widespread requirement for state actors in democratic political systems, with extensive but selective use in the private sector, notably company reporting rules and labeling obligations. Right-to-know laws have been adopted by more than eighty countries (see **Policy diffusion**): they are both an alternative and supplement to other regulatory instruments, and are most apposite where information deficits or asymmetries are related to welfare losses, including environmental degradation (Florini 2007). Recent uptake of right-to-know legislation includes national examples with broad scope, such as in

India and South Africa (covering both public and private sector actors), and also more restrictive applications, notably the Chinese freedom of information legislation designed to promote efficient decision-making (Florini and Jairaj 2014).

Environmental information may be covered within the general provisions of right-to-know legislation, but environment-specific information access is set out in substantive laws prescribing disclosure about particular pollutants or harmful chemicals. In democratic political systems, right-to-know about toxic chemicals normally means different disclosure responsibilities within and outside the workplace. Pollution inventories or registers are a common institutional embodiment of right-to-know norms, applied to the release and transfer of selected chemicals. These inventories are found both in advanced economies (e.g. US Toxic Release Inventory, Australian National Pollution Inventory) and **emerging countries** (e.g. Indonesia's Program for Pollution Control, Evaluating and Rating).

The relation between global and domestic transparency practices structures the transnational diffusion of right-to-know (Bauhr and Nasiritousi 2012; Florini and Jairaj 2014) (see **Policy diffusion**). International environmental law contains multilateral obligations that advance transparency between states, notably rights to notification and prior informed consent (PIC) concerning cross-border risk-bearing activities. The global regulation of hazardous chemicals, wastes, and GMOs has featured frequent clashes between exporting and importing countries over the nature and scope of PIC rules (Langlet 2009) (see also **Hazardous Chemicals Convention** and **Persistent Organic Pollutants Convention**). While few multilateral environmental agreements vest right-to-know entitlements in natural or legal persons, since the 1990s the European Union has created community-wide citizen rights to (environmental) information against both member states and EU administrative bodies.

According to Ludwig Krämer (2012), the most important legal expression of a transnational right-to-know is contained in the information disclosure provisions of the 1998 Aarhus Convention—the Convention of Access to Information, Public **participation** to Decision Making and Access to Justice in Environmental Matters. Negotiated under the auspices of the UN Economic Commission for Europe, the Aarhus Convention reflects the role of the commission in democracy promotion across Central and Eastern Europe. Aarhus information rights are public entitlements across all convention parties, supported by a relatively strong compliance mechanism (see **Compliance and implementation**). They combine passive (request-based) and active disclosure obligations on public authorities: Parties are allowed some discretion in enacting these duties, which has led to discrepancies between states. While the 2003 Kiev Protocol to the convention (on pollutant release and transfer registers) has also created indirect obligations on private owners and operators of polluting facilities, there remains a concern that the treaty is compromised by the absence of a right-to-know entitlement against private sector entities generating major environmental impacts (Mason 2014).

Scholarship on transparency indicates that it is more likely to work when it is embedded in the decision processes of both disclosers and recipients (Fung et al. 2007; Mol 2008). This creates challenging conditions for broad right-to-know obligations—a burden compounded for access to information on transboundary environmental risks and harm. In a global political economy dominated by market liberal imperatives, environmental transparency is weakened by the propensity of private sector disclosers (e.g. transnational corporations) to oppose any expansion of environmental reporting beyond voluntary measures.

## References

Bauhr, Monika and Naghmeh Nasiritousi. 2012. "Resisting Transparency: Corruption, Legitimacy and the Quality of Global Environmental Politics." *Global Environmental Politics* 12(4): 9–29.

Florini, Ann (Ed.). 2007. *The Right to Know: Transparency for an Open World.* New York, Columbia University Press.

Florini, Ann and Bharath Jairaj. 2014. "The National Context for Transparency-based Global Environmental Governance." In *Transparency in Global Environmental Governance*, Eds. Aarti Gupta and Michael Mason, forthcoming. Cambridge, MA, MIT Press.

Fung, Archon, Mary Graham, and David Weil. 2007. *Full Disclosure: The Perils and Promises of Transparency.* New York, Cambridge University Press.

Krämer, Ludwig. 2012. "Transnational Access to Environmental Information." *Transnational Environmental Law* 1(1): 95–104.

Langlet, David. 2009. *Prior Informed Consent and Hazardous Trade.* Alphen, Kluwer Law International.

Mason, Michael. 2014. "So Far but No Further? Transparency in the Aarhus Convention." In *Transparency in Global Environmental Governance*, Eds. Aarti Gupta and Michael Mason, forthcoming. Cambridge, MA, MIT Press.

Mol, Arthur P.J. 2008. *Environmental Reform in the Information Age: The Contours of Informational Governance.* Cambridge, Cambridge University Press.

# TREATY NEGOTIATIONS

## Daniel Compagnon

*Sciences Po Bordeaux, France*

In international studies, the dominant conceptualization of global treaty making is based on rational choice models of international cooperation derived from game theory. They analyze the distribution of gains and costs among participating countries (Barrett 2003), and focus on how to reach an optimal negotiation equilibrium maximizing benefits and minimizing costs of participation. Somehow they merely corroborate intuitive ideas such as the larger the number of parties the harder it is to get a substantial agreement (Barret 2003: 355–356). What was originally labeled the "law of the least ambitious program" (Underdal 1980; Hovi and Sprintz 2006) might highlight the difficulty in dealing with the **tragedy of the commons** and **global public goods** when almost all UN member states are involved, but does not account for successes in building more robust global **regimes**—such as the **ozone regime**. It is often the complexity of global environmental issues, such as climate change, that tend to paralyze the multilateral process rather than the number of parties.

We focus hereafter on another approach based on an empirical, actor-oriented perspective: it addresses issues, negotiation phases, and negotiator's tactics in the formation and governance of international environmental regimes. Prominent in this field, Chasek's phased process fits multilateral negotiations characterized by a very large number of participating states, multiple interlinked issues, and various types of actors located either at the core or at the periphery of the process. These include **epistemic communities, nongovernmental organizations, business and corporations**, and the media (Chasek 2001). Ahead and after well-publicized UN conferences there is a continuous stream of preparatory committees, specialized working groups, conferences of parties (COPs) sometimes every year, not to mention a number of ad hoc meetings. This has been going on for years, even decades for several conventions. Thus global regimes are altered and sometimes strengthened through additional protocols to the initial framework convention—a pattern followed for the **ozone, climate change**, and **biodiversity regimes**—as member states' positions evolve, **negotiating coalitions** emerge and disintegrate, and new issues and ideas arise.

In environmental treaty making epistemic communities play a crucial role in framing problems and solutions. The leadership of **influential**

**individuals** such as UNEP executive directors, conference chairs, or even executive secretaries (see **Secretariats**) often salvage some negotiations from doom. Non-state actors have also gained a growing influence since 1992, not only in agenda setting but also in subsequent negotiation phases (Betsill and Corell 2008). State delegations include non-state actors representatives to enhance national expertise although the latter have no access to closed-doors meetings (Chasek 2001: 198). Access to negotiations and effective engagement remain difficult for the poorest countries which can hardly cope with so many meetings and complex agendas, and which often lack the relevant expertise and resources (see **Least developed countries**).

Behind the bitter diplomatic haggling till the last hour dubbed "negotiation by exhaustion" emphasized by the media (see **Summit diplomacy**) there is a more discrete side. This deliberative dimension is rooted in the logic of arguing, aiming at building a consensus, and is facilitated by the penetration of the "empowered spaces" by ideas and actors from the "public spaces" (see **Global deliberative democracy**), also including recurrent interactions within networks of government negotiators (Orsini and Compagnon 2013). This "network diplomacy" is common in the field of the environment but also in trade issues and other areas of "low politics." It differs notably from the traditional "club diplomacy" where a handful of professional diplomats secretly make decisions over war and peace. Through social learning such networks sometimes overcome prevailing deadlocks. Many case studies emphasize the importance of procedural flexibility, personal understanding between negotiators meeting regularly over the years, and ad hoc mechanisms to resolve differences in final bargaining phases, including innovative techniques to promote consensus (Davenport et al. 2012). For example, the chair of the final negotiating session of the Biosecurity Protocol in Montreal in 2000 used colored teddy bears bought in the subway, to draw the order of speech for representatives of negotiating blocks. It eased the tension and allowed the last row of discussion to proceed smoothly.

Although the treaty at the end might not be totally satisfactory and compliance remain low, the negotiation process might nevertheless have created a shared world vision, within which arguing over the best solutions is legitimate, in a way that effectively influences policymaking at national level.

## *References*

Barrett, Scott. 2003. *Environment and Statecraft: The Strategy of Environmental Treaty-Making.* Oxford, Oxford University Press.

Betsill, Michelle and Elisabeth Corell (Eds.). 2008. *NGO Diplomacy: The Influence of Nongovernmental Organizations in International Environmental Negotiations.* Cambridge, MA, MIT Press.

Chasek, Pamela S. 2001. *Earth Negotiations: Analyzing Thirty Years of Environmental Diplomacy.* Tokyo, United Nations University Press.

Davenport, Deborah, Lynn M. Wagner, and Chris Spence. 2012. "Earth Negotiations on a Comfy Couch: Building Negotiator Trust through Innovative Process." In *The Roads from Rio: Lessons Learned from Twenty Years of Multilateral Environmental Negotiations,* Eds. Pamela Chasek and Lynn M. Wagner, 39–58. London and New York, RFF Press/Routledge.

Hovi, Jon and Detlef F. Sprinz. 2006. "The Limits of the Law of the Least Ambitious Program." *Global Environmental Politics* 6(3): 28–42.

Orsini, Amandine and Daniel Compagnon. 2013. "From Logics to Procedures: Arguing within International Environmental Negotiations." *Critical Policy Studies* 7(3): 273–291.

Underdal, Arild. 1980. *The Politics of International Fisheries Managements: The Case of the Northeast Atlantic.* New York, Columbia University Press.

# UNITED NATIONS ENVIRONMENT PROGRAMME

## Steffen Bauer

*German Development Institute, Germany*

The United Nations Environment Programme (UNEP) is the most visible and lasting institutional achievement of the 1972 United Nations Conference on the Human Environment and considered to be the United Nations' "leading global environmental authority that sets the global environmental agenda, that promotes the coherent implementation of the environmental dimension of **sustainable development** within the United Nations system and that serves as an authoritative advocate for the global environment" (UNEP 1997: §2).

Since it was formally established as a minor UN bureaucracy with a small headquarters in the Kenyan capital Nairobi, i.e. remote from the United Nations hubs in New York and Geneva, it has come to epitomize the status attributed to environmental governance in the context of the United Nations: the notion of "environment" arrived late on the international policy agenda, it occupies limited institutional space within the convoluted United Nations system, and it is considered an issue of low politics in intergovernmental relations (Bauer 2013: 320). Still, UNEP has come to represent "the closest thing there is to an overarching global institution for the environment" (DeSombre 2006: 9).

At the same time a considerable gap prevails between the high expectations that the United Nations' "leading global environmental authority" finds itself confronted with and its limited capability to help solve the world's manifold ecological crises. This gap is all the more striking as UNEP has proved an effective agenda setter and negotiation facilitator in international environmental politics. As such it has been instrumental to the genesis of numerous multilateral environmental agreements, notably the framework convention of the **climate change regime** and the **desertification convention**, and is indeed administering many of these treaties as well as corresponding **treaty negotiations**, including in the **biodiversity**, the **ozone**, the **persistent organic pollutants**, and the **hazardous waste regimes** as well as other more specific and regional treaties (see **Secretariats**).

As the **effectiveness** of the respective **regimes** varies considerably, so do scholars' attributions regarding UNEP's contribution to their relative success or failure. For instance, while some denounce its incapacity to effectively coordinate international biodiversity governance (e.g. Andresen and Rosendal 2009), others praise its instrumental leadership in having brought about and seen through global efforts to halt depletion of the ozone layer (e.g. Downie 1995).

Taking UNEP's mandate as a yardstick means to acknowledge that it was originally conceptualized to provide the international community with leadership and guidance on global and regional environmental matters by (1) assessing and monitoring the state of the environment (see **Assessment**), by (2) serving as a norm-building catalyst for international environmental policy and law, and by (3) coordinating all of the United Nations' environmental activities, even as key UN agencies are superior to UNEP either hierarchically or politically (Bauer 2013: 324). While fulfilling the coordination function has never seemed realistic in the first place, UNEP has been remarkably successful on the first two counts: it established itself as both the United Nations' environmental consciousness and as a catalyst for environmental multilateralism. By and large this is achieved by raising awareness for the environmental challenges facing the international community—e.g. through UNEP's flagship Global Environment Outlook reports—and by the promotion of environmental law at international, regional, and even national levels (ibid.: 325).

To a considerable extent, this is a function of the bureaucratic authority vested in the UNEP secretariat and the leadership thus exerted (Bauer 2009) (see **Influential individuals**). It enables UNEP to act as an efficient knowledge broker at the nexus of science and environmental

policymaking, and as a negotiation facilitator in tenacious intergovernmental processes. Accordingly, UNEP's influence is most visible along the
cognitive and normative dimensions of international environmental
governance. Somewhat ironically, UNEP's evident success in advancing
issue-specific multilateral environmental institutions is counteracted by
the concomitant proliferation of separate decision-making bodies: As
distinct environmental treaties typically take on a life of their own, UNEP's
ineptitude to coordinate international governance on a systemic level is
only compounded further (Andresen and Rosendal 2009; Bauer 2009).
Moreover, the proliferation of multilateral environmental agreements
has intensified the pace, density, and complexity of UNEP's portfolio
while at the same time spreading thin its modest resources.

The resulting inefficacy of UNEP is not exactly an original insight.
Even the Secretary-General's High-level Panel on System-wide
Coherence in the Areas of Development, Humanitarian Assistance, and
the Environment acknowledges that "a substantially strengthened and
streamlined international environmental governance structure" would
be required to reverse the trends of global environmental degradation (UN
2006: para. 31). To this end, scholars and practitioners have long debated
the pros and cons of elevating UNEP, i.e. a small program subordinate
to the UN Economic and Social Council, to the status of a full-fledged
specialized agency or **World Environment Organization**, albeit to
limited avail (Biermann and Bauer 2005). Indeed, it took forty years for
the international community to eventually expand UNEP's exclusive
Governing Council into a United Nations Environment Assembly with
universal membership in the wake of the 2012 Rio+20 summit.

Ultimately, the reach of UNEP as a central actor of global environmental governance remains confined by its organizational history in the
context of the United Nations institutional complexity and the unresolved
structural issues this encompasses, notably along the North–South divide
(e.g. Ivanova 2012). The latter especially reflects the prevailing tension
between the prerogative of sovereign states to exploit their national
resources on the one hand and their responsibility to consider the global
impacts of their corresponding socioeconomic activities on the other
hand.

## References

Andresen, Steinar and Kristin Rosendal. 2009. "The Role of the United Nations
Environment Programme in the Coordination of Multilateral Environmenal
Agreements." In *International Organizations in Global Environmental Governance*, Eds.
Frank Biermann, Bernd Siebenhüner, and Anna Schreyögg, 133–150. London,
Routledge.

Bauer, Steffen. 2009. "The Secretariat of the United Nations Environment Programme: Tangled Up In Blue." In *Managers of Global Change: The Influence of International Environmental Bureaucracies*, Eds. Frank Biermann and Bernd Siebenhüner, 169–201. Cambridge, MA, MIT Press.

Bauer, Steffen. 2013. "Strengthening the United Nations." In *The Handbook of Global Climate and Environment Policy*, Ed. Robert Falkner, 320–338. Chichester, Wiley-Blackwell.

Biermann, Frank and Steffen Bauer (Eds.). 2005. *A World Environment Organization: Solution or Threat for Effective International Environmental Governance*. Aldershot, Ashgate.

DeSombre, Elizabeth R. 2006. *Global Environmental Institutions*, London, Routledge.

Downie, David L. 1995. "UNEP and the Montreal Protocol." In *International Organizations and Environmental Policy*, Eds. Robert V. Bartlett, Priya A. Kurian, and Madhu Malik, 171–185. Westport, CT, Greenwood Press.

Ivanova, Maria. 2012. "Institutional Design and UNEP Reform: Historical Insights on Form, Function and Financing." *International Affairs* 88(3): 565–584.

United Nations. 2006. *Delivering as One: Report of the Secretary-General's High-Level Panel on System-Wide Coherence in the Areas of Development, Humanitarian Assistance, and the Environment*. New York, United Nations.

UNEP, Governing Council. 1997. *Nairobi Declaration of the Heads of Delegation*. Nairobi, UNEP.

# WETLANDS CONVENTION

## Royal Gardner

*Stetson University, United States*

The Convention on Wetlands of International Importance especially as Waterfowl Habitat, known as the Ramsar Convention, is a wetland conservation treaty with more than 165 parties. Concluded in Ramsar, Iran, in 1971, it entered into force in 1975. As an early multilateral environmental agreement, its obligations are general in nature (Bowman 1995). Each party is expected to comply with three primary duties (referred to as the three Ramsar pillars) (see **Compliance and implementation**): designation and conservation of at least one site as a Wetland of International Importance (called a Ramsar site); the wise use (sustainable use) of all wetlands within its territory; and international cooperation with respect to wetland matters. The Ramsar Convention endorses ecosystem approaches to protecting the environment. Indeed, Ramsar parties have defined wise use as "the maintenance of their ecological character, achieved through the implementation of ecosystem approaches, within the context of sustainable development."

Ramsar parties meet approximately every three years at a Conference of the Parties (COP), the Convention's primary policymaking body (see also **Treaty negotiations**). The COP considers and adopts resolutions, traditionally on a consensus basis. While the consensus-based approach ensures the positive support of the greatest number of parties, it can also result in watered-down resolutions. These resolutions are afforded different treatment by various parties. Some parties, such as the United States, view Ramsar resolutions as aspirational and non-binding (Gardner and Connolly 2007). Other parties consider resolutions adopted by consensus to have legal effect within their domestic regimes. For example, in a case involving the adequacy of an environmental impact assessment for a proposed project in a Ramsar site, the Dutch government stated that COP resolutions unanimously adopted are part of the Netherlands' national obligations and thus legally enforceable (Verschuuren 2008; Gardner and Davidson 2011).

The Ramsar Convention is not formally affiliated with the UN. The Ramsar **secretariat**, which facilitates the day-to-day coordination of Convention matters, is based in Switzerland in the headquarters of IUCN, which was an early proponent for the creation of the Convention. During treaty negotiations, when due to the financial implications no country volunteered to host the Secretariat (originally referred to as the Ramsar Bureau), IUCN agreed to do so until the parties, by a two-thirds majority, selected another organization or government. Some parties advocate moving the Secretariat under the auspices of the **United Nations Environment Programme**, suggesting that this would provide Ramsar a greater profile in their countries. Although COP-11 in Bucharest reached consensus for IUCN to remain the institutional host of the Secretariat, the issue is likely to be revisited.

The Ramsar Convention lacks a formal enforcement mechanism and its **effectiveness** is difficult to quantify (see also **Compliance and implementation**). While Ramsar sites are among the largest network of protected areas, many sites remain under threat from on-site and off-site actions. More generally, wetlands continue to suffer a high rate of degradation. The situation, however, would likely be worse in the absence of the Convention. Those parties that implement the Convention through national wetland policies or similar instruments find positive outcomes for wetlands (Gardner and Davidson 2011).

### References

Bowman, M.J. 1995. "The Ramsar Convention Comes of Age." *Netherlands International Law Review* 42(1): 1–52.

Gardner, Royal C. and Kim Diana Connolly. 2007. "The Ramsar Convention on Wetlands: Assessment of International Designations within the United States." *Environmental Law Reporter* 37(2): 10089–10113.

Gardner, Royal C. and Nick Davidson. 2011. "The Ramsar Convention." In *Wetlands—Integrating Multidisciplinary Concepts*, Ed. Ben A. LePage, 189–203. Dordrecht, Springer.

Verschuuren, Jonathan. 2008. "Ramsar Soft Law is Not Soft at All." *Milieu en Recht* 35(1): 28–34.

# WORLD BANK

## Susan Park

*The University of Sydney, Australia*

Created in 1944, the International Bank for Reconstruction and Development (IBRD) or "World Bank", is a multilateral financial institution lending approximately US$20–30 billion annually to its member states. Bank funds come from member state capital that is "callable" or "paid-in," from international capital markets, and income from interest and loan repayments. Loans are provided for projects such as roads, railways, and dams. From the early 1980s the World Bank began to increase its program loans. Known as Structural Adjustment Loans (SALs, now called Policy Based Loans) these aimed to restructure borrowers' economies based on neoliberal economic tenets.

The World Bank has a weighted voting system based on members' capital, and a formula of basic and proportional votes (a "one dollar, one vote" system). All 188 members are represented and voting is consensual but the World Bank has reacted to the "shareholder activism" of the powerful United States which was driven by pressure from civil society in advocating for environmental and social safeguards, gender equality, project quality, transparency (see **Transparency**), accountability, and reducing poverty.

Pressure from environmentalists has been crucial for the World Bank's incorporation of environmental concerns. The debate focused on whether the Bank can become green or whether it has merely green-washed its operations. The World Bank initially established an environmental unit in 1970 for a mixture of economic arguments in favor of limiting environmental destruction, political support for environmental policies, and intellectual engagement by the then World Bank President Robert McNamara, yet the "push" for a comprehensive re-evaluation of the Bank's environmental impacts came from mass environmental campaigns in the 1980s such as the Narmada Sadar Sarovar dam in India. This led to increasing the number of environmentalists on staff, the amount of lending for environmental projects, monitoring and evaluation of environmental safeguards, and ensuring that people whose local environment was adversely affected by a World Bank funded project could seek redress. The World Bank also became an implementing agency to the Global Environment Fund.

Scholars argue that the greening resulted from increased oversight by the Bank's member states and targeted action by Bank management that aligned with the culture and incentive structure of Bank staff (Nielson et al. 2006). Haas and Haas (1995) argued that the World Bank analyzed how environmental concerns fit within its aims through a re-evaluation of its beliefs about cause and effect, resulting in a change of the organization's goals to employ new environmental criteria. They distinguished learning from adaptation, arguing that only the **United Nations Environment Programme** and the Bank were capable of the former. This separated the organization's complex learning from tactical responses to pressure to reform. Yet tactical concessions are often seen to be the first step in a process of norm adherence (Park 2010).

Yet Wade (1997) argued that while the Bank had shifted from "environment versus growth" to "**sustainable development**" it had not changed its internal incentive system, thus undermining its environmental rigor (which Goldman 2005 calls "green neoliberalism", see also **Liberal environmentalism**). Environmental activist Bruce Rich (1994) agreed that the Bank green-washed its operations because its environmental criteria had not been implemented properly and the Bank's loan approval culture prevented sustainable development. Ongoing controversies over the Bank's role in deforestation and large-scale dams, its ban on lending for nuclear power, and its failure to adequately shift towards renewable energy challenge the Bank's green image. In comparison Gutner (2002) found that the World Bank was a greener bank, because it "finances projects with primary environmental goals and attempts to integrate environmental thinking into the broader set of strategic goals it develops." Evidence of this is the Bank's role in the Clean Development Mechanism. Green financing, like that undertaken by the International Finance Corporation, is having an impact on how the World Bank reviews its environmental policies.

## References

Goldman, Michael. 2005. *Imperial Nature: The World Bank and Struggles for Social Justice in the Age of Globalization.* New Haven, CT, Yale University Press.

Gutner, Tamar L. 2002. *Banking on the Environment: Multilateral Development Banks and Their Environmental Performance in Central and Eastern Europe.* Cambridge, MA, MIT Press.

Haas, Peter and Ernst Haas. 1995. "Learning to Learn: Improving International Governance." *Global Governance* 1(3): 255–284.

Nielson, Daniel, Michael Tierney, and Catherine Weaver. 2006. "Bridging the Rationalist-Constructivist Divide: Re-engineering the Culture at the World Bank." *Journal of International Relations and Development* 9(2): 107–139.

Park, Susan. 2010. *World Bank Group Interactions with Environmentalists: Changing International Organisation Identities.* Manchester, Manchester University Press.

Rich, Bruce. 1994. *Mortgaging the Earth: The World Bank, Environmental Impoverishment and the Crisis of Development.* Boston, MA, Beacon Press.

Wade, Robert. 1997. "Greening the Bank: The Struggle over the Environment 1970–1995." In *The World Bank: Its First Half Century,* Eds. Davesh Kapur, John Lewis, and Richard C. Webb, 611–734. Washington, Brookings Institute.

# WORLD ENVIRONMENT ORGANIZATION

## Frank Biermann

*Vrije Universiteit Amsterdam, Netherlands, and Lund University, Sweden*

A "world environment organization" does not exist. Yet proposals to create an international agency on environmental protection have been debated now for over forty years (overviews in Biermann and Bauer 2005). These proposals use a variety of names for such a new world environment organization, such as "Global Environment Organization," "United Nations Environment Organization," or "United Nations Environmental Protection Organization." What all proposals have in common is the argument for setting up a new specialized intergovernmental organization within the system of the United Nations that would focus on environmental policies.

The first proposal for a world environment organization dates back to US foreign policy strategist George F. Kennan (1970), who argued for an International Environmental Agency encompassing "a small group of advanced nations." Several authors supported this idea at that time. As one outcome of this debate, the United Nations established in 1973 the **United Nations Environment Programme**. The creation of a UN environment program was a more modest reform than the strong international environmental organization that some observers had called for then.

Since then, various authors have published proposals arguing for the establishment of a world environment organization to replace, or "upgrade," UNEP (for example, Biermann 2000; Desai 2000; Runge 2001). Virtually all proposals for a world environment organization can be categorized in three ideal type models, which differ regarding the degree of change that is required.

First, the least radical proposals advise upgrading UNEP to a specialized UN agency with full-fledged organizational status. Proponents of this approach have referred to the World Health Organization or the International Labor Organization as suitable models. The new agency in this model is expected to facilitate norm-building and norm-implementation processes (see **Compliance and implementation**). This strength would in particular derive from an enhanced mandate and better capabilities of the agency to build capacities in developing countries, for example by giving the new agency an operational mandate at country level similar to other major international organizations. This differs from UNEP's present "catalytic" mandate that prevents the program from engaging in project implementation. Furthermore, additional legal and political powers could come with the status of a UN special agency. For example, its governing body could approve by qualified majority vote certain regulations that could be binding, under certain conditions, on all members (comparable to the International Maritime Organization), or could adopt drafts of legally binding treaties negotiated under its auspices (comparable to the International Labor Organization).

Second, some observers argue for a more fundamental reform to address the substantive and functional overlap between the many international institutions in global environmental governance (see **Institutional interactions**). These advocates of a more centralized governance architecture call for the integration of several existing agencies and programs into one all-encompassing world environment organization. Such an integration of environmental regimes could loosely follow the model of the **World Trade Organization**, which has integrated diverse multilateral trade agreements.

The third and most far-reaching model is that of a hierarchical intergovernmental organization on environmental issues that would be equipped with enforcement powers vis-à-vis states that fail to comply with international agreements, for example along the lines of an "environmental security council." Support for such a powerful agency, however, remains scarce and largely restricted to a few nongovernmental organizations.

More skeptical voices and critics of a new organization have also come forward. Calestous Juma for example has argued that such proposals divert attention from more pressing problems and fail to acknowledge that centralizing institutional structures is an anachronistic paradigm. Sebastian Oberthür and Thomas Gehring (2005) argued also that cooperation theory would advise against a new agency. Konrad von Moltke (2005) and Adil Najam (2005) proposed as an alternative decentralized institutional clusters to deal with diverse sets of environmental issues rather than entrusting all problems to one central organization.

Politically, the idea of a world environment organization today finds the support of several governments. Notably, at the 2012 UN Conference on **sustainable development** a specialized agency status for UNEP was supported by the member states of the European Union and of the African Union as well as a number of other developing countries. Resistance has remained strong, however, from the United States, Japan, Russia, and even Brazil, which had earlier been a supporter of a world environment organization but now seemed afraid of an imbalance in favor of the environmental pillar of sustainable development. These countries argued that this question requires further debate and analysis (Vijge 2013). As one outcome of these recent debates, the **United Nations Environment Programme** has been further strengthened.

## References

Biermann, Frank. 2000. "The Case for a World Environment Organization." *Environment* 42(9): 22–31.

Biermann, Frank and Steffen Bauer (Eds.). 2005. *A World Environment Organization: Solution or Threat for Effective International Environmental Governance?* Aldershot, Ashgate.

Desai, Bharat. 2000. "Revitalizing International Environmental Institutions: The UN Task Force Report and Beyond." *Indian Journal of International Law* 40(3): 455–504.

Kennan, George F. 1970. "To Prevent a World Wasteland: A Proposal." *Foreign Affairs* 48(3): 401–413.

Najam, Adil. 2005. "Neither Necessary, nor Sufficient: Why Organizational Tinkering Will Not Improve Environmental Governance." In *A World Environment Organization: Solution or Threat for Effective International Environmental Governance?*, Eds. Frank Biermann and Steffen Bauer, 235–256. Aldershot, Ashgate.

Oberthür, Sebastian and Thomas Gehring. 2005. "Reforming International Environmental Governance: An Institutional Perspective on Proposals for a World Environment Organization." In *A World Environment Organization: Solution or Threat for International Environmental Governance?*, Eds. Frank Biermann and Steffen Bauer, 205–234. Aldershot, Ashgate.

Runge, C. Ford. 2001. "A Global Environment Organization (GEO) and the World Trading System." *Journal of World Trade* 35(4): 399–426.

Vijge, Marjanneke J. 2013. "The Promise of New Institutionalism: Explaining the Absence of a World or United Nations Environment Organization." *International Environmental Agreements: Politics, Law and Economics* 13(2): 153–176.

von Moltke, Konrad. 2005. "Clustering International Environmental Agreements as an Alternative to a World Environment Organization." In *A World Environment Organization: Solution or Threat for Effective International Environmental Governance?*, Eds. Frank Biermann and Steffen Bauer, 175–204. Aldershot, Ashgate.

# WORLD TRADE ORGANIZATION

**Fariborz Zelli**

*Lund University, Sweden*

Surrounding the establishment of the WTO in 1994, scholars discussed whether the new organization would contribute to a shift of global environmental governance toward more **market**-based mechanisms (see **Liberal environmentalism**).

The over sixty conventions under the auspices of the WTO indeed include a series of provisions that may conflict with environmental standards, e.g. with trade restrictions due to unsustainable process and production methods. According to the most favored nation clause, a WTO party has to grant any trade advantage it concedes to any one country to all other parties. The national treatment principle prohibits the discrimination of foreign goods or services in comparison to "like" domestic goods or services.

The WTO treaties also include clauses that qualify the applicability of these and other non-discrimination principles. The GATT grants "general exceptions," including for measures "necessary to protect human, animal or plant life or health" and for the "conservation of exhaustible natural resources" (Article XX). Yet, the abstract phrasing of principles and exceptions leaves considerable room for interpretation—and for legal tensions.

Attempts to address this uncertainty were made at WTO political bodies such as the Committee on Trade and Environment. The committee inter alia covers the relationship to multilateral environmental agreements (MEAs) and the reduction of trade barriers to environmental goods and services. But various efforts, mostly tabled by the EU and Switzerland, to discuss broader exceptions of WTO rules in favor of MEAs were turned down by the US and developing countries who feared eco-protectionist consequences.

Given the inconclusiveness of these debates, the WTO's environmental role has been mainly defined through judicial decisions. The unprecedented WTO **dispute resolution mechanism** has come to cover a series of disputes over domestic environmental laws, from **fisheries governance** and species protection to natural resources conservation, air pollution, and health standards. While early rulings strictly prioritized free trade principles there is a notable trend in more recent decisions towards accommodating environmental norms (Howse 2002).

One example: in the 1991 tuna–dolphin dispute, a GATT panel had still interpreted US import bans on Mexican yellowfin tuna—whose fishing methods had violated US standards for dolphin protection—as a breach of the national treatment rule. In the 1998 shrimp–turtle dispute, however, the WTO Dispute Settlement Body widened its understanding: not only the final product, but process and production methods requirements in a product's life cycle should be taken into account, if such requirements are rooted in multilateral agreements, e.g. the **biodiversity regime** (Charnovitz 2008; Pauwelyn 2009).

Aside from the Dispute Settlement Body's growing practice of referencing other treaties, MEAs themselves have so far not been directly subject to WTO dispute settlement. This may be surprising, given considerable **institutional interactions**, e.g. trade restrictions on hazardous waste, endangered species, and ozone-depleting substances, under the **hazardous wastes regime**, the **CITES**, and the Montreal Protocol of the **ozone regime** respectively. Since these restrictions discriminate against non-members or non-compliers of these MEAs, they may get into conflict with the WTO's most-favored nation principle. Moreover, the Biodiversity Regime's Cartagena Protocol on Biosafety may collide with WTO rules due to its stringent precautionary restrictions and respective requirements for information-sharing prior to trading genetically modified organisms.

Another example with legal conflict potential involves the **climate change regime**, since its framework convention does not specify exhaustively the measures parties may take to reach their carbon emissions targets. This leaves the door open for the potential implementation of fiscal measures (subsidies, tariffs, or **taxation**) and regulatory measures (standards, technical regulations, **labeling and certification**) that might discriminate against imported products with greenhouse gas-intensive process and production methods. Scholars have led long-standing discussions on the compatibility of such measures with the national treatment principle and other WTO clauses (cf. Zelli and van Asselt 2010).

Why have these overlaps not entailed a dispute settlement procedure so far? One reply is that MEAs are increasingly referenced in WTO rulings as acceptable specifications. This practice qualifies the argument of the WTO's instrumental role in a shift toward **liberal environmentalism**. However, some scholars criticize that the Dispute Settlement Body has taken only those external norms into account that suit its own neoliberal worldview (Kulovesi 2011). Others again took a closer look behind the scenes of **treaty negotiations**, and discovered a certain self-censorship or "chill" effect that avoided more trade-restrictive approaches (Eckersley 2004).

## *References*

Charnovitz, Steve. 2008. "The WTO as an Environmental Agency." In *Institutional Interplay: Biosafety and Trade*, Eds. Oran R. Young, W. Bradnee Chambers, Joy A. Kim, and Claudia ten Have, 161–191. Tokyo, United Nations University Press.

Eckersley, Robyn. 2004. "The Big Chill: The WTO and Multilateral Environmental Agreements." *Global Environmental Politics* 4(2): 24–50.

Howse, Robert. 2002. "The Appellate Body Rulings in the Shrimp/Turtle Case: A New Legal Baseline for the Trade and Environment Debate." *Columbia Journal of Environmental Law* 27(2): 489–519.

Kulovesi, Kati. 2011. *The WTO Dispute Settlement System: Challenges of the Environment, Legitimacy and Fragmentation*. Dordrecht, Kluwer Law International.

Pauwelyn, Joost. 2009. *Conflict of Norms in Public International Law: How WTO Law Relates to Other Rules of International Law*. Cambridge, Cambridge University Press.

Zelli, Fariborz and Harro van Asselt. 2010. "The Overlap between the UN Climate Regime and the World Trade Organization: Lessons for Climate Governance Beyond 2012." In *Global Climate Governance Beyond 2012*, Eds. Frank Biermann, Philipp Pattberg, and Fariborz Zelli, 79–96. Cambridge, Cambridge University Press.

# INDEX

Aarhus Convention xvi, 39, 89, 144, 225; *see also* information (access to), justice
Aarhus Protocol *see* heavy metals
aboriginal peoples *see* indigenous peoples
access and benefit sharing xvi, 13–14, 67, 196; *see also* genetic resources
accountability 17, 44, 89, 117, 136, 147, 149 165, 234
acid rain 70, 171, 207, 215
adaptation 1–2, 27, 54, 65–67, 71, 97, 115, 127, 182, 205, 209
advocacy networks 70; *see also* nongovernmental organizations, social movements
Africa 25, 49, 92, 114–115, 127, 150, 183; *see also* African Group, African Union
African Group 115–116, 132; *see also* Africa, African Union
African Union 198, 238; *see also* Africa, African Group
agency 148, 154, 159, 171, 174, 189, 190, 197, 223
Agenda 21 xvi, 29–30, 144, 202
Agreement on Application of Sanitary and Phytosanitary Measures 161–162
agriculture 3, 40, 50, 95, 97, 111, 115, 149, 165; *see also* farmers, Food and Agriculture Organization
aid 2–5, 52, 105, 131, 144; *see also* International Aid Transparency Initiative, Millennium Development Goals, Paris Declaration on Aid Effectiveness
air pollution *see* transboundary air pollution regime

Alliance of Small Island States 115–116, 131–133
Amazon *see* forest
Antarctic Treaty regime xvi, 5–7, 35, 102, 114
anthropocene 51, 83
anthropocentrism 58, 94
AOSIS *see* Alliance of Small Island States
Arab Group 132
Arctic 7–8, 137–138, 145, 150
ASEAN *see* Association of Southeast Asian Nations
Asia 62, 92, 95, 114, 127, 198, 216–217
assessments xvi, 3–4, 7, 9–10, 25, 32–33, 65–66, 129, 141–142, 162–164, 184, 188, 200, 210, 216, 230, 233
atmosphere 27, 36, 74, 143, 205, 213
audits 11–12, 19, 165, 176
Australia 62, 100, 106, 132, 157, 225; *see also* JUSCANZ
awareness 13, 26, 75, 98, 100, 135, 182, 199, 230

Bali Action Plan 28, 167–168
Bamako Convention xvi, 92; *see also* hazardous wastes
Basel Convention xvi, 91–92, 99; *see also* hazardous wastes, prior informed consent
BASIC 28, 68, 132; *see also* Brazil, China, India, South Africa
benefit sharing *see* access and benefit sharing
Bhopal 43, 90
BINGOs *see* business
biocentrism *see* ecocentrism
biodiversity regime *see* Convention on Biological Diversity

biofuels 9, 137; *see also* energy
biosafety xvi, 14, 68, 161–162, 240
biotechnology 67, 196; *see also*
    biosafety, GMOs
Bolivia 132
Bonn Convention xvi, 41
boundary organizations 9, 13, 16–17,
    50, 52, 78, 184, 186, 197
Brazil 6, 62, 67, 132, 148, 238;
    *see also* BASIC, BRICS, IBSA
BRICS 68; *see also* Brazil, China,
    India, Russia
British Petroleum 43
Brundtland, G. H. 100
Brundtland Report 61, 100, 120, 195,
    201, 203
burden-sharing 32–33
bureaucracy 30, 144, 190, 229;
    *see also* secretariats
business 6, 10–11, 18–21, 42–45, 52,
    61, 63, 70–71, 76–77, 90, 92, 111,
    117, 124, 134–135, 142, 144,
    147–148, 152, 158, 165–167, 170,
    176–177, 180, 184, 193, 195–196,
    202–203, 207, 220, 226–227;
    *see also* British Petroleum,
    corporate social responsibility,
    Dow chemicals, Dupont, Exxon
    Valdez, Natura, World Business
    Council for Sustainable
    Development

California effect *see* race to the top
CAMPFIRE 97
Canada 7, 27–28, 90, 96, 100, 117,
    132, 152, 163; *see also* JUSCANZ
cap and trade 27, 121, 123–124, 205;
    *see also* market-based instruments
capacity building 38, 92, 115, 131,
    135, 141, 152, 208–209
capitalism 23, 45–46; *see also* liberal
    environmentalism, market-based
    instruments
carbon market *see* cap and trade
Caribbean Group 132
carrying capacity 21–23, 88, 157,
    181, 202, 210, 213, 216
Carson, R. 98
Cartagena Protocol on Biosafety
    *see* biosafety
catastrophes *see* disasters

certification *see* labeling
chemicals xvi, 90–91, 129, 140–141,
    148, 150–151, 174, 180, 225;
    *see also* pesticides, Rotterdam
    Convention
Chernobyl *see* nuclear accident
children 93, 144
China 6, 8, 32, 62, 67–68, 110, 124,
    129, 131–132, 153–154, 222, 225;
    *see also* BASIC, BRICS
chlorofluorocarbon 19, 102, 123,
    140–143; *see also*
    hydrochlorofluorocarbon, ozone
    regime
CITES *see* Washington Convention
cities 22, 77, 98, 109, 180, 217, 221
civil society organizations *see*
    nongovernmental organizations
Clean Air Act 123
Clean Development Mechanism
    27–28, 124, 235; *see also* climate
    change regime
Climate Action Network 78
climate change regime xvi, 1, 4, 8,
    10, 16, 26–29, 32, 39, 50, 66–68,
    77–78, 99, 102, 115–116,
    121–122, 124–125, 127, 132, 138,
    143, 159, 162, 167, 171, 174, 186,
    189–190, 197, 205–206, 208,
    219–220, 230, 240; *see also* Clean
    Development Mechanism
climate Convention *see* climate
    change regime
Club of Rome 21–22, 99, 157
coal *see* fossil fuels
Coase, R. (Coase, Coasean) 63, 123
code of conduct 43, 54, 90, 165
Cold War 6, 8, 181, 192, 201, 215;
    *see also* wars
collective action 19, 61, 76, 85, 139,
    170
Colombia 132
command and control *see* regulatory
    approaches
Commission on Sustainable
    Development 29–30, 68, 176
common but differentiated
    responsibility 4, 31–34, 107, 121,
    202
common heritage of mankind 6,
    34–36, 195, 206